AQA History

AS
Unit 1

Tsarist Russia, 1855–1917

Sally Waller

OXFORD
UNIVERSITY PRESS

Great Clarendon Street, Oxford, OX2 6DP, United Kingdom

Oxford University Press is a department of the University of Oxford.
It furthers the University's objective of excellence in research, scholarship,
and education by publishing worldwide. Oxford is a registered trade mark of
Oxford University Press in the UK and in certain other countries

British Library Cataloguing in Publication Data
Data available

978-1-4085-0311-9

10 9 8 7 6 5

Printed in Spain

Acknowledgements

Illustrations: Bob Moulder (c/o Graham Cameron Illustration), Thomson
Digital, David Russel Illustration

Page make-up: Thomson Digital

Although we have made every effort to trace and contact all
copyright holders before publication this has not been possible in all
cases. If notified, the publisher will rectify any errors or omissions at
the earliest opportunity.

Links to third party websites are provided by Oxford in good faith
and for information only. Oxford disclaims any responsibility for
the materials contained in any third party website referenced in
this work.

Contents

Introduction

The publisher has worked hard to ensure that this book offers you excellent support for your AS course and helps you to prepare for your exams. You can be confident that the range of learning, teaching and assessment practice materials has been checked and is matched to the requirements of your specification.

How to use this book

The features in this book include:

Timeline

Key events are outlined at the beginning of the book. The events are colour-coded so you can clearly see the categories of change.

Learning objectives

At the beginning of each section you will find a list of learning objectives that contain targets linked to the requirements of the specification.

Key chronology

A short list of dates usually with a focus on a specific event or legislation.

Key profile

The profile of a key person you should be aware of to fully understand the period in question.

Key terms

A term that you will need to be able to define and understand.

Did you know?

Interesting information to bring the subject under discussion to life.

Exploring the detail

Information to put further context around the subject under discussion.

A closer look

An in-depth look at a theme, person or event to deepen your understanding. Activities around the extra information may be included.

Sources

Sources to reinforce topics or themes and may provide fact or opinion. They may be quotations from historical works, contemporaries of the period or photographs.

Cross-reference

Links to related content within the book which may offer more detail on the subject in question.

Activity

Various activity types to provide you with different challenges and opportunities to demonstrate both the content and skills you are learning. Some can be worked on individually, some as part of group work and some are designed to specifically 'stretch and challenge'.

Question

Questions to prompt further discussion on the topic under consideration and are an aid to revision.

■ Summary questions

Summary questions at the end of each chapter to test your knowledge and allow you to demonstrate your understanding.

Study tip

Hints to help you with your study and to prepare for your exam.

Practice questions

Questions at the end of each section in the style that you may encounter in your exam.

Learning outcomes

Learning outcomes at the end of each section remind you what you should know having completed the chapters in that section.

■ Web links in the book

Because the publisher is not responsible for third party content online, there may be some changes to this material that are beyond our control. In order for us to ensure that the links referred to in the book are as up-to-date and stable as possible, the web sites provided are usually homepages with supporting instructions on how to reach the relevant pages if necessary.

Please let us know at **schools.enquiries.uk@oup.com** if you find a link that doesn't work and we will do our best to correct this at reprint, or to list an alternative site.

Introduction to the History series

When Bruce Bogtrotter in Roald Dahl's *Matilda* was challenged to eat a huge chocolate cake, he just opened his mouth and ploughed in, taking bite after bite and lump after lump until the cake was gone and he was feeling decidedly sick. The picture is not dissimilar to that of some A level History students. They are attracted to History because of its inherent appeal, but when faced with a bulging file and a forthcoming examination, their enjoyment evaporates. They try desperately to cram their brains with an assortment of random facts and subsequently prove unable to control the outpouring of their ill-digested material in the examination.

The books in this series are designed to help students and teachers avoid this feeling of overload by breaking down the AQA History specification in such a way that it is easily absorbed. Above all they are designed to retain and promote pupils' enthusiasm for History by avoiding a dreary rehash of dates and events. Each book is divided into sections, closely matched to those given in the specification itself, and the content is further broken down into chapters which present the historical material in a lively and attractive form. Each book offers guidance on the key terms, events and issues and blends thought-provoking activities and questions in a way designed to advance students' understanding. The series encourages students to think for themselves and to share their ideas with others as well as helping them to develop the knowledge and skills they will need. This book should ensure that students' learning remains a pleasure rather than an endurance test.

To make the most of what this book provides, students will need to develop efficient study skills from the outset and it is worth spending some time considering what these involve:

- **Good organisation of material in a subject specific file.** Organised notes help develop an organised brain and sensible filing ensures time is not wasted hunting for misplaced material. This book uses cross-references to indicate where material in one chapter has relevance to that in another. Students would be advised to employ the same technique.

- **A sensible approach to note-making.** Students are often too ready to copy large chunks of material from printed books or to download sheaves of print from the internet. These books are designed to encourage students to think about the notes they collect and to undertake research with a particular purpose in mind. The activities given here will encourage students to pick out that which is relevant to the issue being addressed and to avoid making notes on material that is improperly understood.

- **By far the most important component of study is taking time to 'think'.** By encouraging students to '*think*' before they write or speak, be it for a written answer, presentation or class debate, students should learn to form opinions and make judgements based on their accumulation of evidence. These are skills you will need to develop and the beauty of History is that there is rarely a right or wrong answer, so, with sufficient evidence, one student's view will count for as much as the next!

Unit 1

The topics offered for study in Unit 1 are all concerned with issues of 'Change and Consolidation'. They invite consideration of what changed and why, as well as posing the question of what remained the same. Through a study of a period of about 50–60 years, students are encouraged to analyse the interplay of both long and short-term reasons for change and to consider not only how governments have responded to the need for change but also to evaluate the ensuing consequences. Such historical analyses are, of course, relevant to an understanding of the present and through such historical study, students will be guided towards a greater appreciation of the world around them today as well as developing their understanding of the past.

Unit 1 will be tested by a one hour fifteen minute paper which will contain three questions, from which students will need to choose two. Details relating to the style of questions, with additional hints for students, are given below and links to the examination requirements are provided throughout this book. Students should familiarise themselves with the question styles and the marking criteria before attempting any end-of-section practice questions. Like the sportsman, the wise student understands the rules of the game before taking up the challenge!

Answers will be marked according to a scheme based on 'levels of response'. This means that the answer will be assessed according to which level best matches the historical skills displayed, taking both knowledge and understanding into account. Take some time to study these criteria and use them wisely.

Question 1/2/3 (a)

L1: Answers will contain either some descriptive material which is only loosely linked to the focus of the question or some explicit comment with little, if any, appropriate support. Answers are likely to be generalised and assertive. The response will be limited

Unit 1	Question	Marks	Question type	Question stem	Additional hints for students
Question 1, 2 & 3	(a)	12	This question will be focused on a narrow issue within the period studied and will require an explanation.	Why did... Explain why...	Make sure you explain 'why', not 'how' and try to order your answer in a way that shows you understand the inter-linkage of factors and which were the more important. You should try to reach an overall judgement/conclusion.
Question 1, 2 & 3	(b)	24	This question will link the narrow issue to a wider context and will require an awareness that issues and events can have differing interpretations.	How far... How important was... How successful...	This answer will need planning as you will need to develop an idea or argument in your answer and show balanced judgement. Try to set out your idea/argument in the introduction. Then, as you develop your ideas through your paragraphs, support your opinions with detailed evidence. Your conclusion should flow naturally and again provide evidence to support your judgement.

in development and skills of written communication will be weak. *(0–2)*

L2: Answers will demonstrate some knowledge and understanding of the demands of the question. They will either be almost entirely descriptive with few explicit links to the question or they will provide some explanations backed by evidence that is limited in range and/or depth. Answers will be coherent but weakly expressed and/or poorly structured. *(3–6)*

L3: Answers will demonstrate good understanding of the demands of the question providing relevant explanations backed by appropriately selected information, although this may not be full or comprehensive. Answers will, for the most part, be clearly expressed and show some organisation in the presentation of material.

(7–9)

L4: Answers will be well-focused, identifying a range of specific explanations, backed by precise evidence and demonstrating good understanding of the connections and links between events/issues. Answers will, for the most part, be well-written and organised. *(10–12)*

Question 1/2/3 (b)

L1: Answers may either contain some descriptive material which is only loosely linked to the focus of the question or they may address only a limited part of the period of the question. Alternatively, there may be some explicit comment with little, if any, appropriate support. Answers are likely to be generalised and assertive. There will be little, if any, awareness of differing historical interpretations. The response

will be limited in development and skills of written communication will be weak. *(0–6)*

L2: Answers will show some understanding of the demands of the question. They will either be almost entirely descriptive with few explicit links to the question or they may contain some explicit comment with relevant but limited support. They will display limited understanding of differing historical interpretations. Answers will be coherent but weakly expressed and/or poorly structured. *(7–11)*

L3: Answers will show a developed understanding of the demands of the question. They will provide some assessment, backed by relevant and appropriately selected evidence, but they will lack depth and/or balance. There will be some understanding of varying historical interpretations. Answers will, for the most part, be clearly expressed and show some organisation in the presentation of material. *(12–16)*

L4: Answers will show explicit understanding of the demands of the question. They will develop a balanced argument backed by a good range of appropriately selected evidence and a good understanding of historical interpretations. Answers will, for the most part, show organisation and good skills of written communication. *(17–21)*

L5: Answers will be well-focused and closely argued. The arguments will be supported by precisely selected evidence leading to a relevant conclusion/judgement, incorporating well-developed understanding of historical interpretations and debate. Answers will, for the most part, be carefully organised and fluently written, using appropriate vocabulary. *(22–24)*

Introduction to this book

Fig. 1 *Map of the extent of the Russian Empire, 1855*

The nineteenth century was a time of huge industrial and political advance in western Europe. The development of new forms of energy, the spread of railways and the expansion of trade, together with advances in medicine and improvements in public health, helped raise living standards for an increasing proportion of the population. Alongside such change went social and political advances. Standards of literacy increased, the old social hierarchies broke down and an increasing number of people gained the right to vote for a law-making assembly.

Russia, although still considered a 'great' power because of its size and structured society, trailed behind in every one of these developments. Whereas serfdom, whereby the peasants at the bottom of the social hierarchy were 'owned' by their landlords, had disappeared from western and central Europe after the 1848 revolutions, it was not until 1861 that serfs finally acquired their freedom in Russia, and even after this – and right up until 1917 – their civil rights and status in society were very much determined by their position as 'former serfs'.

When Alexander II came to the throne in 1855, Britain, Belgium, France and the states comprising Germany were already well advanced industrially, whereas the Russian economy remained predominantly rural with a ratio of 11:1 village to town dwellers compared with 2:1 in Britain. It was only in the 1890s that Russia began to experience industrial change. So whilst the British death rate had fallen to 18 per 1,000 of the population by 1900, in Russia it was 35, and whilst 83 per cent of the adult population of Britain and France were literate, in Russia only 28 per cent could read and write. Furthermore, with the exception of Turkey and Montenegro, Russia was the only country in Europe still without a parliament in 1900.

There are good reasons for Russia's backwardness. Nineteenth century Russia was a vast Empire of roughly 8 million square miles, twice the size of Europe and a sixth of the globe's surface. It had been acquired through military conquest and colonisation, and was still growing. However, much of this Russian territory was inhospitable (over two thirds lay to the north of the 50th parallel), comprising tundra, forests and vast barren areas especially to the north and east. Consequently, both size and climate placed severe strains on economic development Although mid-nineteenth century Russia was Europe's main exporter of agricultural produce and possessed vast reserves of timber, coal, oil, gold and other precious metals, much of its potential remained untapped and communications between the different parts of the Empire were poor.

Furthermore, within this vast land mass lived many different ethnic groups, each with its own culture, customs, language and, in some cases, religion. Less than half the total population of about 69 million people in 1855 was Russian, and three quarters of the total population lived within European Russia – to the west of the Urals – on less than a quarter of the total land mass.

Fig. 2 *In the 19th century serfdom was the established way of life in rural Russia*

At the beginning of Alexander II's reign, 85 per cent of Russians were peasants and of these the vast majority were serfs. They were tied to their communes or *mirs* where they farmed their allotted strips of land, working and living in conditions which, by western standards, would be regarded as primitive. It was normal for corn to be cut by hand with sickles and for the peasants to share huts with their animals. In such circumstances, it is perhaps unsurprising that most peasants were illiterate but deeply religious, inclined to superstition and deeply hostile to change.

Russia did have some cities and towns, where craftsmen and other urban workers lived, but these were generally small administrative or market centres, although the largest, the capital St Petersburg, boasted 500,000 inhabitants (a little larger than Liverpool in Britain but lagging well behind London's 3,500,000). A 'middle class' was almost non-existent. There was an educated '**intelligentsia**' – often the sons of nobles, and a group which fulfilled the roles of minor government officials, lawyers, doctors and teachers – but for the most part Russian society remained deeply divided between the 10 per cent of landowners who owned 75 per cent of the land, and the rest.

The need to control this vast and diverse Empire, acquired by conquest, had led to the evolution of a powerful **autocratic** structure of government. At the head was the tsar, who took the title 'Emperor and Autocrat of all Russia'. According to the 'Collected Laws of the Russian Empire' compiled by Nicholas I in 1832:

'The Emperor of all the Russias is an autocratic and unlimited monarch; God himself ordains that all must bow to his supreme power, not only out of fear but also out of conscience.'

The tsar was the titular Head of the Russian **Orthodox Church** and was regarded by Orthodox believers as the embodiment of God on earth. The land of Russia was his private property and the Russian people his children. Russians were taught to show devotion to their tsar and accept their conditions on earth as the will of God. The Patriarch of Moscow, who worked in close harmony with the tsar, provided spiritual guidance, while the Over-Procurator of the Holy Synod, a post created in 1721, was a government minister, appointed by the tsar to run Church affairs. The structures of Church and state were thus entwined, as archbishops and bishops at the head of the church hierarchy were subject to tsarist control over appointments, religious education, most of the Church's finances and issues of administration.

The tsar's imperial edicts, or *ukase*, were the law of the land. The tsar did, of course, have advisers and ministers, but these were all chosen by the tsar himself and none could do anything without his approval. His main advisory bodies were the Imperial Council or Chancellery, a body of 35–60 nobles specially picked by the tsar to advise him personally and provide their 'expert' opinion; the Committee of Ministers, a body of 8–14 ministers in charge of different government departments; and the Senate, which was supposed to oversee all the workings of government but in practice was largely redundant.

The tsarist regime also depended on the provincial nobility for support. Nobles had not been obliged to serve the state since 1785, although many continued to do so, for example as Provincial Governors, but their sense of obligation remained strong and all landowners were relied upon to keep order on their estates. Furthermore, when circumstances demanded, tsars might choose to appoint a special committee to carry out an investigation or prepare a report. Such committeees were usually headed by trusted nobles but, even so, there was no need for the tsar to take any notice of their findings.

The civil servants who made up the bureaucracy were paid noble officials, selected from a 'Table of ranks' which laid down the requirements for office. There were 14 levels, from rank 1, held by members of the Ministerial Council, to rank 14, which qualified the educated for minor state office, for example, collecting taxes or running a provincial post office. Each rank had its own uniform, form of address and status, which included hereditary nobility at the higher levels. This bureaucracy was riddled by internal corruption and incompetence but through it orders were passed downwards from the centre to the governors of the 50 provinces and in turn to the district governors and the commandants of towns. It was a one-way operation, with no provision for suggestions to travel upwards from the lower ranks.

As well as his civilian officials, the tsar also had at his disposal the world's largest army of about 1.5 million conscripted serfs, each forced into service for 25 years and made to live in a 'military colony'. This huge army and much smaller navy absorbed about 45 per cent of the the government's annual expenditure. The higher ranks of the military were prestigious posts, reserved for the nobles who bought and sold their commissions, but for the lower ranks discipline was harsh and army life tough. This army could be called upon to fight in wars or to put down internal risings and disturbances. The tsar also had the service of elite regiments of mounted cossacks, with special social privileges, which acted both as a personal bodyguard to the tsar and as police reinforcements.

■ **Key terms**

The Orthodox Church: following a split in the Christian Church in the 11th century, the Eastern Orthodox Church had developed its own beliefs and rituals. In 1453, when Constantinople fell to the Turks, Moscow became its spiritual capital.

To maintain the autocracy, the country had developed into a police state. The police state prevented any freedom of speech, of the press and of travel abroad. Censorship existed at every level of government and was carried out by the state and the Church as well as by the police. The state security network was run by the 'Third Section' of the Emperor's Imperial Council. Its agents kept a strict surveillance over the population, enforcing a rigid control and ensuring that any subversive activites were exposed. Political meetings and strikes were forbidden and the Third Section had unlimited powers to carry out raids, arrest and ensure the imprisonment or exile of any suspected of anti-tsarist behaviour, sometimes merely on the word of an informer.

Key terms

Indirect taxation: taxes on goods that were bought.

This governmental structure was financed from from taxes and dues, largely borne by the peasantry. For instance, the nobility and clergy were exempt from the Poll Tax, which had been introduced in 1719 in order to defray the costs of maintaining Russia's large army and was levied, at the same rate, on every male peasant in the Empire, rich or poor. Other **indirect taxation**, which included taxes on such 'essentials' as vodka and salt, also hit hard at the peasantry. In total, the peasants, urban workers and tradesmen provided about 90 per cent of the imperial revenue.

This autocratic system of government was not without critics. The intellectual 'westerners', influenced by an eighteenth century cultural movement, the Enlightenment, which had encouraged a questioning of established customs and practices, favoured changes in government and society along western lines. However, their calls were rejected, not only by the tsarist establishment, but by Slavophile philophers who believed that Russia should follow its own unique and superior path, based on a peasant society and the teachings of the Russian Orthodox Church. As early as the reign of Alexander I (1801–25), a representative assembly to advise the tsar, and possibly one with law-making powers, had been considered. However, while Alexander had pondered the idea, but not put it into practice, his brother Nicholas I (1825–55) had totally rejected such a thought. A military uprising against his rule in December 1825 by rebels, later known as 'the Decembrists', encouraged him to follow a path of repression and he deliberately sought to distance Russia from the west where the liberal ideas he most feared were spreading. He believed in 'Orthodoxy, Autocracy and Nationalism'. Severe restrictions were imposed on Russia's other nationalities and Jews were required to reside in 'The Pale'. Whilst leading intellectuals argued for an end to serfdom and a civil society based on the rule of law, Nicholas tightened censorship and set up the Third Section. His reign culminated in military defeat in the Crimea, and it took this to act as a wake-up call to a country which had for long ignored the need for change.

A closer look

The *Decembrists*

A revolt or uprising took place on 14 December 1825 – hence the rebels' name. Russian army officers led about 3,000 soldiers in a protest against Nicholas I's assumption of the throne after his elder brother Constantine removed himself from the line of succession. The Decembrists were interrogated, tried, and convicted. The leaders: Kakhovsky; Pavel Pestel; the poet Kondraty Ryleyev; Sergey Muravyov-Apostol; and Mikhail Bestuzhev-Ryumin were hanged. Other Decembrists were exiled to Siberia, Kazakhstan, and the Far East.

Cross-reference

Tsarist policies in terms of the various nationalities, including the Jews, within the Empire are discussed in more detail on pages 70–71.

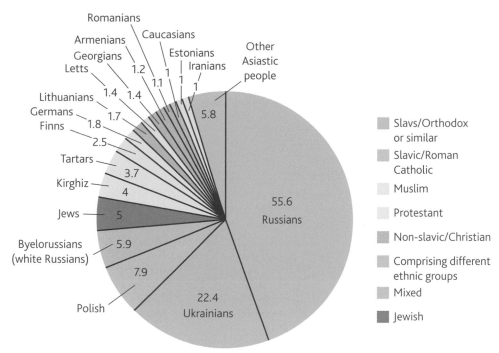

Romanians
Armenians
Georgians
Letts
Lithuanians
Germans
Finns
Tartars
Kirghiz
Jews
Byelorussians
(white Russians)
Polish

Caucasians
Estonians
Iranians
Other
Asiastic
people

1.2
1.4
1.4
1.7
1.8
2.5
3.7
4
5
5.9
7.9

1.1
1
1

5.8

55.6
Russians

22.4
Ukrainians

Slavs/Orthodox
or similar

Slavic/Roman
Catholic

Muslim

Protestant

Non-slavic/Christian

Comprising different
ethnic groups

Mixed

Jewish

Fig. 3 *Ethnic groups within the Russian Empire, taken from the first national census of 1897*

Thus, when Alexander II took the throne in 1855, Russia was facing
a dilemma – how to match the other European powers in economic
development without weakening the autocratic structure which held the
Empire together. Russian history from 1855–1917 was to be a struggle
between progress and control. The gains of industrialisation were offset
by an escalation of workers' discontent created by over-rapid urbanisation,
and the transition to a modern society was to to bring into prominence
revolutionary movements which went even further than the liberal
intelligentsia in their criticisms of autocracy. Successive governments were
forced to choose between modernisation and maintaining political control
over society in order to protect themselves. This conundrum still faced
Lenin in 1917, as much as it had faced Alexander II in 1855.

Fig. 4 *Alexander II came to the throne amidst great pomp and ceremony in 1855*

Timeline

1855	1856	1861	1862	1862–74	1863	1864
Alexander II becomes tsar.	*Treaty of Paris* ends Crimean War.	Abolition of serfdom.	Creation of Ministry of Finance and State Bank. Taxation collection reformed.	Reforms in the Navy and Army.	Polish Revolt. Education extended throughout country and to women. Universities given greater freedom.	*Zemstva* formed as part of local government reforms. Judiciary reformed.

1883	1886	1886	1887–92	1889	1891–02	1892–1903
'Emancipation of Labour' founded by Plekhanov.	Revival of People's Will by students of St Petersburg University.	Abolition of Poll Tax.	Ivan Vyshnegradsky Minister of Finance.	Land Captains introduced.	Widespread famine.	Sergei Witte, Minister of Finance, introduces rapid industrialisation programme.

1903	1903	1903	1904	1904	1905	1905
Witte dismissed in reaction to unrest caused by economic slump.	Split of Social Democrats at their Brussels Congress into Bolsheviks (led by Lenin) and Mensheviks (led by Martov).	Union of Liberation founded by Pyotr Struve.	Struve initiates liberal campaign of political banquets. Minister of the Interior, Plehve, assassinated by the Socialist Revolutionaries.	War breaks out between Russia and Japan over Korea and Northern Manchuria.	**January** 'Bloody Sunday' massacre leads to revolutionary upheavals.	**August** *Portsmouth (USA) Peace Treaty* with Japan.

1914	1915	1916	1917	1917	1917	1917
1 August Germany declares war on Russia. **26 August** Russia defeated at the battle of Tannenberg.	**6 September** The tsar assumes command of the armed forces and suspends the Duma.	**June–October** Brusilov Offensive produces some advances. **30 December** Murder of Rasputin.	**January–February** Strikes and civil unrest in Petrograd. **23 February** International Women's Day March in Petrograd turns into a workers' demonstration.	**27 February** Troops refuse to fire on demonstrators and join the revolutionary movement.	Formation of the Petrograd Soviet. **1 March** First Provisional Government is formed.	**2 March** The tsar abdicates. **3 April** Lenin returns and formulates his April Theses.

1865	1870	1873	1874	1877–78	1881	1883
Relaxation of censorship.	Introduction of the *Duma*.	Censorship laws tightened.	Military Service is reformed. Populists begin to '*Go to the People*'.	Russo-Turkish war.	Assassination of Alexander II.	Creation of Peasant Land Bank.

1894	1897	1898	1901–05	1901	1902	1903
Death of Alexander III; accession of Nicholas II.	Russia adopts the Gold Standard.	Foundation of Russian Social Democratic Workers' Party.	Economic slump follows world-wide depression and failed harvests; agrarian and industrial unrest.	Lenin publishes '*What is to be Done?*'.	Commission on Agriculture set up.	Main section of Trans-Siberian Railway completed.

1905	1905	1906–11	1907	1911	1912	1912
August The tsar promises a constitution.	**October** The St Petersburg Soviet is formed; The tsar authorises elections to a State Duma.	Stolypin carries through programme of agrarian reform.	Second Duma meets and is dissolved after four months. Stolypin alters electoral laws.	**November** Stolypin is assassinated.	Lena Gold Fields Massacre – renewed industrial unrest.	Fourth Duma elected.

1917	1917	1917	1917	1917	1918
3–4 July Anti-government demonstrations in Petrograd – the 'July Days'. **27–30 July** Kornilov's coup fails and Red Guards are given arms.	**September** Trotsky becomes chairman of the Petrograd Soviet; Bolshevik majorities in Petrograd and Moscow soviets.	**24–25 October** Bosheviks take over key buildings in Petrograd.	**25–27 October** Provisional Government members arrested; Bolshevik Coup announced at the second Congress of Soviets; Congress adopts decree on peace and decree on land and appoints the first Soviet government.	**December** Establishment of the Cheka.	**January** The Constituent Assembly is forcibly dissolved.

1 'The Tsar Reformer' – Alexander II

In this chapter you will learn about:

■ the reasons why Alexander II embarked on a programme of reform

■ the Emancipation of the Serfs

■ the other reforms that were passed during the reign

■ the impact and limitations of those reforms for Russian society.

Fig. 1 *Alexander II, the 'Tsar Reformer'*

■ **Activity**

Thinking point

As you read this chapter, think about what Chicherin wrote in Source 1 and see if you agree with him. At the end of this chapter, write a commentary to support or correct him.

Alexander set out to remodel completely the enormous state which had been entrusted to his care; to abolish an age-old order founded on slavery; to replace it with civic decency and freedom; to establish justice in a country which had never known the meaning of legality; to redesign the entire administration; to introduce freedom of the press in the context of unbroken authority; to call new forces to life at every turn and set them on firm legal foundations; to put a repressed and humiliated society on its feet and to give it the chance to flex its muscles.

1

So wrote the liberal Boris Chicherin (1828–1904), summing up what he believed were the progressive ideals of the 'Tsar-reformer' Alexander II, who came to power in 1855. Chicherin was attempting to prove that the liberal spirit of the 1860s had been subsequently perverted by the tsars Alexander III and Nicholas II and that, had Alexander's work been upheld, Russia might well have developed into a western-style society. Therefore, his views need to be treated with caution. They do, however, indicate some of the many areas where Alexander II attempted to bring change.

■ **Motives for reform**

The impact of the Crimean War

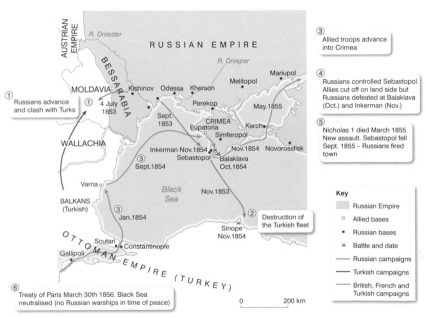

Fig. 2 *Map of the Crimean War*

As Nicholas I lay dying in 1855, he addressed his son, Alexander, with the words, *'I hand over to you my command, unfortunately not in as good order as I would have wished'*. Russia had just suffered two disastrous defeats in the Crimean war against Britain, France, Turkey and Piedmont-Sardinia at Balaclava in October 1854 and at Inkerman in November 1854. The fortress of Sebastopol, Russia's great naval base on the Black Sea, had fallen to its enemies. The country was in a state of shock and humiliation.

The Crimean War, undertaken in a spirit of utmost confidence, had proved a disaster in many respects. It had shown Russia's military and administrative inadequacies, disrupted much-needed trade through the Black Sea, provoked peasant uprisings, and thrown the gap between Russia and the West into sharp relief. The war was concluded by the Treaty of Paris in 1856 which not only reduced Russia's influence in the Black Sea area, but also declared the Black Sea a 'neutral zone', preventing its use by Russian warships in times of peace. The Russian belief that it was one of the 'great powers' of Europe was certainly brought into question.

■ **Exploring the detail**

The Crimean War

The Crimean War (1853–56) was provoked by Russian plans for expansion in the Turkish-controlled Balkan area. In 1853, the Russians demanded the right to protect the Christians there, and when the Turks rejected this, war broke out. The British and French, wary of Russia's ambition and concerned for their own interests, came to Turkey's defence and attacked the Crimean peninsula where the Russians had an important naval base at Sebastopol. In the ensuing war, which was marked by incompetence on both sides, the Russians suffered a defeat at Inkerman in November 1854 and in September 1855, they abandoned Sebastopol.

Fig. 3 *The Russians abandoning Sebastopol*

■ **Cross-reference**

A Key profile of Dmitrii Milyutin is on page 21.

The shameful defeat and peace treaty led members of the Russian intelligentsia and some of the more enlightened officials to raise questions about the state of Russian society and, in particular, its reliance on an army of serf conscripts. General Dmitrii Milyutin, who eventually became minister of war 1861–81, took the view that the army had to be modernised. However, before this could be done, a new way of enlisting soldiers was needed. Russia's inadequate communication system and its lack of railways were also held responsible for the wartime failures. Clearly if the system of serfdom were changed and the communications network opened up, there was also a possibility of developing Russia's economic potential. The need to reform in order to strengthen the state and prevent a repetition of the recent disaster found willing ears among the St Petersburg 'Party of Progress', the loose title given to the more liberal civil servants who frequented the salons of the Tsar's aunt, the Grand Duchess Elena Pavlovna, or gathered around his brother, the Grand Duke Constantine.

■ **Did you know?**

Problems of the Crimean War

There was only one musket for every two Russian soldiers and Russian weaponry was out-dated and far inferior to that of the British and French. Battle tactics had their limitations for both sides, but the Russians were far more dependent on brutal discipline to impel their soldiers into action. Furthermore, Russia had no railway system to transport troops or supplies to the front line and two thirds of the men in some Russian battalions died from starvation or sickness before even reaching the front lines.

Alexander II's own views

Alexander was no 'liberal' in the broad sense of the term. He was fully committed to maintaining the tsarist autocracy and upholding his 'God-given' duties. However, he believed that part of this responsibility involved enhancing the power and prestige of Russia and restoring the country's dignity as a leading power of Europe. He accepted that Russia needed to change and believed that by granting limited freedoms and reforms, he would help to stimulate a more dynamic economy, without altering the basic political framework of his rule.

Alexander had had the opportunity to witness at first hand some of the problems which Russia faced. He had taken control of government during his father's frequent absences abroad and had worked for over ten years in the Council of State, serving on various committees, including one on serfdom and another on the railways. He had also travelled around the Empire and had even visited Siberia, gaining some first hand knowledge of conditions of life there. Such experience had taught him that for Russia to modernise it needed to move away from its reliance on serfdom. Although he was mindful of the dangers of extreme change, he believed that some practical steps could and should be taken to lead Russia along the road towards economic modernisation.

In this, he was supported by other leading members of his family, his brother, the grand Duke Constantine and his aunt the grand Duchess Elena Pavlovna. He was also surrounded by a number of 'enlightened bureaucrats' who pressed for change and reform along western lines. Nicholas Alexander Milyutin, Alexander II's minister for internal affairs, 1859–61 (and brother to Dmitrii), for example, was anxious to carry through reform and had a good deal of influence in imperial circles.

■ Cross-reference

A Key profile of Nicholas Alexander Milyutin is on page 21 .

Alexander set the tone of his reign when he addressed the Moscow nobility in 1856. Unfortunately the original text of his speech has not survived, but of the three slightly-varying copies that have, one reads:

■ Activities

Source analysis

1 What do you understand by the phrases 'from above' and 'from below'?

2 Source 2 appears contradictory at first reading. Why do you think Alexander spoke to the nobles in this 'roundabout' way?

> There are rumours abroad that I wish to grant the peasants their freedom; this is unjust, and you may say so to everyone to right and left; but a feeling of hostility between the peasants and landlords does, unfortunately exist, and this has already resulted in several instances of insubordination to the landlords. I am convinced that sooner or later we must come to it. I believe that you too, are of the same opinion as I; consequently, it is far better that this should come about from above, rather than from below.

2

■ Cross-reference

The Decembrists' plot to assassinate Nicholas I in December 1825 is outlined in the Introduction, page 4.

Alexander's first actions on coming to power seemed to confirm his determination to rule in a more enlightened manner. He released political prisoners and even pardoned those who had been involved in a plot to assassinate his father (the Decembrists). He relaxed controls on censorship, lessened restrictions on foreign travel and university entrance, cancelled the debts of those in arrears with their taxes and restored some of the liberties of Poland and the Catholic Church.

Political considerations

There is little doubt that Alexander's 'enlightened' views were also influenced by political considerations. His father Nicholas I had maintained a reactionary and authoritarian regime, yet for all his spies and repression, he had been unable to prevent the emergence of a new ferment of social and political thought which helped politicise the Russian intelligentsia and breed undercurrents of disloyalty. Furthermore, it was becoming increasingly difficult to maintain the standard of vigilance and control that Nicholas had demanded.

The incidence of peasant unrest, for example, had steadily increased in the decade up to the Crimean War as landowners had tried to drive their peasants to produce more, and protests against the military conscription escalated. There had been more than 300 separate peasant risings plus murders of landowners and bailiffs had grown more common, so threatening the social stability of the countryside.

Furthermore, the Russian social structure seemed to be doing nothing to help the nobility, on which the tsarist autocracy depended. Nobles' incomes were falling and, whilst they remained dependent on their serfs, they had no incentive or training to put their talents to other uses, for example business ventures.

Economic considerations

There were many economic reasons why reform was necessary but it was above all the recognition of Russia's need to catch up with the West in order to reassert her great power status that persuaded men within the ministry of internal affairs, as well as a large number of landowners, that serfdom was acting as a brake to economic progress.

Serfdom was widely seen as the principal handicap to Russia's industrialisation since it prevented the movement of workers to factories, limited capital accumulation and kept the internal market demand low. The removal of serfdom was also essential if modern methods were to be developed in agriculture, for there was no incentive for the peasants to innovate or develop their land when the landowners could take the profits of their labours. It had not gone without notice that in areas where peasants were able to engage in paid work or, as in Siberia, where free peasant labour was the norm, peasants were more productive.

However, it was not just a question of incentive. Russia's population had doubled in the first half of the nineteenth century and, no matter how hard they worked, the conservative and inefficient agricultural system made it hard for the serfs to produce enough to feed themselves *and* provide a surplus for their landowners. Productivity levels remained stagnant, causing a crisis of supply. Serfs, who were forced to hand over grain at harvest time, were left unable to accumulate reserves to feed their families through the winter months, which led to recurrent bouts of famine.

Nor was the system effective for the landowners, or state. In serf-dominated areas, the landowning nobility was falling into ever greater debt as it tried to maintain its traditional lifestyle on a reduced income. Changes in agricultural practices in western Europe had increased the competitiveness of the European markets, making it harder for the nobles to sell grain and make a profit. Consequently, nobles were being forced to take out **mortgages** on estates which had previously been owned outright by their families By 1859, 66 per cent of serfs had been mortgaged as security for nobles' loans from the State Loan Bank, while peasants were also unable to pay their taxes – the Poll Tax and obrok. By 1855, the government had a debt of 54 million roubles.

Moral and intellectual considerations

Pressure for reform among intellectuals had begun long before 1855, although its members were divided between those who believed

> **Cross-reference**
>
> Peasant taxes are explained on page 14.

> **Key terms**
>
> **Mortgage:** this involves borrowing money by providing a guarantee. In this case a landowner's serfs provided the guarantee for a state loan. If the borrowed money and additional interest was not repaid, the state could seize the serfs.

Fig. 4 *Intellectuals were well aware of the problems caused by serfdom. What do you think this picture is trying to say?*

Cross-reference

More detail on Alexander Herzen can be found on page 35.

Activity

Extension activity

Research and discover more about the life and works of Turgenev and his contemporaries such as Tolstoy (1828–1910) and Dostoevsky (1821–86). All these thinkers and novelists were concerned with the state of Russian society and a dip into their writings enhances an appreciation of 19th century Russia.

Russia should become more westernised and those who favoured a unique 'Russian' way. Members of the intelligentsia such as Alexander Herzen and Ivan Turgenev wrote copiously and persuasively about the need to change Russian society. They argued not only that owning (and treating) people like cattle was immoral but also that it was detrimental to the moral fibre of the upper classes, making them callous, apathetic and indolent. Fashionable in the 1860s were the Nihilists, who claimed to believe in nothing save the need to rescue Russian society from its backwardness. In 1862, Turgenev popularised the term in his novel *Fathers and Sons* in which the main character, Bazároff, who considered himself a 'Nihilist', wanted to educate the people:

'What sort of person is Bazároff?' Arkády laughed. 'Would you like to have me tell you, my dear uncle, what sort of person he is?'

'Pray do, my dear nephew.'

'He is a Nihilist.'

'What?' asked Nikolai Petróvitch; and Pavel Petróvitch elevated his knife with a bit of butter sticking to the blade, in the air, and remained motionless.

'He is a Nihilist,' repeated Arkády.

'A Nihilist' said Nikolai Petróvitch.'That comes from the Latin, *nihil*, 'nothing,' so as far as I can judge, consequently that word denotes a man who – who recognises nothing.'

'Say, 'Who respects nothing'' put in Pavel Petróvitch, and devoted himself once more to his butter.

'Who treats everything from a critical point of view,' remarked Arkády.

'And isn't that exactly the same thing?' inquired Pavel Petróvitch.

'No, it is not exactly the same thing. A Nihilist is a man who does not bow before any authority whatever, who does not accept a single principle of faith, with whatever respect that principle may be surrounded.'

3

Key profile

Ivan Sergeyevich Turgenev

Ivan Sergeyevich Turgenev (1818–83) was a Russian novelist and playwright. He came from a wealthy landed family and after his university studies in Russia, he attended the university of Berlin, where he developed western ideas. His first success as a novelist, *A Sportsman's Sketches*, published in 1852, is said to have helped to influence educated Russian opinion in favour of the abolition of serfdom. During the rule of Tsar Nicholas I, Turgenev emigrated to Europe, but he returned to Russia in 1861 when he heard of the Emancipation Edict. His most famous novel, *Fathers and Sons* was published in 1862. In this, as in all his novels, he addressed the problems of contemporary Russian society.

A closer look

Westerners and Slavophiles

The critical-thinking minority among the Russian intelligentsia had spent much of the century pondering the political and social direction that Russia should follow. This group divided broadly into two categories: the Slavophiles and the Westerners. The former believed Russia had a unique culture and heritage centred on the prevailing peasant society and the tenets of the Orthodox Church, which should be preserved as the country modernised. The latter adopted the view that Russia should forget some of its traditions, which were holding it back, and absorb modern western values. This included not only economic and military reform but also reforms to 'civilise' society by providing representative assemblies, reducing the stranglehold of the Orthodox Church and establishing civil liberties.

Summary question

Explain why Alexander II decided to embark on a series of reforms when he came to power in Russia.

The emancipation of the serfs, 1861

Fig. 5 *The expectations of gain from the abolition of serfdom*

Study tip

When dealing with 'Explain why' questions, you will need to consider both general and specific motivation, long *and* short-term factors. Think carefully how you will plan your answer before you start writing. You may like to start with a spider diagram of factors and 'weave a web' to show the interconnections between them.

What was serfdom?

A serf was a bonded labourer. Over half of all serfs in the mid-nineteenth century were privately owned, whilst others were 'state serfs', who lived on the tsar's own lands and generally enjoyed slightly more freedom than their counterparts. The serfs were further subdivided into those paying rent (*obrok*) and those who paid with their labour (*barschina*). Those paying *obrok* had some freedom to practise a trade, but the lord would vary their rent depending on how profitable their trade might be. This stunted enterprise as there was little incentive to be too successful simply to pay more rent. Those paying *barschina* normally worked for their lord for three days a week, although if he decided at important times of the year to increase this burden there was no complaints procedure which could be followed. Most serfs belonged to local village communes called *mirs* that were run by the village elders who decided how the land should be distributed and what farming activities should take place and when.

Whilst in winter there might be little to be done apart from feeding livestock, in the short spring and summer months there was often a huge burden of work for all serfs, particularly those working a lord's strips of land as well as their own. Serfs could be bought and sold, were subject to corporal punishment and were not allowed to marry without their landlord's permission. Although the relationship between the master and serf was often good and cruelty was the exception, nevertheless, the lord could do almost anything except murder a serf. Serfs were also liable for conscription into the army.

Sometimes a landowner would decide to take serfs into domestic service. A number of domestic serfs was a status symbol for an aristocrat, implying that he had sufficient serfs on his estates and could afford luxuries. It might also provide better conditions for the serfs, whose work could range from that of a housemaid or cook to a gardener, handyman or carriage-driver. However, such employment also left them landless and totally dependent on their master.

Early attempts to reduce serfdom

In 1803 Alexander I had made it legal for landowners to sell land to their peasants. However, only about 100,000 peasants had bought their freedom in this way before 1855. Between 1816 and 1819, the Baltic states of Estonia, Livonia and Kurland had abolished serfdom, but had not granted land to the freed peasants. In the 1840s, there had also been an attempt to regulate serfdom in the Ukraine. Even Nicholas I had regarded serfdom as an '*evil palpable to all*' and had convened ten secret committees to discuss the issue, but there had been little change. The 1842 'Law of Obligated Peasants' allowed landlords to negotiate fixed agreements on land-holding and obligations in a contract, but it also freed the landlord from any obligation to support such peasants in hard times. Only 27,000 had become obligated peasants in Russia by 1858. A decree of 1847 allowed serfs to purchase their freedom and land, if an estate was sold at public auction, but only 964 were able to take advantage of this.

It was traditional, at the end of a war, such as that in the Crimea, which had been brought to an end in 1856, for the tsar to announce the freedom of those serfs conscripted to fight. However, Alexander II delayed doing so. This was not because he did not wish these serfs to have their freedom, but because he was considering a broader all-embracing measure. Nevertheless, this only increased tensions. Alexander asked a small group of nobles to produce suggestions for an emancipation measure as early as March 1856, but when they failed to respond, a secret committee of leading officials was convened in 1857, led at first by the conservative Alexei Fedorovich Orlov, President of the Council of State, but from August, when the tsar had become frustrated by its slow progress, by his own brother, the Grand Duke Constantine. However, the secrecy was soon abandoned and in 1858–59 Alexander himself toured the country making pro-emancipation speeches, while provincial committees of nobles were invited to consider the issue and draw up detailed records of peasant holdings, terms and dues, with a view to putting together an emancipation plan. This involvement in legislation was an unprecedented break with traditional methods of ruling. As one contemporary wrote:

> Until this time it was not the custom of our tsars to speak with the estates about general national interests. They usually flew with lightning speed across the vast expanse of the empire and rarely even bestowed a gracious word or glance upon the subjects who gathered to greet them.

4

It appeared that Alexander's reign was adopting a 'new course', but the reasons were not entirely 'liberal'. Alexander's speeches not only emphasised his commitment to emancipation but also the 'personal bond' between monarch and nobility – making it hard for nobles to oppose the measure without appearing disloyal. The aim was to make the final edict appear a personal and moral gesture from the nobility, rather than simply a legal act. Alexander talked of a process of 'national renewal' and was encouraged by the welcome he received from peasants on his tour. However, the negotiations dragged on, as some vested interests stood out against change. Whilst many landowners accepted that some reform was needed, they naturally sought a measure which was advantageous for them, which usually meant retaining their economic and judicial control over their serfs. Furthermore, fear of peasant uprisings, whilst in some ways an incentive for reform, also provided an argument for those conservatives who believed that the serfs must be kept restrained for fear that to open the door to freedom would lead to a tidal wave of reform which would destroy the tsarist autocracy. Many provincial committees could not agree and some sent in 'majority' and 'minority' reports. Interestingly, Alexander tried to silence the debate by tightening the censorship laws again – a further sign that this measure was not a 'democratic' decision. Against a background of peasant unrest, Alexander finally gave a Commission of 38, led by Nicholas Alexander Milyutin, the responsibilty for drawing up the measure, but even within this Commission there was considerable dissension. A measure was finally produced in October 1860, but it took until February 1861 before the *ukase* (or edict) was ready to be proclaimed as law and even then it did not come into force until Lent.

Activity

Pairs discussion

In pairs, make a list of the problems that faced the committees discussing serf emancipation. Include the arguments that might be used on both sides of the debate.

The terms of the Emancipation Ukase

Fig. 6 *Tsar Alexander II emancipating the serfs in 1861*

The 1861 Emancipation *Ukase* (or decree) was a lengthy legal document which initially only applied to the privately owned serfs living on the land. Over 20 million state serfs – who had already been released from some of their obligations before 1861 – had to wait until 1866 to receive their complete freedom. There were also a further 7 million serfs in different categories, for whom terms were worked out over the following years.

Basic provisions:

■ Serfs were to be released from bondage (ties to landowners) and become free men. They would be free to marry, own property, set up businesses, travel and enjoy legal rights.

■ Each serf family (except domestic serfs) was entitled to keep its cottage and an allotment (land). The amount depended on the area.

■ Landlords would receive compensation for the loss of land from the government in the form of government bonds and peasants were required to pay 'redemption payments' (a form of direct taxation) to the government for the land they had acquired. There were to be 49 annual payments and a 6 per cent interest charge would be added.

■ The freed serfs were to remain within their peasant commune (*mir*) until all their redemption payments had been made. The *mir* distributed allotments, controlled farming patterns and assessed, collected and paid the taxes of all the peasants living within its jurisdiction.

Further details:

■ Peasants were to continue to pay *obrok* or labour service for a further two years before achieving the status of freemen. The landlord was not allowed to alter demands during this period of 'temporary obligation' and the time was to be used preparing inventories of land farmed and dues owed.

■ Landowners were to retain ownership of meadows, pasture and woodland and the land which had been farmed for himself which would be worked by hired labour (usually ex-serfs).

■ Communal open fields were retained in common by the *mir* and could be used by all ex-serfs.

■ Peasants kept the land surrounding the cottage (known as *usad'ba*) and received additional allocations of land according to their position and the decision of the *mir*. They could sometimes buy up additional strips of land.

■ '*Volosts*' were established to supervise the *mirs*. These had their own communal courts (from 1863) and provided for some degree of peasant self-government, replacing the landlords' jurisdiction over serfs.

The abolition of serfdom was a huge undertaking. In theory, the emancipation of the 21 million private landlords' serfs in Russia was supposed to happen over two years, but in practice it took over 20 years. Around 15 per cent of peasants still remained 'temporarily obligated' to their landlords until 1881, when redemption was made compulsory.

The following extract is taken from a biography of Ivan Turgenev by Henri Troyat (Turgenev's profile is on page 12).

> (Turgenev) was in Paris when he heard about the publication of the Imperial Manifesto of 19th February, 1861, emancipating the serfs. It caused him such joy that although he claimed to have no sense of religion, he attended a thanksgiving service at the Orthodox Church. He was eager to get back to Russia and see the thrilling effects of emancipation with his own eyes. Finally on April 21st, 1861 he set out. As soon as he got to Spasskoye (his estate), he tackled the business of organising his peasants' lives. The system was complicated and unpopular with both the landowners, who felt they were being despoiled of a possession justly handed down to them by their forebears, and the *muzhiks* (serfs), who could not see why their masters' lands should not be made over to them *in toto* and without payment of any kind. Turgenev, who had been anticipating an explosion of joy among the latter, was disappointed. Instead of a brotherly drawing-together of liberated serfs and their former masters, he observed a rising tide of mistrust, trickery and hostility on both sides. Each was trying to get the better of the other.

5

■ Activity

Thinking point

Do you think Turgenev's disappointment with the Emancipation *Ukase* is typical of the reaction of those who supported it? Explain your answer.

Activity

Revision exercise

Before reading the next section, study the emancipation terms carefully and complete the following table:

The Impact of the Emancipation *Ukase*

Peasant gains	Peasant losses	Possible problems in implementing the order.

Add to your table, if necessary, as you read through the next section.

The practice of emancipation

Fig. 7 *Celebrations in the streets of Moscow after the emancipation of the serfs*

The Act was not an unqualified success. Both peasants and landowners felt their interests had not been fully met, although at least one intention of the Act – a drive to greater modernisation of the economy – was certainly assisted by this move. As so often happens, there were winners and losers. The 'winners' included those peasants who did well out of the land allocations and were astute enough to buy up extra land from their less prosperous neighbours. These *Kulaks* increased the size of their estates and produced surplus grain to sell for export. Some landowners too found that the compensation offered enabled them to get out of debt and invest more – perhaps in industrial enterprises. The decline of labour services thus contributed to the growth of a money-based economy and encouraged enterprise, so stimulating (although still only to a limited degree) the growth of railways, banking, industry and cities. Furthermore, for those former serfs prepared to sell their lands and forfeit their rights within the *mir*, the opportunity to move to an industrialising city and earn regular wages must have been tempting. In *The Industrialisation of Russia* (1972), M.E. Falkus argued that large numbers of internal passports, allowing peasants to leave the *mirs*, were issued after 1861, which helped the industrial labour supply.

However, for the 'losers' the picture seemed less rosy. Even though the annual amount demanded in redemption payments was roughly equal to what had been paid in feudal dues before the emancipation, many peasants resented the requirement to pay any redemption payments for land which they regarded as their own and which had been in their families for generations. In some cases, they had even been granted less land than they had previously farmed or were required to pay higher dues than previously. Even when they did receive an allocation of land which equalled that held before, it was not always enough to live on once other former 'props' – including the use of common land, the right to graze their cattle on pasture land, to collect firewood and to receive some protection form their landlords in times of hardship – had gone.

Since the local and provincial nobility supervised the setting up of the *volosts* and *mirs*, they were usually in a position to ensure that they received the best land for themselves. They could also set the price of the land (which the peasants had to pay for) above its market value. In some of the less productive areas, this was as much as 90 per cent higher than it should have been. This made the peasants' redemption payments unfairly high, and to meet them some peasants had to continue to work for their old masters, or to rent land from them, paid for with half the crops grown on it. These high redemption payments – and the long-term scale of them – reduced the purchasing power of peasants, so failing to stimulate industrial production through consumer demand as much as intended.

The average peasant plot was about nine acres, and although this varied considerably across the country, it was hardly big enough to enable peasants to adopt new methods and farm efficiently, as the *ukase* had intended. Furthermore, in the more fertile regions of the country, the peasants saw the greatest fall in the size of their holdings. In the Ukraine, for example, they fell by 30.8 per cent in size. Subsistence farming and technical backwardness continued and in 1878 only 50 per cent of the peasantry was capable of producing a surplus. This meant that a large proportion of the rural population was still liable to famine and insufficient investment in the land prevented agriculture developing to a point where it could finance industrialisation.

Some peasants fell into debt and were forced to sell out to the *kulaks*, who became a new source of resentment in the countryside, whilst the landless became labourers and were forced to seek work for a wage. Personal serfs, who received no land, also became dependent on wages and swelled this group. However, industrial development failed to keep pace with the increased numbers of such workers who drifted to the towns in search of work.

The *mir* system also proved to be a highly conservative institution which stood in the way of agricultural innovation. Peasants were required to co-operate together within the commune and land was regularly redistributed as family circumstances changed. (Each male child born in the *mir*, for example, had a right to land.) Such controls meant that peasants did not, in practice, have full civil rights but were legally and economically tied to the commune. Freedom to travel or move (which was possible only with an internal passport issued by the *mir*) was severely restricted. This had a detrimental effect on the development of industry, which required a mobile labour force.

■ Did you know?

Many aspects of later Communist Russia can be traced back to the activities of the *mir*. The meetings of the village assemblies required unanimous binding decisions – a system echoed in Communist times when all party members had to agree a decision and opposition was banned. The *mir*'s control of internal passports was a precursor to the Communist state's control over people's freedom of movement, while the telephone tapping and examination of private mail by Communist secret police would later echo the *mir*, where the community knew all the personal affairs of its members.

The Emancipation *Ukase* was not entirely satisfactory for the landowners either. Many had not wanted it at all and their fears seemed to be fulfilled as unrest in the countryside continued and, in some areas, was even exacerbated by the measure. Disputes broke out over landholding and redemption payments and for some landowners it was a frightening time. In the four months following the decree, there were 647 incidents of riot and it was sometimes even necessary to call in the army to restore order. (The bloody suppression of a peasant riot in Bezdna, in Kazan, left 70 dead.)

Furthermore, although landowners received compensation, the act did not end the spate of noble bankruptcies and the profits they had expected from the measure did not always materialise. Fifty per cent of the money received in government bonds was used to pay off existing debts and by 1905 the nobility had been forced to sell around a third of the land it had owned in 1861, while 50 per cent of that remaining was mortgaged. The loss of land and local political and economic influence led some landowners to sell up and move to the towns, taking with them their resentment of the government whom they blamed for their losses. The majority remained in the countryside where some found fulfilment in the new *zemstva* and were increasingly attracted by the intellectual movement opposing tsarist autocracy.

Cross-reference

The new *zemstva* will be discussed below, pages 22–3.

Activities

Group activities

1   Divide into three groups to consider the impact of the Emancipation *Ukase* for:
    ■ the tsar and his government
    ■ the nobility
    ■ the peasantry.

You should write a speech and deliver your verdict to the rest of your group. In each case, try to make some positive and some negative comments.

2   In groups of four or five, create an informative wallchart about the emancipation of the serfs in 1861. You should include:
    ■ key reasons for the legislation, with explanations
    ■ obstacles to emancipation before 1861
    ■ factual information about the legislation
    ■ a balanced evaluation of the legislation.

Try to present the wallchart in the most clear and attractive way possible.

Alexander's subsequent reforms and their impact

The emancipation legislation ushered in a whole range of further reforms as its changes to the rights and position of both the peasants and the landowners had wide implications for both society and government. Influential figures, such as the brothers Nicholas Alexander and Dmitrii Milyutin, were anxious to see reform go further, but the widespread disappointment provoked by the terms of the emancipation statute also contributed. Peasants felt cheated while landowners resented their loss of influence. As the relatively free press fanned the flames further and a wave of student protests and riots occurred in St Petersburg, Moscow and Kazan, the government was forced to respond – and this brought a mixture of further reforms as well as repression.

■ **Key profiles**

The Milyutin Brothers

Nicholas Alexander (1818–72) joined the Ministry of Internal Affairs in 1835, after graduating from Moscow University, and he became an influential voice in favour of reform within the Slavophile tradition. By 1859 he had reached the rank of assistant minister and he was largely responsible for drafting the terms of the Emancipation *Ukase* of 1861. He was also involved in the deliberations leading to the establishment of the *Zemstva* although he resigned in 1866, shortly after their establishment.

Dmitrii (1816–1912) opted for the career of a soldier and trained in a military academy, but after receiving a major wound whilst fighting, he became a professor within the academy. He earned a reputation as a military scholar and it was he who analysed the reasons behind Russia's defeat in the Crimean War. He was an obvious choice for Alexander II's minister of war from 1861–81, and in this position he carried through some major army reforms. He was made a count in recognition of his services and in 1898 became Russia's last Field Marshal.

Military reforms (1874–75)

Military reform was a priority. Not only had the disaster of the Crimea highlighted the need for changes to traditional practices, emancipation had also removed the means of conscripting serfs to provide for the rank and file. Consequently, Dmitrii Milyutin, the minister of war 1861–81, set about a wholesale reorganisation of the armed forces to remove abuses that had become apparent during the Crimean campaign and to create a smaller, more professional, more efficient and less expensive army.

- Service in the army could no longer be given by the courts as a punishment.
- Military colonies (where conscripts were forced to live) were abandoned. Better provisioning and medical care was established.
- Length of service was reduced from 25 years to 15 years (with just 6 years actually in the army and 9 years in the reserves).
- Conscription was made compulsory for all classes (including nobles) from the age of 20 – although education could reduce the length of service.
- Corporal punishment and flogging were abolished and military punishments made less severe.

Other improvements:

- Modern weaponry was introduced, iron-clad steamships built and strategic railways constructed so as to improve the transport of troops and provisions.
- Military Colleges were set up (accepting non-noble recruits) to provide better training for the officer corps. Privates could rise to officer rank by merit.
- Fifteen regional commands were established, the military code was reviewed and changes made to procedures in the military courts. A new code of conduct was drawn up for the soldiers and sailors.

Despite some determined opposition from the nobility and merchants, Alexander gave his assent to the reforms in 1874 and they were put into

War against Turkey 1877–78

In an attempt to recover the losses of the Crimean War, in 1877, the Russians went to war in support of the Balkan states which were fighting against Turkish rule. In March 1878 after some hard fighting, Russia concluded the Treaty of San Stefano with Turkey. This freed Romania, Serbia, and Montenegro from Turkish rule, gave autonomy to Bosnia and Herzegovina, and created a large Bulgaria under Russian protection. Alarmed by such Russian gains, Britain and Austria-Hungary forced Russia to accept the Treaty of Berlin (July 1878), which split up the new Bulgaria.

■ Activities

Discussion points

1 Why do you think 'nobles and merchants' in particular opposed the military reforms?

2 Why do you think the Russian army performed badly in the wars of 1877–78, 1904–05 and 1914–17, despite the military reforms?

■ Key terms

Electoral Colleges and representation: In a system of electoral colleges individuals vote for others who then cast votes on their behalf. In this case, the peasants would elect members of an 'electoral college'. The electoral college would vote for nominee(s) to sit on the *zemstvo*. The nobles, townspeople and Church did the same. Proportionately, the nobles, which dominated the *zemstva*, had more influence than the peasants.

effect from 1875. They did, as intended, create a smaller but better-trained army and in turn reduced the very heavy government expenditure which the army had incurred. Literacy within the army began to improve, with mass army-education capaigns in the 1870s–90s, although there were still substantial numbers of illiterate peasant recruits who could not benefit from the training on offer. Furthermore, although the system was fairer, the well-to-do found substitutes to serve in their place and the officer class remained largely composed of aristocrats. It therfore remained, in essence, a peasant conscript army and the problems of supply and leadership were by no means fully resolved. When the military was tested in the war against Turkey (1877–78), victory took far longer than expected. Furthermore, Russia was also to suffer defeat on land and at sea, at the hands of the Japanese in 1904–05 and again by Germany in 1914–17.

Local government reforms (1864–70)

Fig. 8 *Despite the abolition of serfdom, peasants sought further reform: police visit the home of a suspected dissident*

Although the emancipation of the serfs had been proclaimed by imperial decree, the changes it brought about needed to be effectively administered to ensure that the legislation was put into practice at a local level. What is more, the abolition of serf-owners' rights over the local population left a void which had to be filled. As well as possessing local legal and judicial control, the serf-owners had, for example, been responsible for the construction of local roads, the provision of fencing and the repair of bridges, so new provision had to be made for such tasks. New institutions of local government also provided an opportunity to respond to the demands of the liberal nobles for greater representation in government.

A Commission was appointed in 1860, chaired at first by Nicholas Alexander Milyutin and subsequently by Pyotr Valuev, minister for internal affairs, and in 1864 the following changes were put into effect:

■ There was to be a system of elected local councils, both at district (*Uezd*) and provincial levels, known as *zemstva* (singular *zemstvo*).

■ The *zemstva* were to be elected bodies, chosen through a system of '**electoral colleges**'. There would be separate electoral colleges for nobles, townspeople, Church and peasants, but votes would be arranged in a way that allowed the nobility to dominate.

■ The *zemstva* were to have a range of powers to make improvements to public services such as roads, schools, public health and gaols as well as to develop industrial projects.

■ *Zemstva* were to administer poor relief in times of hardship.

In 1870 this reform was extended to towns, when *dumas* (elected town councils) were set up in urban areas.

These reforms established a degree of representative government at a local level, but the hopes of reformers that Alexander would go on to grant a representative National Assembly were not fulfilled. Nevertheless, most landowners and officials approved the limited changes. The nobility retained many of the positions of authority in these new organisations, which partly compensated them for their loss of power over their serfs and even some radicals accepted these developments as a first step on the path of change. Certainly the *zemstva* were generally to prove a valuable addition to local government, not least because they were composed of men who understood the locality and its needs. They were particularly effective in the fields of education and welfare, extending and improving local provision as a matter of pride.

Since they tended to be filled by liberal-minded professional people, such as doctors, lawyers, teachers and scientists, they were also to provide a forum for debate about and criticism of the central government and they were to be at the forefront of demands for reform in the later 19th and early 20th centuries. However, despite allowing some limited peasant representation, they were never truly 'people's assemblies' and there was a tendency for them to preserve the interests of those who sat on them.

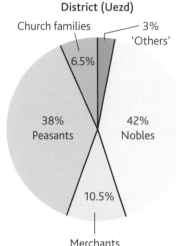
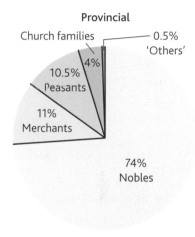

Fig. 9 *Representation in the* zemstva, *1865–67*

The powers of the *zemstva* and *dumas* also remained limited. They had no control over state and local taxes and the appointment of officials and maintenance of law and order remained with the Provincial Governors, appointed by the tsar, who could also overturn their decisions if he chose. Furthermore, they only spread slowly. By 1914, only 43 of the 70 provinces of Russia had actually established a provincial assembly.

Judicial reforms (1864)

Under Nicholas I, the codification of Russian law (reducing the number of laws, bringing them up-to-date and clarifying their meaning) had begun. There was therefore already work in progress for the Ministry of Justice, but the new freedom given to the serfs demanded a further overhaul of the law, particularly that concerning property rights and contracts. The landowning class also wanted protection from any backlash and challenge from the newly emancipated population, whilst emancipation made a change to the corrupt and secretive system of local justice necessary.

Before emancipation a serf had possessed very little chance of obtaining justice. He was always presumed guilty, unless proven innocent and he was given no chance to defend himself. His case was simply looked at by a judge examining written evidence, usually prepared by the landowner and police. There was no jury, no lawyers and no examination of witnesses, and the judge's decision was final. This system of Russian law had been subject to heavy criticism from the intellectuals for its inequality and slowness – another instance of Russia's backwardness in comparison with the West.

After three years' consideration by the Council of State, the minister of justice, Dmitrii Zamyatnin, introduced a new legal system in 1864. It consisted of local courts under justices of the peace for minor offences, and district courts, judicial chambers and the Senate for graver ones. It was modelled on systems in the West, especially in terms of openness and procedure.

- The principle of equality before the law (as opposed to separate courts for different classes) was established.
- Criminal cases at district level were to be heard before barristers and a jury, selected from lists of property owners above a certain level, drawn up by the *zemstva*. Judges were appointed by the tsar.
- Proceedings were to be open to the public and conducted orally. The accused could see the judge and employ a defence counsel.
- Judicial chambers were courts of appeal for cases heard in district courts and responsible for jurisdiction in certain high crimes – with judges appointed by the tsar.
- Judges were given better training and pay (so they were less open to bribery).
- The senate heard appeals and was the court of first instance for the most dangerous crimes.
- Local courts with magistrates dealt with minor offences and could not impose a sentence of more than one year's imprisonment. These magistrates were elected every three years by the *zemstva*. They were to be independent from political control.
- *Volost* courts were established to deal with 'peasants leaving serf dependence'. They dealt with minor offences, and judges in these courts were peasants, who had to be literate and without convictions. They were elected for three years by the peasants.
- *Volost* courts could give reprimands, fines of up to 300 roubles and prison sentences of between three months and a year.
- Freedom of the Press was extended to legal reporting, which was now to be recorded verbatim in a government newspaper called The *Russian Courier*.

The system established was clearly much fairer and less corrupt than that known previously and helped establish the rule of law in Russia. Opening up the courts to the public was particularly popular and cases sometimes attracted large numbers. Laywers could become 'celebrities' and the career attracted numbers of the growing intelligentsia. However, open courts also gave articulate lawyers an opportunity to criticise the regime and the use of the jury system could undermine government control. In 1878, for example, Vera Zasulich was acquitted of terrorism. After this it was established that political crimes and those by high ranking officials were to be tried by special procedures under the Ministry of Internal Affairs. Revolutionaries were routinely dealt with by the Third Section until 1880 and still faced arbitrary arrest and trial in special courts.

There were other limitations too. Trial by jury was never established in Poland, the western provinces and the Caucuasus, while ecclesiastical and military courts were excluded from the reforms and the peasantry in the *volost* courts were still treated differently from those of higher status.

A closer look

The case of Vera Zasulich, 1878

Vera Zasulich (1849–1919) was the daughter of an impoverished noble who became involved in radical politics. Her trial, in 1878, followed others a year earlier, when the government had tried to make an example of those arrested for revolutionary activities. The trials were widely and sensationally reported by the free press and provided a platform for the radicals to air their views and justify their actions in public. In July 1877, a political prisoner, Alexei Bogolyubov refused to remove his cap in the presence of General

SAINT-PÉTERSBOURG. — Tentative d'assassinat contre le général Trepov, chef de la police. — (Dessin de M. Meaulle, notre correspondant à Saint...)

Fig. 10 *Vera Ivanovna Zasulich, a leading terrorist, shoots and wounds Police Chief Trepov in retaliation for his brutality. She was later tried but acquitted by a sympathetic court*

Trepov, the Governor of St Petersburg. In retaliation, Trepov ordered that Bogolyubov be flogged with sticks, which outraged the revolutionaries and sympathetic members of the intelligentsia. A group of six revolutionaries plotted to kill Trepov but Zasulich acted first. She shot and seriously wounded him but at her widely publicised trial, despite her obvious guilt, a sympathetic jury found her 'not guilty' in an attempt to stand up to the authorities. She fled before she could be rearrested and went on to become a Populist.

Cross-reference

For more on the Populist movement, look ahead to pages 38–39.

Educational reform (1863–64)

While Alexander's authority emanated from his special relationship with God, which gave the Russian Orthodox Church a privileged position in Russian society, the need to educate Russians in order to 'catch up with the West' ran counter to the conservatism of the Church, which had been the key force in the education of Russian students in both schools and universities. The abolition of serfdom increased the need for basic literacy and numeracy among peasants trying to run their newly-acquired private smallholdings. Although suspicion of mass education beyond a basic level prevailed, nevertheless the establishment of the *zemstva* provided an opportunity for changes in the control and development of education, as well as an opportunity to rationalise the funding of educational institutions.

The liberal-minded Alexander Golovnin was minister for education from 1862–67 and under his direction:

- The universities were given the opportunity to govern themselves in 1863, appointing their own staff, subject to the approval of the Ministry of Education.

- In 1864, responsibility for schooling was transferred from the Church to the *zemstva*.

■ Primary and secondary education was extended throughout the country – and 'modern schools' established at secondary level for those who did not want the traditional classical education offered in the '*gymnazii*'. Students could progress from both to university.

■ Schools were declared 'open to all' regardless of class and sex (allowing women to attend secondary school for non-vocational education from 1870).

The number of primary schools rose from 8,000 in 1856 to 23,000 in 1880, and the number of children in primary education from 400,000 to over a million. However, the primary curriculum, with the aim of *'strengthening religious and moral notions and spreading basic knowledge'* was still restricted. At secondary level students had a choice of study in classics or modern subjects, although these still largely remained the preserve of the professional and upper classes. The number of students in the universities grew – from 3,600 to 10,000 by the 1870s – but this had the side effect of increasing the number of radical and militant thinkers. Indeed, the education reforms were so 'successful' that after 1866, it was deemed necessary to reassert government control.

Censorship reform (1858–70)

In accordance with the greater 'liberalisation' of the new reign, there was an initial relaxation of press censorship, which, under Nicholas I, had extended to all books and newspapers.

■ In 1863 censorship was placed under the contol of the Ministry for Internal Affairs.

■ 1865 the press and book publishers received a new codification of regulations which reduced some of the restrictions (e.g. advance approval for all titles) which had previously existed concerning published material.

■ Foreign publications could be sold in Russia, with government approval.

■ The Ministry of Internal Affairs could stop publications and fine publishers but the new legal system provided a fairer court system in which to challenge censorship.

■ In 1865 the press was allowed to print editorials with comment on government policy for the first time.

Such changes encouraged a growth in the numbers of books, journals and newspapers on sale in Russia. The numbers of books published, for example, grew from 1,020 in 1855 to 1,836 in 1864 and 10,691 by 1894. However, editors were still subject to a degree of censorship – particularly since there were still both military and Church censors and the government was very wary of anything that suggested subversion (although they sometimes made mistakes, as when Chernyshevsky's book of 1864, *What is to be done?*, inciting peasants to rebellion, was allowed to be published!). Nevertheless, the growth in critical writing encouraged a clampdown in the 1870s and by the end of Alexander's reign, censorship had become much tighter again.

Economic reforms (1860–78)

Alexander wanted to restore Russian prestige and win international respect though imperialism and military success. To achieve this, the Russian economy needed a huge boost in order to provide funds, not only for the military but also for other areas of the Russian state and society.

Cross-reference

Chernyshevsky is discussed further on page 35.

Mikhail von Reutern (minister of finance, 1862–78) produced some of Alexander's most successful reforms during his long tenure of this post.

- The Treasury was reformed. A new system for collecting taxes, establishing budgets and auditing the accounts of government departments was put in place.
- Tax-farming (whereby groups bought the right to collect certain taxes) was abolished.
- Banks and credit facilities were extended with the establishment of a state bank in 1860, municipal banks in 1862 and a savings bank in 1869.
- Liberal trade policies and lower tariffs were introduced.
- Government subsidies were offered to enable private entrepreneurs to develop the railways.
- Foreign investment in Russia was encouraged with a government-guaranteed annual dividend.
- Other industrial initiatives were encouraged. These included supporting the development of the cotton industry (seizing the opportunity created by the American Civil War 1861–65 to capture former American markets), and the beginning of mining in the Donets Coalfield.

Key profile

Mikhail von Reutern

Mikhail von Reutern (1820–90) was a German from the Russian Baltic landowning class who rose to become minister of finance 1862–78. He believed that state money and control should direct economic change and he used his position to carry these beliefs into action. He particularly encouraged the development of railways – selling contracts to many of his own friends and acquaintances. He became Chairman of the Council of Ministers in 1881.

Although slow, industrial development became noticeable under Alexander II and agriculture also enjoyed a boom. Not all of this was because of government initiative, but the framework laid down by Reutern and other reforms, such as emancipation, certainly encouraged and supported the expansion. For example, former tax farmers looked to invest elsewhere while government subsidies and trade treaties stimulated growth.

However, despite the improvements, Russia's economy remained comparatively weak. The budget was not subject to public scrutiny and there was no fundamental reform of the taxation system. Sixty-six per cent of government revenue still came from indirect taxation, which placed a heavy burden on the peasantry. Furthermore, a third of all government expenditure went on the repayment of debts and the Russian currency – the rouble – was subject to wild variations in its value. Although the output of grain and industrial goods had begun to increase, there were still severe limitations, not least the limited domestic market, which was not helped by the slow speed in the increase of railway construction during Alexander's reign.

Fig. 11 *The Church was an important instrument of government*

Church reforms (1867–69)

The Orthodox Church had a close bond with the tsarist regime. Its influence over the peasantry had been hugely beneficial to the regime as a means of controlling the masses. However, in 1858 a report on the poverty and ineptitude of the rural clergy had been written by Ivan Belliustin. Largely as a result of these revelations, the minister of internal affairs, Pyotr Valuev, set up an Ecclesiastical Commission to look into the Church organisation and practice in 1862. It was important to the government in the uncertain times following emancipation that the Church maintained the respect of the people, and helped implant loyalty to the state. If the Church were open to criticism, or did not toe the official line, it was feared that the authority of tsardom would be weakened.

The bureaucracy was slow to act and by the time the Commission set out its proposals in 1868, the **reactionary** Dmitrii Tolstoy had become a primary influence. The 1868 reforms allowed talented, educated and charismatic priests to gain promotion to key positions in the Church hierarchy, but little was done to address the initial concern about clerical poverty or the suitability of rural priests to do their job.

Alexander's reign began with a relaxation of restrictions in Poland, on Catholicism, the Polish language and other overt displays of Polish national identity. Similarly, in Finland, the Finnish language was encouraged, a representative assembly accepted as a semi-independent government, and other concessions were made. Even the Jews had some relaxation of the laws curtailing their activities. However, after 1863, the policies on Poland and the Jews were reversed, although Finland enjoyed its new freedoms until the reign of Alexander III.

■ Cross-reference

Dmitrii Tolstoy is profiled on page 32.

■ Key terms

Reactionary: the term used to describe someone who is backward-looking and wants to restore the past.

■ Cross-reference

See the *Did you know?* box on page 30 for more on the Polish revolt.

Summary question

Evaluative thinking and summary essay question

While there were clearly limitations to these reforms, there was an extraordinary amount of positive change. However, whether these changes were perceived as hugely beneficial or deeply unsettling depended on the perspective of those affected. This activity requires you to weigh up these different perspectives and to step outside modern perceptions of reform, looking at the changes from, for example, the point of view of the contemporary peasants, landowners, priests, military commanders, radical university students, the tsar and government officials. You will need to think carefully about how the reforms impinged on these people's lives – their concerns, their suspicions and their perspectives on new government initiatives.

1 Divide into pairs or groups. Each should consider the effects of the reforms of Alexander II's reign for *one* of the groups listed in the table below.

The impact of reforms on:	Positive	Negative
Military Reform		
Local Government Reform		
Judicial Reform		
Educational Reform		
Economic Reform		
Church Reform		

2 In a whole group session, discuss and justify your various suggestions.

3 Write a response to the question: 'How successful were Alexander II's reforms in transforming Russian society?'

2 Hopes betrayed; reaction and opposition

Did you know?

There had been a revolt in Poland in 1863 which explains why the tsar's immediate presumption was that his would-be assassin was a disaffected Pole.

On April 4th 1866, Tsar Alexander II was just stepping out of his summer garden when a shot was fired. Whether it was a quick-witted peasant, Ossip Komissarov, who had lept forward and struck the arm of the assassin forcing the bullet to go astray, as the 'official' version of events later claimed, or whether it was simply a shout from a guard which distracted the would-be assassin, as the latter claimed, we shall never know, but the bullet missed. The tsar was saved but severely shaken. 'Are you Polish?' he demanded of the gun-wielding peasant who was rapidly apprehended. 'No, a pure Russian', he replied. That a 'pure Russian' should be attempting to assassinate his beloved tsar was bad enough, but when it later turned out that Dimitrii Karakozov was not a peasant at all, but an erstwhile student of noble blood, the scenario grew worse still. Had all the tsar's reforming instincts led only to this? The poet Tiutchev even penned a poem:

> Everything, everything in us has been insulted by this shot,
> And there is no escaping the insult:
> A disgraceful stain lies, alas,
> On the whole history of the Russian people

While the tsar proceeded directly to Kazan Cathedral to thank God and pray for his miraculous escape, public displays of rejoicing outside the Winter Palace, endless anthems in the theatres and a semi-party atmosphere on the streets helped reaffirm the sense of popular devotion on which the autocracy relied. Alexander thanked his ministers the next day for, *'that devotion and those feelings that are constantly expressed to me in all difficult cases from you, the nobility, as from all other estates'.* Komissarov was granted hereditary nobility; the ministers sat down to reflect on what had gone wrong.

The extent of reaction before 1881

The attempt on his life undermined Alexander's confidence in his mission. Only a year earlier his eldest son and heir had died and his wife, suffering from tuberculosis, had withdrawn from public appearances. The tsar had sought consolation at the hands of a mistress, Caterina Dolgoruki, who was to bear him four children (and whom he eventually married in 1880, with rather indecent haste, 40 days after the death of his first wife). This liaison both mentally and physically distanced him from the reforming elements within his own family – his brother the grand Duke Constantine and the Grand Duchess Elena. Alexander subsequently grew ever more aloof and he became less inclined to resist those who urged him to adopt a harsher line.

The assassination attempt gave conservatives and churchmen the ammunition with which to attack reformist

Fig. 1 *No-one could feel safe from the activities of the tsarist secret police*

policies which they had never liked. According to the modern historian, Richard Pipes:

> The Emperor faced the solid opposition of the rank and file of the bureaucracy as well as that of his son and heir-apparent, the future Alexander III. The radicals unwittingly assisted this conservative party. Every time they made an attempt on the life of the tsar or assassinated some high official, opponents of political reform could press for more stringent police measures and further postponement of basic reforms. The terrorists could not have been more effective in scuttling political reform had they been on the police payroll.

1

At court, reactionary ministers hinted that the tsar's reforming instincts had gone too far, weakening the props which the imperial monarchy relied on – the Church and the nobility. They argued that the state needed to be purged of the 'foreign influences' which were undermining it – both the dangerous and uncontrollable 'western' ideas which were spreading through the liberal universities and being discussed in the press and, more literally, the ethnic minorities and their different religions which were seen as diluting Russian strength.

The conservatives were not against all the changes that Alexander II had initiated. Reutern's reforms of the economy and Milyutin's of the army, for example, were seen as essential to the future of Russia and these two ministers were allowed to continue in their positions. However, in more controversial areas, Alexander was persuaded to make a spate of new appointments in 1866, replacing those more liberally inclined with staunch reactionaries. The changes included:

- The replacement of the liberal Golovnin by Dmitrii Tolstoy as minister for public instruction.
- The appointment of Pyotr Shuvalov as head of the Third Section (The Secret Police).
- The appointment of Alexander Timashev to replace Pyotr Valuev as minister of internal affairs.
- The promotion of Konstantin Pahlen to minister of justice.

Education

A tight control over education was regarded as essential if western liberal ideas were to be eradicated and the growing flow of criticism of the autocracy stemmed. The conservatives feared that an educated populace would be a rebellious one and Count Dmitrii Tolstoy seemed the ideal person to reinstate tight controls over schools and universities. He was a staunch Orthodox believer and had a reputation as a pillar of conservatism.

Under his leadership, the *zemstva*'s powers over education were reduced and the Church was restored to a position of prominence in rural schools, while the higher schools, or *gymnazii*, were ordered to follow a traditional classical curriculum and abandon their experimentation with the natural sciences. From 1871, only students from these traditional *gymnazii* were allowed to progress to universities, while those at the modern technical schools were limited to higher technical institutions, where they would not be exposed to the 'corrupting' influence of the universities.

Government control was also extended over what could be taught in universities and here too, more liberal courses were replaced by a traditional curriculum. Subjects that encouraged critical thought such as Literature, Science, Modern Languages and History were forced out, while Maths, Latin, Greek and Divinity, which were all believed to discourage the contemplation of the future of society, were encouraged. In 1873 the Ministry of Internal Affairs was given the right to forbid certain topics from discussion and censorship was tightened once again in the later 1870s. A strict control over student activities was also exercised, including a ban on extra-curricular student organisations.

Consequently, although there was an extension in public education throughout this period and more teacher training colleges (under state control) were set up, education came to be seen as yet another way of enforcing tsarist control, rather than as a way of helping people to better themselves. Tolstoy reluctantly accepted Moscow University's decision to organise lectures for women, but he used the government's right to veto university appointments wherever he felt it necessary and any academics or students who wanted greater freedom to pursue their own studies were forced to attend universities abroad.

Key profile

Dmitrii Tolstoy

Count Dmitrii Andreyevich Tolstoy (1823–89) was of noble birth and, after university, entered state sevice, firstly in the Ministry of the Navy and then as Over-Procurator of the Holy Synod in 1865–80. In 1866 he also became a member of the State Council and he held the post of minister of public instruction (Education) between 1866 and 1880. From 1882 to 1889, Tolstoy was the minister of internal affairs and Chief of the Gendarmerie. He was elected President of the St Petersburg Academy of Sciences in 1882 and wrote a number of books on Russian history.

The police and the law courts

Fig. 2 *Prisoners were subject to cruel treatment on their way to exile in Siberia*

Pyotr Shuvalov worked to strengthen the police and stepped up the activities of the Third Section who were responsible for rooting out subversion, while Konstantin Pahlen ensured that the judicial system made an example of those accused of political agitation. Even radicals who fled the country and settled in Switzerland or Germany were liable to be tracked down by the Third Section and recalled to face justice.

Pahlen held some open 'show' trials which members of the public were invited to witness, with the intention of deterring others from similar activity, but the whole experiment backfired. The 'Trial of 50' and the 'Trial of 193', both set up to prosecute those arrested for involvement in revolutionary populist activities, were a resounding failure for the minister. At the latter 153 of the 193 defendants were acquitted and the others received only light sentences from a sympathetic jury.

The passionate speeches given by the defence were reported word for word in the press and this gave the revolutionaries plenty of publicity. The government was made to appear incompetent, so, in 1878, it was announced that political crimes would be transferred from the civil courts to the military, where cases could be heard, and sentences passed, in secret.

Attitude to ethnic minorities

Accompanying these reactionary policies came a harsher policy towards the ethnic minorites within the Russian Empire. A rebellion in Poland in 1863, which was only crushed after fierce fighting in 1864, persuaded the authorities that non-Russian peoples were a danger to the Empire and this gave rise to the policy of Russification. Although this did not flourish as 'official' state policy until the reign of Alexander II's successor, Alexander III, a more hostile attitude towards the Poles, Finns, Jews and other minority races became apparent in the years after 1866. Not surprisingly, the consequence of such action was the growth, rather than the lessening, of the number of discontented intellectuals within Russia and a spread of opposition with a large student input.

For the reformers, the changed climate proved an anti-climax. According to Milyutin:

> Count Shuvalov has terrified the Emperor with his daily reports about frightful dangers to which, allegedly, the state and the sovereign himself are exposed. Under the pretext of the protection of the Emperor's person and of the monarchy, Shuvalov interferes in everything and all matters are decided in accordance with his whisperings. He has surrounded the Emperor with his people. All new appointments are made at his instructions. What a devastating and disgusting contrast with the atmosphere in which I entered the government 13 years ago! Then, everything was striving forwards; now everything is pulling backwards.

2

The late 1870s proved a time of political crisis in Russia as the Russo-Turkish war of 1877–78 failed to bring a swift victory and a poor harvest, resulting in famine in 1879–80, was coupled with the beginnings of an industrial recession. Searches and arrests were stepped up and new governor-generals were set up in 1879 with emergency powers to prosecute in military courts and exile political offenders.

In 1879 and again in February 1880 there were further attempts on the tsar's life. Alexander II was severely shaken by these demonstrations of disloyalty and decided to set up a commission under General Loris-Melikov to investigate how best to reduce revolutionary activity.

Loris-Melikov made some immediate ministerial changes and instituted a series of concessions, such as the release of political prisoners, the relaxation of censorship the removal of the salt-tax and a lifting of restrictions on the activities of the *zemstva*. The Third Section was also abolished and its powers transferred to the regular police, although a special section which became known as the *Okhrana* was created, and soon became just as feared and oppressive.

Loris-Melikov produced a report in 1880, designed to meet the demands of the *zemstva* for an extension of representative government at national level. It considered the inclusion of elected representatives of the nobility,

Cross-reference

The trials of 1877 and the trial in 1878 of Vera Zasulich is outlined on pages 24–25.

The spread of discontent among intellectuals and students, including Populist activities, will be discussed on pages 38–39.

Russification is discussed in more detail on page 70–71.

The war against Turkey is outlined on page 22.

The 1880 attempt on the Tsar's life is described later on page 41.

Activity

Research and talking point

Find out as much information as you can about the work of the security services in Russia at this time. You should focus on the Third Section, the methods they used, the trials and detention of suspects, and their treatment of political prisoners in the tsar's prisons. Compare this to the treatment of political prisoners in other societies either in the past or the present day. How effective are such methods of control? Are such methods justifiable in any circumstances?

■ **Key terms**

Constitution: a set of rules by which a country is governed, i.e. regarding where power lies and which bodies should make laws and how.

■ **Activity**

Here are three assessments of the reforming activity of Alexander II's reign:

1. bold and adventurous

2. half-hearted and over-cautious

3. inadequate and misdirected.

Choose one of these as your theme and write an obituary for Alexander II in which you assess the reforms of his reign.

of the *zemstva*, and of the town governments in the discussions of the drafts of some state decrees. The project became known as the 'Loris-Melikov's Constitution', although it was not really a **constitution** for the running of the state at all.

Alexander II signed the report in the morning of March 13, 1881 and called for a meeting of the Council of Ministers to discuss the document. The same day the tsar was killed by a bomb.

■ Opposition to the tsarist regime

The reforms of Alexander II's reign were not only controversial in court circles, they also stimulated those who, from excitement or disappointment, saw the possibility of further change and were willing to use extremist tactics to achieve their ends. Opposition forces ranged from the mostly mildly-behaved *zemstva* which contained many of the liberally-minded intelligentsia, through the universities, the stronghold of the student radicals, right down to the merchants, small businessmen and the more prosperous peasantry. The *kulaks* in particular contained within its ranks some who, having obtained their freedom, were all the more more resentful of the remaining restrictions. Once the press was able to report more freely, criticism increased and when the regime tried to restrict publications once more in the later 1870s, censorship, which had previously been tolerated, became another source of discontent.

The intelligentsia

Although the intelligentsia was relatively tiny, since there existed so few literate and educated Russians at this time, their size and influence grew in the 1870s. The development of the law courts, as a result of reform, had produced an unexpected crop of professionally trained lawyers, skilled in the art of persuasion and ready to question and challenge autocratic practices. Similarly, the development of the *zemstva* (and later dumas) provided a new forum for debate, whilst the move towards greater independence and growth in the universities had led to a greater understanding among students and lecturers of the state of the country. Opposition was at its most acute among these intellectuals who were not only knowledgeable about western developments and had maybe travelled abroad, but also read, wrote in the press, went to the theatre and were determined to change what they believed to be outmoded and inhibiting Russian ways.

Some of the younger generation of the 1860s where inspired by the Nihilist movement. They wanted to sweep away everything from the past so that a new society could be born. The Nihilists believed in reason and science and were hostile not only to the tsar but to the Russian Orthodox Church. In 1862, a group of students published a manifesto, 'Young Russia' in which they argued that revolution was the only way forward:

> Society is at present divided into two groups that are hostile to one another because their interests are diametrically opposed. The party that is oppressed by all and humiliated by all is the party of the common people. Over it stands the landowners, the merchants, the government officials – in short all those who possess property, either inherited or acquired. At their heart stands the tsar. They cannot exist without him, nor he without them. There is only one way out of this oppressive and terrible situation which is destroying contemporary man and that is revolution – bloody and merciless revolution.

■ **Cross-reference**

The Nihlist movement is introduced on page 12.

3

The need for action was also encouraged by the works of a number of socialist intellectual thinkers, including Mikhail Bakunin. Bakunin has sometimes been described as an anarchist (a person who believes in no central government) because of his belief that the state crushed individual freedom and should therefore be removed. However, he was also a socialist in that he believed in the superiority of the peasant and suggested that state and private ownership of land should be replaced by collective ownership and that income should be determined by the number of hours worked. Bakunin was greatly influenced by Alexander Herzen, whom he met at university in Moscow. Like Bakunin, Herzen believed that Russia's existing social and political system had to go and that the peasant should be at the centre of a new social structure. However, he differed from Bakunin in preferring a system of socialism based on the *mir* within a central governmental regime. Another influential intellectual of the period was Chernyshevsky whose radical journal *The Contemporary* had an even wider circulation among intellectuals than Herzen's *The Bell*. He also placed his faith in the peasants as the revolutionary class and expressed his views in his book, *What is to be done?*, while imprisoned for his activities.

Fig. 3 *Mikhail Bakunin, the radical revolutionary*

All of these thinkers had one thing in common – they believed that the Russian state had to change and that there needed to be more individual freedom. In 1869, Mikhail Bakunin and Sergei Nechaev's *Catechism of a Revolutionary* was published in Switzerland but secretly smuggled into Russia. This exhorted opponents of autocracy to be merciless in their pursuit of revolution, laying aside all other attachments – family, friends, love, gratitude and even honour – in order to find the steely resolve to pursue a revolutionary path. The work included the famous lines:

> The Revolutionary is a doomed man. He has no private interests, no affairs, sentiments, ties, property nor even a name of his own. His entire being is devoured by one purpose, one thought, one passion – the revolution. Heart and soul, not merely by word but by deed, he has severed every link with the social order and with the entire civilised world; with the laws, good manners, conventions, and morality of that world. He is its merciless enemy and continues to inhabit it with only one purpose – to destroy it.

4

'Young Russia' called for radical change and when, in June 1862, a series of fires in St Petersburg destroyed over 2,000 shops, there were rumours that the radical students were responsible. A commission was appointed to investigate but came up with no better recommendation than that Sunday Schools should be closed. In 1863, 'the organisation' was set up by students at Moscow university and more calls for reform were heard after the setting up of the *zemstva* in 1864. The St Petersburg *zemstvo* almost immediately demanded a central body to co-ordinate the regional *zemstva*, but the tsar stood firm against the proposal. The increase in repression from 1866 onwards only increased the *zemstva* demands for constitutional change and heightened student idealism and determination.

Did you know?

Chernyshevsky's *What is to be done?* became very famous and inspired Lenin, who took the same title for one of his own works.

The beginnings of Marxism

Amidst this ferment of ideas, the views of Karl Marx began to circulate among the young extreme revolutionaries. Bakunin provided the first translation of the *Communist Manifesto* in Russian, in 1869, while the first volume of *Das Kapital* was published there in 1872.

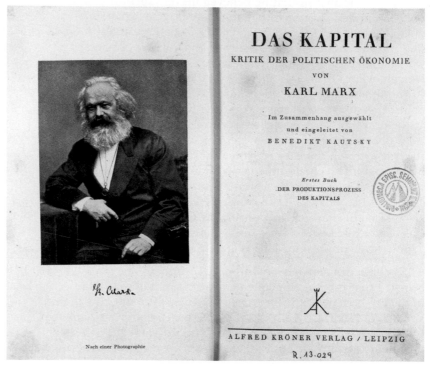

Fig. 4 *Das Kapital, showing a photograph of the author, Karl Marx*

Question

What changes would have to occur before Marxist ideas would find a wider audience within Russia?

Stage 1

Primitive Communism

Men performed the same economic function – hunter-gatherers. They worked together in order to survive. There was no private property and there were no classes. Eventually the most successful hunter-gatherer-warrior gained power and control over the others.

Stage 2

Imperialism

The strong man/Emperor ruled. He began by owning all the land but when threatened by outsiders, he would grant land to others in return for military services. A new land-owning aristocracy was therefore created.

Stage 3

Feudalism

Land was owned by the aristocracy who exploited the peasantry who worked it. There was a surplus of food which the aristocracy sold to others – creating a class of merchants and capitalists who wanted to share political power.

Stage 4

Capitalism

The wealthy merchants and factory owners (bourgeoisie) obtained political power and exploited the workers (proletariat). As the proletariat became politically aware they would rise up and overthrow the bourgeois government.

Stage 5

Socialism

There would be a 'dictatorship of the proletariat' as workers' organisations re-distributed food, goods and services fairly according to need, and profits were shared by all. The middle classes would come to understand that equality was superior to private ownership.

Stage 6

Communism

Everyone would join together for the common good. Money and government would no longer be needed and society would be class-less. As all countries reached this stage the world would become state-less and competition (and wars) would cease.

Fig. 5 *Marxist stage theory*

The theories of Karl Marx were based on the idea that all history was composed of class struggles. Marx had predicted that a struggle between the working class 'proletariat' and the factory-owning capitalist 'bourgeoisie' would ultimately herald, after a short dictatorship of the proletariat, the perfect 'communist' society in which everyone would be equal. Marxist teaching proved attractive intellectually, but in the 1870s its message seemed largely irrelevant to a predominantly rural state, with hardly any proletariat and still fewer bourgeoisie. Marxist discussion remained the preserve of a limited number of underground reading circles and societies.

Activity

Research task

Russian intellectuals in the second half of the nineteenth century were influenced by a host of writers and thinkers both from abroad and within Russia. As well as Marx, these included: foreigners, such as Engels, Mazzini, Blanqui, and Russians, such as Herzen, Nechayev, Lavrov, Bakunin and Chernyshevsky. Try to find out more about these thinkers and the views which they put forward.

Key profile

Karl Marx

Karl Marx (1818–83) was a German Jew who studied law and worked as a journalist. He moved from Germany to France in the early 1840s, but his writings on the social and economic conditions of Paris led to his expulsion from the city and he settled in Belgium. He wrote *The Communist Manifesto* with his friend Friedrich Engels in 1848, immediately prior to the European revolutions of 1848–49. After moving to London, he wrote his major work *Das Kapital*. The first volume was published in 1867 and subsequent ones (after Marx's death) in 1885 and 1894.

The Populists

In 1871, Sergei Nechyev, a radical of peasant extraction, who had been in exile with Bakunin in Switzerland, returned illegally to St Petersburg. He was dedicated to revolution and to carrying out Herzen's plea of 1869 to 'go to the people'. Although he was soon forced to flee again, after the murder of a student who disagreed with him, he inspired a circle of young revolutionaries, the 'Chaikovsky circle', which produced many pamphlets and smuggled in books officially banned in Russia in the years 1869 to 1872. This, in turn, led Pyotr Lavrov to lead a group of around 2,000 young men and women, mainly from the nobility and intelligentsia, in 1874, and 'go to the people'. These became known as the *narodniks* after the Russian '*v narod*' meaning 'to the people' or, in English, Populists.

Key terms

Socialist ideas: a belief that society should be egalitarian. In the 19th century this meant taking from the rich to give to the poor to create a more equal and fair society. The Populists believed, in particular, that the land should be shared among the peasants.

The Populists aimed to win over the peasantry to their **socialist ideas**, by stirring up their resentment against their lack of land and the heavy tax burden they still carried, despite emancipation. They believed that the future of Russia depended on land redistribution and the development of the peasant commune and some even tried dressing and talking like peasants to persuade the villagers of their importance to Russian society. This 'Populist' (*narodniki*) movement had an almost religious zeal about it, but the romantic illusions of the young were soon shattered by scenes of peasant hostility. The peasants' ignorance, superstition, prejudice and deep-rooted loyalty to the tsar ensured that by the autumn of 1874, 1,600 had been arrested.

A closer look

Mikhail Romas – a Populist

Mikhail Romas tried to put his populist ideas into action, sailing 30 miles down the River Volga to a small peasant village where he tried to organise a co-operative selling fruit and vegetables to a nearby town in return for cheap manufactured goods. He could have spared himself the effort. The peasants were suspicious. They could not understand why the prices in his co-operative store were so much cheaper than those offered by other merchants. Some richer peasants, who had made their own deals with urban merchants, filled one of his firewood logs with gunpowder, causing a minor explosion. Any poorer peasants who showed an interest in Romas' goods were intimidated and a poor peasant who had been acting as his assistant was brutally murdered. His mutilated body was left, in several pieces, along the bank of the river, as a warning to others. Eventually peasants blew up the shop (and half the village) by setting light to the kerosene store and then blamed Romas for the fire. Angry peasants set upon him and he was forced to flee for his life.

Activity
Creative thinking
Design a poster or write a short pamphlet encouraging fellow students to join the Populist cause and 'go to the people'. You should make it clear what you hope to achieve and what this will entail.

There was a second attempt to 'go to the people' in 1876, but when this proved no more successful than the first, some of those who had evaded capture, chose to adopt a new strategy. They set up 'Land and Liberty' (*Zemlya i volya*) in 1877, which was a more radical and better organised group which accepted the anarchic view of Bakunin that Russia's land should be handed over to the peasants and the State should be destroyed. Although the Narodniks had originally set out to win over the people in a low-key fashion, the thousands of arrests and the show trials which were held in 1877–78, at a time of war with Turkey, resulted in heightened tension. Members of Land and Liberty set out to find work within the peasant communes – as doctors, teachers or workmen and to use their positions to stir up the peasants in resistance to the tsar's officials and state demands. However, a mixture of repression and peasant apathy made it clear that this approach was never going to achieve its aims of a revolutionary peasant uprising.

 Cross-reference
For the show trials of 1877, return to Chapter 1, pages 32–33.

The movement did succeeed in carrying out some assassinations – General Mezemtsev, head of the Third Section was assassinated in St Petersburg in 1878, as was Prince Kropotkin. What worried the authorities in particular was the public sympathy won by such assassins and the way they seemed able to escape with popular support. There were even some talks between *zemstva* and the Land and Liberty organisation to try to place more pressure on the autocracy for constitutional reform.

Dmitrii Milyutin, minister of war, saw all too clearly the state of the country, yet none within court circles seemed able to respond to the growing opposition:

April 20th 1879

It must be acknowledged that our entire government structure demands basic reform from top to bottom. The structure of rural self-government, of the zemstva, of local administration, as well as of institutions on the central and national level have outlived their time. They should all take on new forms in accordance with the spirit of the great reforms carried out in the sixties. The higher strands of government think only of protective police measures. I am convinced that the present leaders in government are powerless, not only to solve the problem, but even to understand it.

5

Fig. 6 *Revolutionaries operated under the threat of hanging if caught*

In 1879 Land and Liberty split into two different groups:

■ **Black Partition** (*Chernyy peredel*) organised from St Petersburg by Georgi Plekhanov and other colleagues. It was so called because it wanted to share or partition the black soil provinces of Russia among the peasants. It continued to work peacefully among the peasantry, spreading socialist propaganda and trying to bring reform without resorting to violence. It developed ties with students and workers and published radical materials. It was severely weakened by arrests in 1880–1881, when it ceased to exist as a separate organisation. Plekhanov and some of the early leaders grew more attracted to Marxism and created the first Russian Marxist organisation called Emancipation of Labour in Geneva in 1883.

■ **The People's Will** (*Narodnaya Volya*) was ably led by Timofei Mikhailov who successfully planted a spy in the tsar's Third Section to keep the group informed of the secret police's activities and so evade harassment and arrest. This was a bigger group than Black Partition and it advocated violent methods, undermining government by assassinating officials. In 1879 it declared that the tsar had to be removed – although it did offer to withdraw the threat if the tsar agreed to a constitution, which he did not, of course. After a number of unsuccessful attempts against Tsar Alexander's life, including a bomb planted under a train (the wrong one), an attempt to blow up a St Petersburg bridge as the tsar's carriage passed over it, the placing of a mine in the basement of the Winter Palace (below the dining room), by a revolutionary posing as a carpenter, which killed 12 people and wounded 50 more – but not the Tsar who was in another room – their aim was finally achieved in March, 1881.

■ **Cross-reference**

The development of Marxism, and the Emancipation of Labour organisation are discussed in more detail on pages 36–37 and page 60.

Key profiles

Georgi Plekhanov

Georgi Plekhanov (1856–1918) was a revolutionary thinker who was attracted by the Populist movement and became a leader of Land and Liberty and Black Partition. He was exiled from Russia in 1880 and settled in Geneva where he made contact with western thinkers and studied the works of Marx and Engels. Abandoning his former belief in the peasantry, he was attracted to the Marxist idea of worker-led change and co-founded Emancipation of Labour in 1883 with Lev Deutsch and Vera Zasulich (for more details on Zasulich, see Chapter 1 page 25). This was to merge with other socialist groups to form the Social Democratic Labour Party in 1898. In 1903, Plekhanov became a Menshevik and he remained an exile until 1917, when he briefly returned to Russia, but despite his contribution to Russian Marxism, he disapproved of the Bolsheviks and died in Finland. Plekhanov was known as the 'Father of Russian Marxism'.

Timofei Mikhailov

Timofei Mikhailov (1860–1881) was the son of a peasant who moved to St Petersburg to work in a factory there. He became involved in revolutionary politics and in March 1881 was arrested for taking part in the assassination of Alexander II. He was hanged a month later.

■ **Activity**

Thinking and analysis

Draw a Venn diagram of two overlapping circles. Label one circle 'Black Partition' and the other 'The People's Will'. In each circle, describe the main features of that movement and where the circles overlap, fill in what the two groups had in common.

■ A closer look

The assassination of Tsar Alexander II

The *Okhrana* had become aware of a new plot to assassinate the tsar in February 1881 but although they arrested one of the ringleaders, they could glean no information from him. On March 13th, 1881, Alexander II was travelling from Michaelovsky Palace to the Winter Palace in St Petersburg. He was in a closed carriage, followed by six Cossacks on horseback and a group of police officers in sledges, and with another armed Cossack alongside the coach-driver. Members of the People's Will with concealed bombs had positioned themselves along the route. When the carriage reached a street corner, near the Catherine Canal, one terrorist gave the signal to two others to throw their bombs at the tsar's carriage. Both missed and landed amongst the Cossacks. The tsar was unhurt but got out of the carriage to check on the injured men. As he approached the wounded Cossacks, another terrorist threw a further bomb. This time, Alexander was killed instantly and the assassin also died in the blast.

Fig. 7 *The assassination of Alexander II*

The significance of the opposition to 1881

Although the radical opposition to Tsar Alexander II was largely confined to the circles of the intelligentsia and university students, nevertheless, some ominous developments had taken place during the reign. Revolutionary thinking, including Marxism, had begun to take a more definite form within Russia, suggesting alternative ways of organisation in both government and society. Furthermore, whilst Alexander II had been prepared to concede a series of 'reforms from above', even moderate educated Russians of the type found in the *zemstva* had begun to demand 'reform from below' whereby some form of representative government would limit the absolute power of the tsar and his advisers.

The emergence of Populism had taken radical opposition away from the debating chambers and underground meeting rooms into the heart of the countryside. Although it had been largely repulsed by the conservative peasants themselves, it had made others, including the government, more aware of the depth of feeling of its opponents and of the potential for change within the Russian state. Furthermore, the humiliation of the open trials and the hopelessness of the secret police had all served to reinforce the idea that the tsarist regime had lost direction and authority.

The opposition of the right was also of consequence. Such reforms as had been granted had promoted the hostility of conservative bureaucrats, nobles and landlords. These reactionary forces had, in some ways, proved more difficult to contain than the radical opposition, as these were the men on whom the tsar relied to run the state and maintain its stability. In giving in to some of the right-wing opposition pressure from 1866, he had also weakened his own position. He had given a taste of reform and raised expectations but he had failed to fulfil these.

The last years of Alexander's reign saw him retreat more and more from public life, dependent on his relationship with Caterina Dolgoruki and alienated from members of his court and the sympathies of high society too. The opposition forces which he had raised on both sides of the spectrum had thwarted any hope of Russia's peaceful evolution into a modern constitutional state. The ultimate success of the assassins in 1881 was a sign of the determination of the People's Will to show their resolve in the face of the increased tendency to repression demanded by the right and it opened the path for an even more repressive reign under Alexander II's son, Alexander III.

Activity

Revision exercise

Use the following chart to compare the ideas and actions of the liberal intelligentsia and Populists.

	Liberal intelligentsia	Populists
Aims		
Supporters		
Methods		
Key influences (books and personalities)		
Achievements by 1881		

Learning outcomes

In this section you have considered the reasons behind the reforming impulses of the reign of Alexander II and the impact of the reforms which were carried out on various groups within Russian society. You have also seen how the changes, although limited in extent, opened the way for further demands and increased criticism of the tsarist autocracy. The degree of reaction and opposition before 1881 have also been explored and in the next section you will see how the changes set in motion by Alexander II were to have enormous repercussions for future rulers of the Empire and, in particular, Tsar Nicholas II.

Practice questions

(a) Explain why Alexander II emancipated the serfs in Russia in 1861.

(12 marks)

Study tip To answer part (a) you will need to make a list of relevant factors. Remember that the question is not about the terms of the emancipation but the reasons behind it. Try to group your factors into the short-term and long-term factors and don't forget to show the inter-relationship between them.

(b) How successful was opposition to the tsarist regime between 1861 and 1881 in achieving its aims?

(24 marks)

Study tip In part (b) you will firstly need to consider what the ams of the opposition movement were – and you are likely to want to divide the movement into different sections and its aims into short and long-term objectives. Before you begin to write, try to establish what your argument will be, so that the answer flows to a natural conclusion.

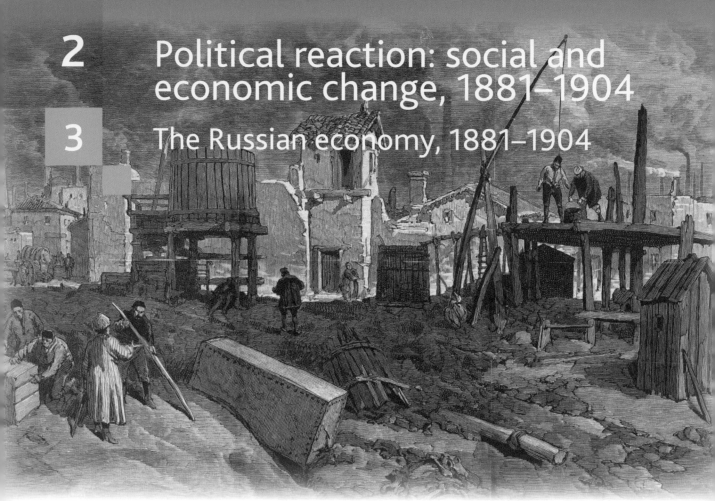

Fig. 1 *The Russian economy was transformed in the 1890s as rural areas were opened up with the development of new industry*

In this chapter you will learn about:

- the impact of industrialisation in Russia

- the work of the finance ministers, Ivan Vyshnegradsky and Sergei Witte

- the continuing problems of the rural economy before 1905.

■ The impact of industrialisation in Russia: the work of Vyshnegradsky and Witte

Economic development, 1881–1904

The transformation of the Russian economy had begun in the reign of Alexander II in response to the humiliation of defeat in the Crimean war of 1854–56. This had led to the development of a railway building programme and a limited spread of factories – some state-owned and geared to the manufacture of armaments, and others in the hands of foreigners. However, by 1881, Russia's economic development still lagged far behind that of western Europe and there was a huge gulf between Russia's potential, given its vast supplies of natural resources and manpower, and the country's actual levels of achievement.

It was not, therefore, until the reign of Alexander III that a real 'industrial revolution' took off and its development owed much to Alexander III's and Nicholas II's finance ministers, Ivan Vyshnegradsky (1887–92) and Sergei Witte (1892–1903).

The former, appointed in 1886, strove to improve Russian finances and build up the country's gold reserves. To achieve this he increased indirect taxes and mounted a drive to swell grain exports. He also reduced imports by increasing tariffs, and in the Tariff Act of 1891 duties were increased so that Russian iron, industrial machinery and raw cotton were heavily protected against outside competition. By 1891 import duties had reached 33 per cent. He also negotiated some valuable loans to kickstart growth, for example, from the

French in 1888. On the surface, the policy appeared very successful. Between 1881 and 1891, grain exports increased by 18 per cent, as a percentage of total Russian exports, and by 1892, the Russian budget was in surplus.

However, this remarkable export drive was achieved at the expense of the peasants. They bore the brunt of heavy indirect taxation which reduced their limited purchasing power. At the same time, the price of goods rose because of the import taxes and their grain was being requisitioned by government to sell abroad. Many peasants were left with no reserve stores and often hungry. It was put about that Vyshnegradsky said, '*We ourselves shall not eat, but we shall export*', and one of the results of this policy was witnessed in 1891 when a bad harvest brought widespread famine, in which many thousands died. Vyshnegradsky was dismissed in 1892, largely because of this national disaster which had been exacerbated by his own policy.

Key profile

Sergei Witte

Sergei Witte (1849–1915) came from a Georgian family, enobled by state service, with Dutch blood on his father's side. He attended Odessa University and worked for the Odessa Railway from 1871–77 where he became an expert on railway administration and wrote a book on rail tariffs in 1883. In 1889 he joined the Ministry of Finance in order to develop a new railways department and in 1892, was promoted, firstly to minister of communications, and then, minister of finance, a post he held until 1903. Although he was an able and forward-thinking administrator, the results of his measures invited controversy. He was the author of the 1905 October Manifesto and became Russia's first 'constitutional' prime minister that year, but was forced to resign after six months. He opposed the entry of Russia to the First World War on economic grounds, and died shortly afterwards, in 1915.

Sergei Witte took over as minister of finance to Alexander III in 1892 and continued to hold this post under Nicholas II to 1903. Witte was totally committed to economic modernisation, seeing it as the only way of preserving Russia's 'great power' status. Despite the strong feelings roused by Vyshnegradsky's policies, Witte believed that the former minister's policies were essentially the correct ones and that economic development was the only way in which standards of living would ultimately be raised. Furthermore he believed that economic development would curb unrest and revolutionary activity as everyone prospered.

Witte identified three key problems that were holding back economic development:

- insufficient capital
- lack of technical and managerial expertise
- insufficient manpower in the right places.

Since there was no entrepreneurial class in Russia, he believed that industrialisation needed to be directed 'from above'. This arrangement is sometimes referred to as 'state capitalism' and it meant continuing

Fig. 2 *Sergei Witte*

Activity

Thinking point

Do you think Witte was correct in his analysis of Russia's needs and the likely outcome of a programme of economic modernisation?

the policies of his predecessor with protective tariffs, heavy taxation and forced exports to generate capital. Consequently, the government raised domestic loans to finance enterprises such as railways, as well as investing directly in enterprises, from national revenue.

However, a shortage of capital led Witte to continue to seek additional loans from abroad and he appreciated the need to the need to stabilise the Russian currency and raise interest rates in order to increase foreign investment and business confidence. A new rouble was brought in, in January 1897, backed by the value of gold. This would prevent the Russian currency from fluctuating wildly in value and would preserve its worth, relative to the value of other currencies. Investors knew roubles could be redeemed for bullion at any time and so were far more likely to risk sinking their capital in Russian enterprises. The policy appeared to work. Foreign capitalists saw an opportunity to make money in Russia and foreign investment increased considerably, as can be seen in Table 1.

Table 1 *Foreign investment, 1880–1900*

Year	Foreign investment in millions of roubles
1880	98
1890	215
1895	280
1900	911

Much of this investment went into the mining and metal trades, while a substantial amount supported the oil industry and banking. France proved the biggest investor supplying a third of all the foreign capital, but Britain provided 23 per cent, Germany 20 per cent, Belgium 14 per cent and the USA 5 per cent too.

Witte also encouraged foreign experts and workers – engineers and managers from France, Belgium, Germany, Britain and Sweden to oversee industrial developments and advise on planning and techniques. Under their guidance and expertise, Russia was rapidly forced into an industrial revolution, with the growth of the railways, a strong concentration on 'heavy' industry and the establishment of huge factories in expanding industrial cities.

Industrial growth

Railways

In the 1880s, the state began to buy up private railway companies and the construction of new long-distance state railways began. By the mid-1890s, 60 per cent of the whole railway system was state-owned and by 1905 this proportion had increased to nearly 66 per cent. The huge acceleration of railway building can be seen in Table 2.

Table 2 *Annual average railway construction, 1881–95*

Years	Kilometres
1881–85	632
1886–90	914
1891–95	1292

By 1905, Russia had 59,616 kilometres of railways, which, although still small in comparison with the size of the country, nevertheless indicates that a major engineering feat had been accomplished. This

Fig. 3 *A train of tankers carrying oil from the oil wells at Baku*

had many implications. The railways helped open up the Russian interior and allowed more extensive exploitation of Russia's raw materials. For example, a rail link between the Donbass coalfields and the iron ore depositis in the Krivoi Rog area of the Ukraine transformed that area, while the Batum–Baku railway of 1883 linking the Caspian and Black Seas greatly increased oil production from the rich oilfields at Baku by providing an outlet for exportation. These developments were aided by overseas investment from the Nobel brothers and the Rothschilds. Other railway lines linked major areas of industrial production such as Moscow and Nizhni Novgorod, while still more connected important industrial and agricultural areas with markets or ports, for example the lines from Kurk or Kharkov to Odessa enabled the grain-growing areas to send their produce to the Black Sea ports, so reinforcing the export drive.

The very building of the railway lines themselves was also a stimulus to the development of the iron and coal industries and encouraged the founding of new industrial areas along their length. Transport costs fell, bringing down the price of goods, while the government gained new revenue from freight charges and passenger fares. Other forms of transport also developed, but less impressively. River and sea navigation were improved, with an increase in the number of steam ships, but most overseas trade was still carried in foreign ships and Russia's roads remained poor.

The most acclaimed development was the impressive construction of the Trans-Siberian railway line, which crossed Russia from west to east. Its building provided a huge industrial stimulus whilst the psychological boost it provided, both at home and abroad, was perhaps even greater.

Did you know?
Foreign Investment and the Baku Oil Fields

The growth of oil production in Baku was based upon high quality crude oil, cheap available manpower, and the quick and effective development and implementation of technical improvements. Foreign capital also increased toward the end of the 19th and the beginning of the 20th centuries – primarily from the Nobel, Rothschild and Vishau families. In 1898, the Azerbaijani oil industry of Baku exceeded the US oil production level. At that time, approximately 8 million tons were being produced. In 1901, Baku produced more than half of the world's oil (11 million tons), and 95 percent of all Russian oil.

The Trans-Siberian Railway

This began in 1891, and was completed in 1902, although sections were still incomplete in 1914. It linked central European Russia and Moscow with the Pacific Ocean at Vladivostok via the Chinese Eastern railway in Manchuria, and ran for 7,000 kilometers. It brough massive economic benefits – in part through its construction – with massive government orders for coal and metals. There were also economic and strategic advantages to the development of western Siberia. The eastern regions became like America's Wild West as peasants were encouraged to emigrate and prospect there, away from the overpopulated areas of western Russia. Siberia had no tradition of serfdom, and the distance from the capital meant that there were fewer restrictions on life. In this respect it was an attractive option for peasants who were happy to take the challenge. Farming in the region increased, supplying the towns and cities of the West, and also foreign countries. Strategically, the railway could be used to transport troops and other military supplies to the more lawless or vulnerable outlying parts of the empire. But it promised more than it delivered.

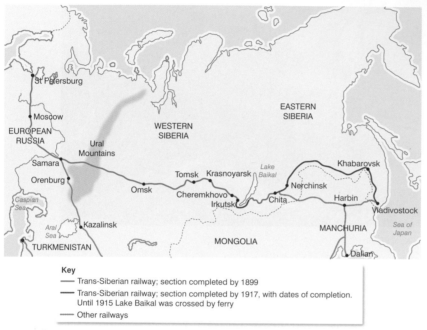

Key

— Trans-Siberian railway; section completed by 1899

— Trans-Siberian railway; section completed by 1917, with dates of completion. Until 1915 Lake Baikal was crossed by ferry

— Other railways

Fig. 4 *The Trans-Siberian Railway*

Fig. 5 *A gushing oil fountain at Baku. The development of the oil fields was essential to the Russian economy*

Heavy industry

In the early stages of industrial growth to the 1880s, the lighter industries, particularly textiles, had led the way. By the time Witte came to power, the total industrial output of the textile trades was one and a half times greater than that of coal mining, oil, minerals, and the metal trades put together. Witte believed that, by concentrating production in key areas and by developing large factory units of over 1,000 or so workers, big increases in heavy goods production could be achieved.

His policies are mirrored in Table 3.

Table 3 *Factories and factory workers, 1887–1908*

Year	Number of factories	Number of factory workers
1887	30,888	1.3 million
1908	39,856	2.6 million

Although textiles still dominated, accounting for 40 per cent of the total industrial output in 1910, there was still some impressive growth in heavy industry, as shown in Table 4.

Table 4 *Production (millions of metric tons)*

	1880	1890	1900	1910
Coal	3.2	5.9	16.1	25.4
Pig-Iron	0.42	0.89	2.66	3.0
Crude Oil	0.5	3.9	10.2	12.1

The main areas of industrial development were around St Petersburg and the Baltic coast, Moscow and the provinces of Vladimir, Nizhni Novgorod and the Urals to the east, the Donbas (Donets basin) and Krivoi Rog ironfields of the south eastern Ukraine and south western Russia, the Baku coalfields on the Caspian Sea and in Poland.

Coal from the Donbas region supplied the ironworks in nearby Donetsk, set up in in 1872 to exploit the rich ironfields of the Krivoi Rog. The Caspian sea port of Baku began pumping oil in 1871 and output grew tremendously. Moscow overtook St Petersburg as an industrial centre, because of its position as the hub of the entire rail network and the main link between Europe and the East. However, St Petersburg grew too, particularly in the engineering sector with the expansion of the Putilov Works.

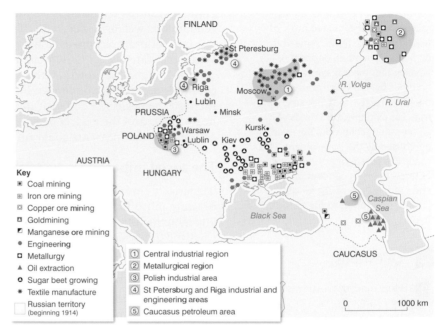

Fig. 6 *Key areas of industrial development*

■ A closer look

The Putilov works

The Putilov factory was first established as a state-run iron foundry in 1789, but moved to the southern side of St Petersburg in 1801 and passed through state and private hands several times before Nikolai Ivanovich Putilov, a retired official from the Naval Ministry, purchased the plant in 1867 as a rail factory. The company provided for nearly a quarter of all state orders for locomotives, wagons, and rails. Putilov died in 1880, but between 1885 and 1900, the Putilov works expanded enormously by shifting production away from mass production of rails, with its high costs of raw materials and production, towards goods that could be produced in smaller quantities but with greater profitability, such as machinery, artillery and products made of high quality steel. The result was that the factory's workforce grew by two thousand in a mere three years (1891–4). By 1903 the firm was able to take on a massive expansion of armaments production that ensured the company's survival through the First World War.

Russia's rate of annual growth, at more than 8 per cent per annum 1894–1904, was the highest of any industrial country in the last decade of the nineteenth century, although it had begun from a very low base

Cross-reference

The social cost of Russia's industrial expansion is discussed in the section below.

Exploring the detail

The state and the economy

By the early 20th century the state controlled 70 per cent of all Russian railways and also owned most of Russia's forests, fields, mine and oil fields. Around 25 per cent of government income came from its holdings by 1903. The state also bought directly from industry, so that, for example, two thirds of all metallurgical production was purchased by the government. This made the prosperity of the private entrepreneurs dependent on the state and may account for their limited opposition to the autocracy itself.

Questions

1 How industrialised was Russia by 1904?

2 How successful were the finance ministers of the period 1886–1903 in transforming Russia economically?

3 How important was the spread of the railway network to the growth of the Russian economy by 1904?

Exploring the detail

Factory entreprenueurs

As industry began to develop in Russia in the 1860–80s, most private industrial enterprises had been in the hands of the traditional nobility. It was not until the 1890s, that non-nobles found a new niche as factory-owners, supervisors and foremen. This is another potential reason why harsh discipline and disregard for workers' well-being became more marked. These new figures had none of the old noble 'paternalism' which made them feel morally obliged to look after their workers.

compared with other countries. Russia moved up the league table of industrialised nations from 1887–97, to become the world's fourth largest industrial economy.

This growth helped bolster an increase in Russian exports and foreign trade. Both imports and exports grew in quantity and value. Russia traded mainly with Germany, closely followed by Britain, and also with the Netherlands, China and the USA, but the bulk of the export trade was in grain rather than industrial goods and even here, the increase in grain export fell short of Witte's predictions.

However, all this relentless drive for industrial expansion came at an economic as well as a social cost. The building of the Trans-Siberian railroad, for example, proved a huge drain on finances. Indeed, under Witte, the state budget more than doubled, eating into the profits of the country's economic growth. Other economic downsides included the country's dependence on foreign loans, which had to be paid back with interest, the neglect of domestic and lighter industry in the drive for heavy goods and the neglect of agricultural modernisation, driven by the assumption that peasants could simply be forced into producing more.

The social impact of industrialisation

The drive to industrialisation brought about major social changes as it began to move Russian society away from a land based society towards one more focused on money, capital and wages. It bred both a new middle class and a new urban working class and such developments were to have profound political repercussions.

The middle class

The growth of industrialisation saw more cross the threshold into 'middle management' as small workshop owners and traders seized the new opportunities. Some re-emerged as the larger factory owners, while professionals, such as bankers, doctors, teachers and administrators, were also in greater demand as society grew more complex. The middle class of professional men and merchants had always been small in Russia and did not change the basic division of Russian society between the small upper strata of nobility and the broad mass of 'peasant stock'. Indeed 'middle classes' made up no more than half a million in 1897 and in the census of that year, were classified alongside the hereditary and non-hereditary nobility. However, government contracts, for example to build railways and state loans to build factories, provided tremendous opportunities for the enterprising.

The growing middle classes found their natural home on the councils of the *zemstva*, where they were able to influence local decision making. However, they had no voice in central government before 1905 and whereas in most western states the moderate liberal-minded middle class became a backbone of the establishment, in Russia the reverse was the case. Revolutionary leaders often came from this very background.

The urban working class

In Russia's major cities, the arrival of new large factories, in addition to the growing numbers of smaller workshops, swelled the urban population. There were probably around 2 million factory workers in Russia by 1900; 6 million by 1913. Between 1867 and 1917, the Empire's urban population quadrupled from 7 to 28 million and this meant that the lives of many former peasant families underwent a major transformation. They left behind the fields of their fathers and grandfathers and exchanged their old masters for new ones.

Fig. 7 *The 'village' of Moscow in the early 20th century*

Exploring the detail

Understanding statistics

It is difficult to estimate the size of the urban proletariat. The government underestimated figures because it did not wish to cause alarm and undermine political stability, while Lenin and later communists exaggerated them to fit their theories of class revolution. Lenin claimed that there were 64 million 'proletarians and semi-proletarians' by the early 20th century – but he included agricultural labourers, forest workers and those who worked in their own homes. Consequently, a figure of 2–3 million urban workers or 2–4 per cent of the total Russian population is more realistic.

In the 1880s and 1890s, it was still relatively common for some workers to move to the towns temporarily, retaining their land and returning to their villages to help out with the harvest. Some, finding they could scarely subsist on their meagre allocation of land, sold up and joined the bands of migrants who worked in one place, (perhaps on a railway) for a few years, before moving on. Others found regular employment, put down roots and produced children who grew up to think of themselves as urban workers. By 1914, three out of every four people living in St Petersburg were peasants by birth, compared with just one in three 50 years earlier. What is more, half the city's population had arrived in the previous 20 years. The situation in Moscow was much the same and here, an even more 'peasant' atmosphere surrounded the workers' quarters of the city. Livestock roamed the streets and there were numerous outdoor 'peasant' markets, including one in Red Square.

Some impression of the degree of change experienced by these two major cities can be seen in Figure 8.

Did you know?

Red Square, lying between the tsar's fortified castle, known as the Kremlin, and the merchant quarter of the city, known as Kitay-gorod, had been created in the 17th century as Moscow's main city square. It was not only used as a market place, but was also a focal point for public ceremonies and proclamations. Its name 'red' derives from the adjacent St Basil's Cathedral, which was described by a Russian adjective which meant both red and beautiful. It remains to this day – as does Moscow's nickname 'Big Village'.

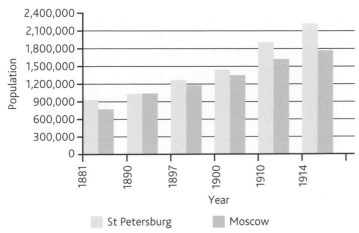

Fig. 8 *The population of two major industrialised cities (St Petersburg and Moscow) between 1881 and 1914*

The facilities needed to provide for this growing urban class were grossly inadequate. Peasants, lured to the towns by the promise of wages and regular employment, often found themselves living in barrack-like buildings, rapidly built, or bought, by the factory owners, and dangerously over-crowded and lacking in adequate sanitation. For the owner, the barracks were an effective means of retaining and monitoring his workers, but for the 'inmates' with little privacy save a rough curtain around their plank bed, they must have seemed like a prison. Workers housed this way had to eat in canteens and wash in communal bath-houses. Even those who managed to find 'private' city accommodation fared little better. In St Petersburg at the turn of the century, for example, about 40 per cent of houses had no running water or sewage system. Excrement was simply set in piles in the backyards and collected by workers with wooden carts at night. It is hardly surprising that 30,000 of the capital's inhabitants died of cholera in 1908–09.

Yet the demand for work and accommodation was such that rents remained high, often taking half a worker's wages. A survey of printers in Saratov in 1900 revealed that food and rent represented three-quarters of the household budget, while clothes, laundry and baths accounted for the rest. A similar survey of St Petersburg in 1904 showed 16 people in the average apartment, six in each room – and even more in the workers' districts. Still, a bed was something. At the bottom of the pile were those who simply lay down in the factory alongside their machines, or lived rough on the streets.

A closer look

A peasant's life in Moscow

Kanatchikov (1879–1940) was a peasant who moved to Moscow from his nearby village. He eventually finished up as a Bolshevik. The account below is his story, as related by Orlando Figes:

Kanatchikov writes: "I wanted to rid myself of the monotony of village life as quickly as possible, to free myself from my father's despotism and tutelage, to begin to live a self-reliant and independent life". It was not long before poverty forced his father to give in to his requests. At the age of 16, Kanatchikov finally left for Moscow to work in the Gustav List metal factory. It was through a group of 15 immigrant workers from his own area that Kanatchikov found a corner of a room in a 'large smelly house inhabited by all kinds of poor folk'. The 15 men who shared a room bought food and paid for a cook collectively. Every day at noon they hurried home from the factory to eat cabbage soup 'from a common bowl with wooden spoons'. Kanatchikov slept in a small cot, shared with another apprentice. His windowless corner was dirty and full of 'bed bugs and fleas and the stench of humanity'. But in fact he was lucky to be in a private room at all. At work, Kanatchikov found himself at the bottom of the factory hierarchy, an unskilled worker, labouring for 6 days every week from 6.00am to 7.00pm for a measly wage of 1.5 roubles a week.

Workers' wages varied tremendously, of course, according to whether they were skilled or unskilled, the occupation followed and the amount of overtime put in, or conversely, the amount deducted in fines. Women, who comprised a fifth of the industrial workforce in 1885, but a third by 1914, were amongst the lowest paid, earning less than half the average industrial wage. According to a female doctor, L. Katerina, working for the *zemstvo* in the central Russian city of Kostroma in 1913:

One cannot but note the premature decrepitude of the factory woman. A woman of 50 who has worked at the factory thirty or more years, frequently looks ancient, She sees and hears poorly, her head trembles, her shoulders are sharply hunched over. She looks about 70 years old. While in the west, elderly workers have pensions, our women workers, having given decades to the factory so that they are prematurely enfeebled, can expect nothing better than to live out their last days as latrine attendants.

2

Conditions were, perhaps, at their worst during the industrial depression of 1900–08, however; even when industry began to revive, the wages of indstrial workers failed to keep pace with inflation. Workers' protests remained comparatively limited, although some strikes did occur – perhaps because strike activity was officially illegal before 1905 and, more likely, because workers had been brought up to expect a hard life as peasants and feared the loss of their job, at a time when many were clamouring for work. Consequently workers could suffer brutish treatment from the factory foreman in a way long since past for their counterparts in western Europe. Witte himself remarked that Russia was lucky to have a labour force of peasant stock for these very reasons.

There were some attempts to alleviate the workers' lot as seen in Table 5.

Table 5 *Workers' legislation, 1885–1912*

Date	Law
1885	prohibited night-time employment of women and children
1886	decreed that workers had to be employed according to contracts overseen by factory boards
1892	employment of children under 12 forbidden and female labour banned in mines
1897	hours of work reduced to 11 and a half per day
1903	expansion of provision for factory inspection
1912	health insurance for workers

> ### Exploring the detail
> **Strike activity**
>
> Between 1886 and 1894 there was an average of 33 strikes per year but between 1895 and 1904 this rose to 176. These occurred despite a new government measure of 1899, which established an elaborate police surveillance system in factories and mines, to arrest strike instigators. A massive strike among the textile workers of St Petersburg in 1896–97 revealed a high degree of unity and discipline and in 1903 alone there were 550 stoppages.

Education also spread with the government's promotion of technical schools and universities, although state investment in education was far less than that in the railways. On the whole, the tsarist government displayed limited concern to improve the workers' lot by legislation and much was only reluctantly conceded. Some, like the tsar's adviser Konstantin Pobedonostev, refused to recognise that any action should be taken and believed it wrong to raise workers' expectations. Others, at least more rationally, feared that if labour costs rose, foreign investors and factory owners, on whom the growing economy relied, would withdraw. Occasionally workers' frustrations spilled over into illegal strike activity – and these became particularly acute in 1904–05, but any such action met with immediate and sometimes violent repression.

It would not be an exaggeration to say that one of gravest mistakes of the tsarist governments was to allow the development of a large and discontented working class in the cities, for it was from here that the impetus to overthrow the regime in 1917 would eventually come.

Konstantin Pobedonostev

Konstantin Pobedonostev (1827–1907) was a former Professor of Law at Moscow State University who was chosen as tutor to the young Alexander (later Alexander III) from 1865. He became very influential at court and his presence behind the throne led to his nickname, 'the Black Tsar'. He probably wrote Alexander III's accession manifesto which reasserted the tsarist autocracy, and, using his position as Over-Procurator of the Holy Synod (Head of the governing body of the Orthodox Church), from 1880, he spoke out forcibly in favour of absolutism, nationalism and anti-semitism, for example referring to Judaism as the 'Hebrew Leprosy'. He also tutored Nicholas II, but lost some influence after the latter's accession in 1894. In 1901, a socialist, Lagovsky, tried to shoot Pobedonostev through an office window, but missed. Pobedonostev retired from public affairs during the 1905 revolution and died two years later.

■ **Activity**

Thinking and analysis

Consider the following consequences of industrialisation in Russia and rank them in order of importance. Justify your order to the rest of your group:

■ a growing middle class

■ a more mobile population

■ industrial workers exposed to dreadful working conditions in factories and mines

■ industrial workers housed in overcrowded barracks and boarding houses with little or no sanitation

■ the growth of cities.

■ The problems of the rural economy

Fig. 9 *The peasants were still the mainstay of the Russian economy*

Whilst much attention was given by Vyshnegradsky and Witte to the development of an industrial economy, the same was not true of agriculture. Although the rural economy provided a livelihood for 80–90 per cent of the Russian population, it was largely ignored or sacrificed in the interests of industrialisation until 1906. Most farming was small-scale and in the hands of former serfs and state peasants, tied to their local *mir* by the redemption dues they were re-paying. In the years of good harvest, the peasants' income remained low because bread prices were kept down – whilst in the bad years, they faced starvation, as occurred in 1891–92 and again in 1898 and 1901.

Exploring the detail

Comparison of grain production

	Country	*Poods*[1] per *desyatina*[2]
Grain production	Russia	45
	Great Britain and Germany	146
Rye production	Russia	54
	France and USA	68

[1] A *pood* was a weight of 16.38 kg
[2] A *desyatina* was an old Russian measurement, little more than one hundredth of a square kilometre

The population explosion in Russia had undermined some of the good intentions of the Emancipation Act of 1861. Russia's population had doubled in the second half of the 19th century to reach 132.9 million by 1900 (and 160.7 million by 1910) and whilst Russian grain production had kept ahead of this population growth, the yields were poor by the standards of the west because of the inefficient farming methods. Population growth had caused the further subdivision of estates and the average holding had fallen from 35 acres to 28 in the years 1877 to 1905. Although the government introduced the Nobles' (1882), and Peasants' (1885) Land Banks to facilitate the purchase and development of larger farms, they sometimes merely increased farmers' debts, which together with high levels of taxation and the competition posed by cheap American grain, made efficient farming impossible.

Quite apart from ignorance, and the suspicion in which some western farming practices were held, until 1905 agricultural output was hampered by the system of the *mir*, in which farmers were bound to work together. The *solcha* or wooden plough was still widely used and medieval rotation systems, which wastefully left land fallow each year, were practised. A lack of husbandry also deprived the soil of manure so that the grain output from American farms was on average one and a half times that of the Russian, whilst that from British farmland was four times as great.

The gap between richest and poorest sections of the peasantry became wider as the wealthier peasant entrepreneurs or *kulaks* took advantage of the position of the less favoured and, sometimes with the help of loans from the peasant banks, bought out their impoverished neighbours.

Kulaks became a small 'capitalist peasant' class – employing labour and perhaps acting as 'pawn brokers' – to a local peasant community by buying their grain in the autumn to provide them with money to tide them over the winter, but only selling it back at inflated prices in the spring, which sometimes meant accepting land in lieu.

Cross-reference

For the Emancipation Act of 1861 see pages 16–17.

Exploring the detail

Land Banks

The Peasants' Land Bank held funds and reserves of land with which to assist peasants who wished to acquire land directly or through purchase from nobles. The Nobles' Land Bank was designed to help nobles with the legal costs involved in land transfer and in land improvement schemes. Interest rates on loans from these banks were kept deliberately low. They helped increase peasant ownership and, between 1877 and 1905, over 26 million hectares passed into peasant hands. However, they also helped prop up some inefficient farms which continued in their traditional ways.

In contrast to the upward mobility of the *kulaks*, the poorest peasants found life getting harsher. Increasing numbers were forced to leave their farms and join the bands of migrant labourers looking either for seasonal farming work or industrial employment. A minority migrated to Siberia, encouraged by government schemes from 1896 to sponsor emigration to the new agricultural settlements opened up by the Trans-Siberian Railway. However, only three quarters of a million, from a peasant population of nearly 97 million, were able to take advantage of this and the scheme was clearly inadequate to alleviate the pressure of a growing population on resources.

Living standards varied in different parts of the country, with more prosperous commercial farming in the peripheral regions such as parts of the Baltic, the Western Ukraine, the Kuban and Northern Caucasus to the south and in Western Siberia. The continuation of land owned by the nobles and backward farming methods was mainly concentrated in the Russian heartland. Orlando Figes, the modern historian, has noted that these were later to become the areas which supported the Bolshevik Revolution from 1917, whilst the more prosperous areas were centres of counter-revolution. There were other reasons for the differences too. Areas of former state peasants tended to be better off than those of the emancipated privately-owned serfs, because they had been granted more land. According to a *zemstvo* survey in the 1880s, two out of every three of the former serfs in the Tambov region were unable to feed the household without falling into debt.

The peasants' lot remained a hard one and despite improvements in health care provided through the *zemstva*, a large proportion of the peasantry was turned down as unfit for military service. Mortality rates in Russia were higher than those in any other European country. In the 1890s the infant mortality rate was 57.4 per cent of all deaths and in some provinces this was much higher. Average life expectancy at the end of the 19th century was 27.25 years for males, 29.83 years for women whilst in England the average age of death was 45.25 years. It would, therefore, not be an exaggeration to say that the economic changes of 1881–1904 failed to improve the lot of the peasantry and may even have affected them for the worse.

Exploring the detail

The nobility

The 1890s saw the nobility's status wane as its economic role declined. Around a third of all nobles' land was transferred to townsmen or peasants between 1861 and 1905. Nobles struggled to meet debts and a fall in agricultural prices at the end of the century made matters worse. Few nobles understood modern money management and cut their living standards and invested for the future. For the government this was a matter of concern. There were sometimes too few nobles left in provincial areas to manage the *zemstva* and other local offices.

Summary questions

1 Explain why Witte tried to transform the Russian economy between 1894 and 1904.

2 How successful were the Russian governments in promoting economic change and modernisation between 1891 and 1904?

The growth of opposition, 1881–1904

Fig. 1 *The execution of the assassins of Alexander II*

Ten days after Alexander II's assassination, the revolutionary group the 'People's Will' sent an open letter to the dead tsar's son, Alexander III.

> Your Majesty,
>
> While fully comprehending your deep sorrow, there is something higher than the most legitimate of personal feelings – the duty to our country, to which all individual sentiments must be sacrificed.
>
> There are but two ways – either revolution or the voluntary transfer of supreme power into the hands of the people. We do not impose conditions, as these have been imposed by history; we merely state them. The conditions are:
>
> - A general amnesty for all political crimes, as those were not crimes, but rather the fulfilment of social duty.
>
> - The summoning of representatives of the whole nation to consider the existing social and economic order and its modification in accordance with the nation's desire.

1

The mourning Alexander III was in no mood for such requests, or for clemency. Within days, 150 members of the opposition movement responsible for the assassination had been arrested. Everywhere there was a clampdown on clandestine meetings, and known centres of trouble were raided by the forces of the secret police. Censorship and security were tightened and the new tsar retired to the fortified castle of Gatchina lest some 'madmen' try to kill him too. Thus a period of reaction and counter-reform was launched that would last until 1904.

■ Revolutionaries and liberals

Populism and the emergence of the Social Revolutionary movement

The assassination of March 13th 1881 effectively ended the Populist movement, as it had been known. However, some of its supporters continued to meet in secret and the acts of terrorism with which it had become associated continued, despite the repression which characterised the reign of Alexander III. In 1886, The People's Will was reformed among students in St Petersburg and in March 1887, a group who made bombs with the intention of asassinating Alexander III was arrested. Two months later, five of these, including Alexander Ulyanov, Lenin's elder brother, were hanged.

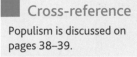

Cross-reference

Populism is discussed on pages 38–39.

Fig. 2 *The radical student Alexander Ulyanov*

■ Key profile

Alexander Ulyanov

Alexander Ulyanov (1866–87) was the son of a government official from Simbirsk and part of Russia's small bourgeoisie. He and his brother Vladimir (later known as Lenin) attended St Petersburg University, where Alexander participated in radical student politics – attending illegal meetings and running propaganda campaigns. Alexander helped re-form the People's Will (*Narodnaya Volya*) in 1886, with a commitment to terrorism, but following his arrest for attempting to assassinate Alexander III, he was hanged.

The assassination of March 13th 1881 was to prove a huge disappointment to the opposition. It yielded no practical benefits, and, on the contrary, led to a wave of arrests, greater police surveillance, the abandonment of Loris-Melikov's proposed reforms and the accession of a tsar, Alexander III, who was determined to enforce reactionary policies. However, it did have some symbolic significance, showing the vulnerability of the autocracy, winning some support overseas and creating martyrs which helped popularise the revolutionary cause.

Populist ideas were preserved in the remnants of the People's Will, and in some of the developing 'self-education' circles, such as the Muscovite Society of Translators and Publishers, which translated and reproduced the writings of foreign socialists, as well as among groups which made contact with radicals in the west. However, police activity, the execution, imprisonment and exile of leaders, a lack of funds and a lack of enthusiasm among the peasants, all reduced the incidences of violent revolutionary activity in the 1890s. Famine too played its part and some radicals turned their energies to relief work among the peasantry during the disastrous years of 1891–92.

■ Cross-reference

To recap on the disastrous years of 1891–92, re-read page 45.

It was following the debates about the competence of the governmnt at the time of the Great Famine, which had highlighted the need to reform the rural economy, that Populist ideas enjoyed a further revival. Populist thinking re-surfaced in the universities, where there were several outbreaks of disorder from 1899, culminating in the assassination, in 1901, of the minister of education, N.P. Bogolepov, by a student named Pyotr Karpovich.

More significant still was the coming together, in 1901, of a number of the new Populist groups, to create the Socialist Revolutionary Party. This was a fairly loose organisation bringing together organisations with a wide variety of views and was never centrally controlled. Its most influential theorist was the intellectual Viktor Chernov (1873–1952), a law graduate from Moscow and editor of the party journal, *Revolutsionnaya Rossiya* (*Revolutionary Russia*). Although the party never held a congress until 1906, its members broadly accepted the basic aspects of Marxist teaching but combined these with Populist ideas, to provide a specifically 'Russian' revolutionary programme. They put forward the view that the interests of peasants and workers – the so-called 'labouring poor' – were identical. Therefore, they argued, they should work together to get rid of autocracy and bring about land redistribution. This set them apart from the pure Marxists, since they emphasised the importance of the peasantry as a revolutionary force and talked of 'land socialisation' rather than 'land nationalisation'. They developed a wide national base, with a large peasant membership, although 50 per cent of their supporters were from the urban working class.

Key profile

Viktor Chernov

Viktor Chernov (1873–1952) had been attracted to the Populist cause and became engaged in revolutionary activity as a teenager. In 1894 he joined the People's Will and was arrested, spending some time in exile. He travelled to Switzerland in 1899 and was to provide much of the intellectual input into the founding of the Socialist Revolutionary Party in 1901. He went on to become the leader of the Socialist Revolutionaries in the Second Duma of 1907 and was minister of agriculture in the Provisional Governemnt of 1917. After the Bolsheviks came to power, he settled in the USA.

The tactics of the Socialist Revolutionary Party were similar to the earlier Populist organisation. They tried to stir up discontent in the countryside and strikes in the towns and to disrupt government by political assassinations. In this they were quite successful, promoting a wave of political terrorism in the early years of the 20th century and carrying out 2,000 political assassinations between 1901 and 1905. These included the assassinations of two ministers of internal affairs: Dmitrii Sipyagin (minister from 1900 to 1902) and Vyacheslav von Plehve, (minister 1902–04), who survived one attack in 1903 and two in 1904 before being killed by a bomb thrown into his carriage.

The Social Democratic movement

In the late 1880s and 1890s, the development of industrialisation in Russia began to make Marxist theories more attractive to Russian intellectuals. In 1883, Georgi Plekhanov, who had been forced into

Exploring the detail

The murder of Bogolepov

Pyotr Karpovich was a student rebel who had twice been expelled from Kazan University. His revenge killing was applauded by a student meeting and as Bogolepov lay dying, a popular demonstration of several thousand people gathered in front of Kazan cathedral in Karpovich's support. This is an early example of a public protest, which was broken up by the police, injuring 60 and leading to the arrests of about 800. It was followed by demonstrations in Moscow and an attempt by another student, one month later, to emulate the achievement by assassinating Pobedonostev. This time, the attempt failed.

Activity

Research task

The Socialist-Revolutionary (SR) Party grew out of the Northern Union of Socialist Revolutionaries founded in 1896 and various local socialist-revolutionary groups, such as the *Workers' Party of Political Liberation of Russia* created in 1899. Among its early leaders were Catherine Breshkovskaya, Victor Chernov, Gregory Gershuni, Nikolai Avksentiev, Alexander Kerensky and Evno Azef.

Try to find out something about these revolutionaries for a short class presentation.

Cross-reference

Von Plehve is profiled on page 72.

Activity

Talking point

What would be the advantages/ disadvantages of a party with a large peasant membership?

Cross-reference

The roots of Marxism in the 1870s and Marxist theory are outlined on pages 36–37.

Georgi Plekhanov is profiled on page 40.

exile after his involvement with the Populist movement, established the Emancipation of Labour group in Switzerland. This was committed to bringing about a proletarian-socialist revolution in Russia and aimed to spread knowledge of Marxism more widely within Russia through propaganda and agitation. The group translated and arranged for Marxist tracts to be smuggled into Russia for the benefit of underground socialist groups and also explained the theories for a Russian audience.

Activity

Challenging your thinking

Using the diagram of Marxism in Chaper 2, pages 36–37, as a basis for discussion, identify the ways in which Marxist theories might have appealed to some Russians in 1881 and the ways they might not. Why did the economic changes of Witte outlined in Chapter 3 make Marxist theory more appealing – and to whom?

In *Socialism and the Political Struggle* (1883) and *Our Differences* (1885), Plekhanov argued that Russian revolutionaries had to accept the inevitability of Marx's 'stages of development' and that Russia was already moving towards the capitalist phase. He therefore stressed that while the first task of the revolutionaries should be to co-operate with the bourgeoisie to fight autocracy, they also needed to accelerate the socialist revolution by working among the Russian workers in the cities. Here, he argued, was the dynamism that would drive the revolution forward; to devote time to trying to rouse the peasantry was misguided and a waste of energy.

The Emancipation of Labour movement made slow headway before the industrial take-off of the 1890s, although Marxist ideas circulated among intellectuals and university students. Plekhanov himself – who remained in exile between 1880 and 1917 – played no active role within Russia. Censorship, tough policing and the limited development of an industrial proletariat had all hindered its activities and in 1884 its German contact, Deich, who was responsible for smuggling Marxist materials into Russia, was arrested by the German police, on a tip-off from the *Okhrana*, However, in the 1890s, as industrialisation speeded up, a number of workers' organisations, illegal trade unions, Marxist discussion circles and other groups sprang up.

A closer look

Repression and the police

Alexander III's government was commited to eradicating revolutionary activity and new legislation was introduced to extend the powers of the police. The Department of Police, responsible to the Ministry of Internal Affairs, supervised the Russian Gendarmerie and the *Okhrana* on which the autocracy relied. The Russian Gendarmerie was the uniformed security police of the Russian Empire, responsible for law enforcement and state security. The Gendarmes investigated political and criminal cases, tracked down fugitives, controlled riots, and assisted local police and officials. The corps was staffed entirely from noble army officers who relied on a network of informers and agents.

From 1882, any area of the Empire could be deemed an 'area of subversion' and police agents could search, arrest, detain, question, imprison or exile not only those who had committed a crime, but any who were thought likely to commit crimes or knew, or were related to, people who had committed crimes. This gave them tremendous power over people's lives, particularly since any such arrested person had no right to legal representation. To enforce this statute, the number of police was increased and new branches of the Criminal Investigation Department were set up. There was also a drive to recruit spies, counter-spies (to spy on the spies) and 'agents provocateurs', who would pose as revolutionaries in order to incriminate others.

Fig. 3 *Heavy-handed treatment by the police*

Although the Gendarmerie operated as the security police in the greater part of the country, the secret police, the *Okhrana*, had offices in St Petersburg, Moscow and Warsaw where they took responsibility for 'security and investigation'. They intercepted and read mail and checked up on activities in the factories, universities, the army and state, detaining suspects and resorting to torture and summary executions. Communists, socialists and trade unionists were particular subjects of their investigations but they also watched members of the civil service and government.

In an attempt to weld these groups together, in 1898 the First Congress of the Russian Social Democratic Workers' Party of the Soviet Union was held in Minsk. Although the Minsk Congress marks the launch of the new Marxist Social Democratic Party (SDs), only nine delegates were present, so it was a very small beginning. As well as choosing a name and electing a three-man Central Committee, it also produced a manifesto (drawn up by Pyotr Struve, who later abandoned Marxism for the liberal movement, declaring that his heart had never really been in it). The manifesto acknowledged a debt to the activities of the People's Will but asserted that Social Democracy would follow a different path to freedom. It asserted that the working classes had been, and were being, exploited by their masters and that the future of Russia would be the product of a class struggle. The manifesto made it clear that the impetus for change had to come from the working men themselves.

The Congress it was broken up by *Okhrana* agents who promptly arrested two of the newly elected Committee. It was not a promising start, but in the years that followed, Vladimir Ilyich Ulyanov (Lenin, 1870–1924), who had been converted to Marxist ideas as a student from 1887, came to play a prominent part in the development of the party.

■ **Exploring the detail**

The first Congress of the Social Democratic Workers' Party

The first Congress of the Social Democratic Workers' Party was held in a private house at Minsk between March 1st and 3rd 1898. The nine delegates included social democrats from Moscow and Yekaterinoslav and representatives of three major socialist groups. From these, a three-man committee was selected – Stepan Radchenko from the Emancipation of Labour, Boris Eidelman from a socialist organisation in Kiev and Alexander Kremer, a leader of the Jewish labour union (Bund) founded in 1897, which had sponsored the congress. Six meetings were held but because of the need for secrecy, no minutes were taken.

■ **Cross-reference**

Pyotr Struve is profiled on page 66.

Fig. 4 *Vladimir Ilyich Ulyanov (Lenin)*

Cross-reference

The title of Lenin's pamphlet *What is to be done?* was taken from Chernyshevsky's book. See page 35

Key profile

Vladimir Ilyich Ulyanov (Lenin)

Vladimir Ilyich Ulyanov (1870–1924), known as Lenin from 1901 after the river Lena in Siberia where he was exiled, came from a well-to-do professional family in Simbirsk. However, his family was ostracised after his brother's execution, following involvement in a plot to assassinate Tsar Alexander III. Lenin was expelled from University in Kazan, for involvement in political rebellion, but he was allowed to take his exams and become a lawyer. Although he practised as a lawyer after his graduation in 1891, Lenin spent much of his time working within underground Marxist societies and eventually became the leader of 'The Elders', a Marxist group meeting in St Petersburg. He wrote pamphlets, organised strikes among the factory workers, and, on a tour of Europe in 1895, met Plekhanov whom he impressed with his devotion to the Marxist cause. His activities in Russia brought him to the attention of the secret police, however, and he was exiled to Siberia in 1895 where he remained until February 1900. He consequently missed the launch of the new Social Democrat Party in 1898 but he wrote a programme for it. After he was released, he went into exile in Switzerland. In 1902 he produced the pamphlet, *What is to be done?*, in which he argued that the party needed to re-direct the workers away from trade unionism towards a revolution which would destroy the tsarist autocracy. He founded a new revolutionary newspaper *The Spark* (*Iskra*) with Plekhanov and others, and helped develop a strong underground party network. His harsh and uncompromising attitude led the Social Democrats to split in 1903 into Bolsheviks and Mensheviks. Lenin remained in exile until 1917, save for a brief return to St Petersburg in October 1905.

The second Party Congress took place in 1903, commencing in Brussels, but subsequently moving to a small congregational chapel in Shoreditch, London. The 51 voting delegates considered a variety of propositions as to how the party should move forward, and were divided on a number of these. While Lenin argued in favour of a strong disciplined organisation of professional revolutionaries to lead the proletariat, others, led by Martov, believed their task should be to develop a broad party with a mass working class membership. Whilst Martov saw members 'co-operating' with other liberal parties, Lenin wanted total dedication to revolution only. Lenin certainly did not have the overwhelming support of the majority at the beginning of the conference and it was only after a number of representatives withdrew that Lenin finally won the vote in favour of a more centralised party structure. Lenin then claimed that his supporters were the majority – in Russian the 'bolsheviki' whilst his opponents, led by Martov, were dubbed the 'mensheviki' – the minority. The terms remained, even though, overall, the reverse was actually true. Over the next few years there was continued argument and rivalry within the embryonic Party about the nature, timing and organisation of the revolution which they were planning and the Bolshevik/Menshevik division hardened so that by 1906 there were effectively two separate Social Democratic parties.

Key profiles

Lev Davodovich Bronstein (Leon Trotsky)

Lev Davodovich Bronstein (Leon Trotsky) (1879–1940) was the son of a well-to-do Jewish farmer from the Ukraine. He rejected a university education in order to devote himself to revolutionary politics. In 1898 he formed a commune of workers and students but their activities were discovered by the secret police and he was imprisoned in Moscow and subsequently exiled to Siberia. He studied Marx, Engels, Plekhanov and Lenin and in 1902 escaped with a false passport in the name of one of the prison guards – Trotsky. He went to London, wrote for *Iskra*, met

Fig. 5 *Leon Trotsky*

Lenin and took a middle road at the time of the split, accepting neither the Menshevik nor Bolshevik position. He returned to Russia in 1905 – and founded a soviet in St Petersburg. He was re-arrested and spent 15 months in prison until he escaped in 1907. He travelled around Europe and began the publication of *Pravda* in 1908. He was in the USA in 1917 when the first Russian revolution of 1917 broke out and he returned to Russia in May and worked with Lenin to win over the masses. He became a Bolshevik in July and was briefly imprisoned after the July days. He subsequently became chairman of the Petrograd Soviet and organised the Military Revolutionary Committee. He was the brains behind the planning of the Bolshevik takeover in the second revolution of 1917 and became Commissar for foreign affairs in the new government. He was unpopular with other Bolshevik leaders for his arrogance and Stalin ensured he did not succeed Lenin. In 1929 he was expelled from the party and murdered by a Stalinist agent in Mexico in 1940.

Julius Martov

Julius Martov (1873–1920) came from a Jewish middle class background. He helped found the Emancipation of Labour and the SD movement. He contributed to the party journal *Iskra* and was editor, 1903–05, after breaking with Lenin. He favoured working through trade unions, co-operatives and soviets to destroy the government. He was not invited to join the Bolsheviks after October 1917 and the Mensheviks were banned in 1918. Martov was exiled in 1920 and died in Germany.

A closer look

The split in the Social Democratic party

The split in the Social Democratic party was to have major consequences for the future of Marxism in Russia. In 1903–04, many members changed sides. While the Mensheviks awaited the bourgeois revolution that they believed had to precede the proletarian revolution, the Bolsheviks suggested the bourgois and proletarian revolution could occur simultaneously. They felt that the party's job was to educate the workers to lead them through the revolution, whilst the Mensheviks believed the impetus had to come from the workers themselves. Bolsheviks also believed that membership should be restricted and members should work within small cells that could escape police notice. The Mensheviks, on the other hand, insisted that memberhip should be open to all and the party should work through the trade unions and other workers' organisations to raise workers' consciousness. They wanted to follow democratic procedures and feared that the approach of the Bolsheviks, who favoured control in the hands of a Central Committee, could lead to dictatorship. These arguments were very damaging and Trotsky devoted much of his energy in trying to reconcile the two groups.

■ Activity

Revision exercise

Complete the chart below to show the main differences between the Russian Marxist groups, the Mensheviks and Bolsheviks:

	Mensheviks	Bolsheviks
Attitude to future revolution		
Role of party		
Decision-making in party		
Membership		

The intelligentsia and the liberals

The third strand of opposition was far more moderate. The liberal intelligentsia continued to press for change and reform, but they did not adopt a revolutionary attitude like the Social Revolutionaries or Social Democrats. They were concerned to promote welfare, education, liberty and the rule of law. Their hope was to reform the autocracy so that the tsar would listen directly to his people and rule in conjunction with them.

From the Slavophile tradition, there were thinkers like the novelist Count Leo Tolstoy, who came from the same noble family as Dmitrii Tolstoy but had very different views. Tolstoy opposed tsarist oppression and the injustice of the legal system, and he expressed his opinions through the moral tracts which he wrote in the 1880s and 1890s. However, he rejected violence and instead urged individuals to live pure and simple lives in order to bring about the moral regeneration of the country. His tract 'What I believe', written in 1883, was banned in 1884 but his work,

Fig. 6 *It was dangerous to keep incriminating documents. If discovered it could lead to exile or even death*

Cross-reference

The Slavophile and Western perspectives are discussed on page 13.

Dmitrii Tolstoy is profiled on page 32.

coming from the pen of a well-respected novelist, certainly contributed to the assault on authority of the autocratic government.

Key profile

Count Leo Tolstoy

Count Lev Nikolaevich Tolstoy (1828–1910) is generally known as Leo Tolstoy and is highly regarded as one of the world's greatest novelists. He began his career in the army and travelled throughout Europe, writing short stories in *Sevastopol Sketches* (1855–56) and the novel *The Cossacks* (1863). He subsequently returned to his family estates where he started a school for peasant children and wrote *War and Peace* (1865–69), a novel set during the Napoleonic Wars, which established his reputation. This was followed by *Anna Karenina* (1875–77), concerning an aristocratic woman who deserted her husband for a lover. Both novels show concern with the meaning of life and, after the second, Tolstoy himself underwent a spiritual crisis. He devoted himself to social reform, advocating simplicity and non-violence. He lived humbly on his great estate and in constant conflict with his wife. In November 1910, unable to bear his situation any longer, he left his estate in disguise. During his flight he contracted pneumonia, and he died a few days later.

Other opposition voices, following the westernising tradition, were heard among the professional 'middle' classes, which had grown considerably in number, thanks to Alexander II's reforms and the modernisation of the country. Through the *zemstva*, there was a new opportunity for liberal thinkers to air their views and since their work brought them into constant conflict with central government directives, they grew increasingly vocal in their criticisms.

Middle class society became more politicised in the years after the Great Famine of 1891–92 when the over-bureaucratic tsarist government showed its incompetence in dealing with the crisis. It had been left to voluntary organisations and the *zemstva* to provide the necessary relief work and this had helped to encourage the view that at least the educated members of society should have some direct say in the nation's governance. Consequently, by the mid-1890s the liberals were growing more vociferous in their demands for a national representative body to advise the government.

Government obstruction, including a reduction in *zemstva* powers under Alexander III, also forced these organisations along a more political path. The Tver *Zemstvo* petitioned Nicholas II to set up an advisory body in 1895, but he merely dismissed it as a 'senseless dream'. This did not deter the liberal nobles, like Prince Lvov, who continued to demand the creation of an all-class *Zemstvo* at district (*volost*) level and a National Assembly, but when Shipov tried to set up an 'All-*Zemstvo* Organisation' in 1896, it was immediately banned. This merely encouraged some of its more radical members to reform at Beseda (Symposium) in 1899 and they continued to meet in secret to discuss matters of liberal interest such as judicial reform and universal education. When, in 1900, the government ordered the dismissal of hundreds of liberals from the elected boards of the *zemstva*, the Beseda representatives assumed the leadership of the liberal constitutionalists attracting a wide-range of support from public figures, town leaders, members of the legal and teaching professions and industrialists.

Cross-reference

To re-read about the Great Famine of 1891–92, return to page 45.

The extract from the speech in which Nicholas II referred to 'senseless dreams' can be found on page 68.

Prince Lvov is profiled on page 96.

In 1903, the Union of Liberation (*Soyuz Osvobozhdeniya*) was founded under the inspiration of Pyotr Struve. Struve had defected from the Marxist movement, opposing its commitment to violent revolution, and had begun to publish a journal, *Osvobozhdenie* (*Liberation*) in Germany, to escape censorship. Struve believed that what Russia needed was a period of 'peaceful evolution' in which to adapt to its new industrialising status. He wanted to see a constitutional system put in place through which the urban workers could campaign legally to improve their conditions.

In 1904, the Union held a grand meeting to which representatives of the *zemstva* and other professional societies were invited. Members declared their intention to work for the establishment of a constitutional government and arranged a series of about 50 society banquets during the winter of 1904, which were attended by members of liberal elite.

The liberals, whether moderate campaigners within the *zemstva* or more radical members of the liberal unions, had limited political influence before 1905. Indeed, the liberals were fortunate to escape the closer attention of the police, which was only achieved because the latter were over-worked coping with the activities of the Social Revolutionaries and Social Democrats who were spreading agrarian and proletarian unrest. Perhaps the most that can be said is that they contributed to the momentum that was building up within the country for political change.

■ Key profile

Pyotr Berngardovich Struve

Pyotr Struve (1870–1944) was a lawyer, economist and philosopher who became interested in Marxism and involved in Populist and Marxist activities in the 1890s. By 1900, Struve had become a leader of the moderate wing of Russian Marxists and when banished from St Petersburg, travelled to Germany and founded *Osvobozhdenie* (*Liberation*) with the help of liberal intelligentsia and the radical part of *zemstva*. In mid-1903, after the founding of the liberal *Soyuz Osvobozhdeniya* (*Union of Liberation*), the magazine became the Union's official publication and was smuggled into Russia, where it enjoyed considerable success. When German police, under pressure from *Okhrana*, raided the premises in October 1904, Struve moved his operations to Paris and continued publishing the magazine there until the October Manifesto proclaimed freedom of the press in Russia.

In October 1905 Struve returned to Russia and became a co-founder of the liberal Constitutional Democratic party. He represented the party in the Second State Duma in 1907, but after its dissolution, he concentrated on writing. With the outbreak of World War I in 1914, Struve adopted a position of strong support for the government and after the Bolshevik revolution of 1917 joined the White movement which opposed the Bolshevik takeover.

■ Cross-reference

The events of 1905 are the subject of Chapter 5.

■ Activity

Creative thinking

Make a large poster depicting the three different types of revolutionary groups of the 1881–1904 period. You could illustrate your poster with photos and illustrations of some of the key personalities and should make clear the different beliefs, methods, and support that each had.

You should explain your poster to the class.

■ Question

Explain why opposition movements spread in Russia in the years 1881–1904.

The rule of the last two tsars, Alexander III and Nicholas II, in the years 1881 to 1904

Key profiles

Alexander III

Alexander III (1845–94) was the second son of Alexander II. He pursued an army career until he became heir to the throne after the death of his elder brother, Nicholas, in 1865. He was tutored by Konstantin Pobedonostev, a firm upholder of autocracy and repression, who taught that any concessions or signs of weakness would be indications of cowardice and failure on his part. He had watched his father die and was so fearful of revolutionary activity that he refused to live in the Winter Palace in St Petersburg and instead spent most of his time at a palace designed like a fortified fortress in Gatchina, which had belonged to his great-grandfather. He was a large but ungainly man, 6 feet 4 inches tall and immensely strong. He could tear a pack of cards in half, bend an iron pole over his knees and crush a silver rouble with his bare hands. He looked an autocrat and had a commanding character. He married a Danish Princess, Dagmar (Maria Feodorovna), and had six children. He died young, of a kidney ailment, possibly brought on by heavy drinking.

Fig. 7 *Nicholas II always lived in the shadow of his father, Alexander III, whose views he tried to uphold*

Nicholas II

Tsar Nicholas II (1868–1918) grew up in his father, Alexander III's shadow and was never rated very highly by him. He was small, naturally reserved and regarded by his father as a dunce and a weakling. He even referred to him as 'girlie'. Nicholas had excellent manners, a good memory and could speak several languages, but he was not a practical man. Politics bored him and he himself admitted that he found it difficult to *'focus his mind'*. When his father died in 1894, Nicholas is said to have said to his cousin, *'What is going to happen to me and to all of Russia? I am not prepared to be a tsar. I never wanted to become one. I know nothing of the business of ruling. I have no idea of even how to talk to the ministers.'* However, he accepted his inheritance as God-given and set out to rule in 'the Romanov way', asserting himself against the demands of the growing reform movement. His reign was to be marked by revolutions in 1905 and February 1917, after which he abdicated.

Cross-reference

Konstantin Pobedonostev is profiled on page 54.

Under the rule of tsars Alexander III (1881–94) and Nicholas II (1894–1917), the cautious reform that had characterised the greater part of the reign of Alexander II came to an end. Alexander III began his reign with the public hanging of those involved in his father's assassination and the rejection of Loris-Melikov's proposals for consitutional reform. Neither he nor his son, who was to become Nicholas II, were prepared to countenance the dilution of the autocracy by a system of representative assemblies. Advised by Konstantin Pobedonostev, the Procurator of the Holy Synod, Alexander produced a manifesto promising to *'reassert the principles of autocracy'*, while his son, tutored by the same hand, was to say in his inaugural speech of 1894:

Activity

Class activity

Prepare a class presentation on Alexander III and Nicholas II. You should try to find out something about their personalities and background before becoming tsar. You might conclude with a summary of the qualities and limitations of each for the position they were to hold.

I rejoice to see gathered here representatives of all estates of the realm, who have come to express their sentiments of loyal allegiance. I believe in the sincerity of these feelings, which have been those of every Russian from time immemorial. But it has come to my knowledge that latterly, at some meetings of the zemstva, voices have been heard from people who have allowed themselves to be carried away by senselesss dreams about the participation of representatives of the zemstva in the general administration of the internal affairs of the state. Let it be known to all that I devote all my strength to the good of my people, but that I shall uphold the principle of autocracy as firmly and unflinchingly as did my ever-lamented father.

2

There are obvious reasons why these tsars were determined to preserve the past. They believed their power was being undermined by western ideas, constitutional theories, secular thinking and urban discontent and they could see no other remedy than to turn the clock back. Nicholas openly declared that he preferred the traditionally slavic Moscow to the westernised St Petersburg and both tsars visited this city often and used it for pompous displays of the power of tsardom.

Under Alexander III, strong centralised control was reasserted, and the nobility and police given a crucial role. In 1889, Alexander III set up a new law for a new office of Land Captains, recruited from the nobility. This meant that whilst the representative *zemstva* and town dumas continued to function, these Land Captains were given wide-ranging powers including the ability to over-ride *zemstva* elections and disregard *zemstvo* decisions. They could even ignore the normal judicial process, overturn the judgements of local courts and impose punishments. Until 1904, they could order the public flogging of peasants for minor offences such as trespass or a failure to pay taxes. Another decree, of 1885, allowed the minister of justice to exercise greater control over the judicial system and reintroduced **'closed' court sessions** without juries for a number of crimes. Furthermore, in 1889, the powers of the magistrates were removed and their duties given to the Land Captains and royally appointed town judges instead.

It is little wonder that the *zemstva* had little faith in the governmental system. Their independence was undermined by the Act of 1890 which changed the election arrangements to reduce the peasants' vote and in 1892 a similar arrangement made it harder for the less wealthy to qualify for a vote in the towns. Both groups were encouraged to concentrate their activities on the social services – education and health in particular – where they performed some valuable work – but nothing could stop the outbursts of hostility, as even Nicholas observed in his speech in Source 2.

Nicholas completely misread the sense of deepening disillusionment presented by the *zemstva* at the beginning of his rule. Had he chosen to abandon autocracy and appeased the liberals by following a path of constitutional government in these early years, the subsequent history of Russia might well have been less turbulent. Instead he dismissed the attempts to create an 'All-*Zemstvo* Organisation' in 1896 and purged the elected boards of the *zemstva* of liberals in 1900.

■ **Key terms**

Closed court session: a trial held in secret to which no observers were permitted and where no reporting was allowed.

■ **Cross-reference**

The attempts to create an an 'All-*Zemstvo* Organisation' in 1896 are outlined on page 65.

A closer look

Marie-Feodorovna, wife of Alexander III and mother of Nicholas II and Alexandra-Feodorovna, wife of Nicholas II

The Empress Marie-Feodorovna (1847–1928) was born Princess Dagmar of Denmark, but in 1865, when she married the future Alexander III, she adopted the Orthodox religion and took her new name. She became an imposing and elegant empress and a domineering mother. She tried to oppose her eldest son Nicholas's marriage to Alix, a minor German princess, for fear this would diminish her own influence over him. However, the couple married in 1894, in St Petersburg, and Alix also accepted Orthodoxy and became Alexandra-Feodorovna (1872–1918). Having been strictly raised by her grandmother, Queen Victoria, from the age of six, when her own mother died, she found it difficult to adapt to life in St Petersburg. Marie-Feodorovna was cold and Alix hated the parties and society which Marie-Feodorovna continued to dominate. The indecisive Nicholas thus found himself sandwiched between a mother who constantly tried to meddle in state affairs and a wife who urged him to act more decisively. However, the devotion which developed between Nicholas and Alexandra led him to ignore the advice of his mother and the imperial couple thus cut themselves off from the broader royal family.

Whereas Alexander III had forced through counter-reforms reasserting the personal authority of the tsar and commanding, as Figes has written, *'like a general at war'*, Nicholas II was far less suited to the position of an autocrat. He failed to develop any domestic policy programme and found it difficult to make up his mind about anything. He changed his ministers repeatedly – fearing any who showed too much independent initiative – and tried to avoid calling the Council of Ministers to prevent its members uniting against him.

The result was that Nicholas feebly tried to preserve the policies of his father, whom he had much admired. This effectively meant ignoring the disturbances created by the growing working class in the towns who, encouraged by the revolutionary groups that developed in the 1890s, began to organise illegal strikes, demanding higher wages, better conditions and a shorter working day. Under Sergei Witte, who earned himself the nickname 'the hangman', more police were recruited, surveillance was stepped up and the army was relied upon to put down disturbances. In 1893, the army was called out 19 times, in 1899, 50 times and by 1902, 522 times. By using martial law, strikers could be arrested and sentenced to death without trial.

Cross-reference
Sergei Witte is profiled on page 45.

Like Alexander III, he was a staunch believer in Orthodoxy and he was happy to continue policies such as the exclusion of lower class children from secondary education and state control over the universities. Thanks to Alexander III's decrees, candidates for university appointment were judged on their 'religious, moral and patriotic orientation', women barred and all aspects of university life, including a measure forbidding students from gathering in groups of more than five, supervised.

Under both tsars, student demonstrations were brutally crushed, even when they had a non-political motive. Indeed heavy-handed police action

Key terms

Nationalism: an intense love of and, in many cases, a belief in the superiority of, one's country. This often included support for its history, religion, language and culture.

Pogrom: this is an old Russian word which means 'round up' or lynching. It originally denoted an assault by one ethnic group on another but after 1881 it gained the special connotation of an attack on Jews.

in St Petersburg in 1901, when a squadron of mounted Cossacks charged into a crowd of students, killing 13, helped radicalise some who might otherwise have been content to return to their studies. Following this particular incident 1,500 students were imprisoned in the Peter and Paul fortress –the first time so many of bourgeois birth had found themselves incarcerated. For lesser offences, students might be expelled or drafted into the army.

Both Alexander III and Nicholas II were believers in '**Nationalism**', and this was spread through a state policy of 'Russification'. This involved forcing the Russian language and culture on peoples of other ethnic origins and and endorsing widespread anti-semitism which produced a number of **pogroms** against Jews.

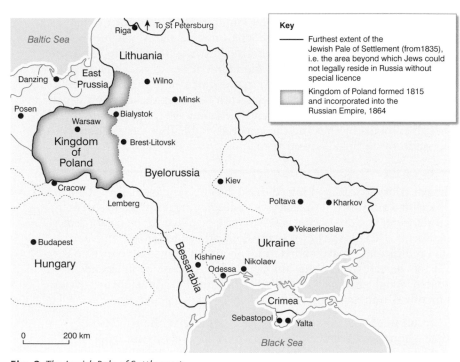

Fig. 8 *The Jewish Pale of Settlement*

A closer look

Russification

Russification became an official policy in the reigns of Alexander III and Nicholas II. Pobedonostev was a particularly ardent supporter and rampant anti-semite (hater of Jews). Both Poland and Finland suffered attempts to destroy their national culture as well as provinces, such as Byelorussia, Georgia and the Ukraine. The use of the Russian language was enforced and risings of ethnic peoples mercilessly surpressed. The racial group that suffered the most from this intense nationalism was the Jews who, since 1736, had only been allowed to live in an area of western Russia known as, 'The Pale of Settlement'. Anti-Jewish pogroms broke out in 1881 in Yelizavetgrad in the Ukraine, where there was a large Jewish population, and they soon spread to other towns. The governing authorities made little attempt to intervene and it is likely that the *Okhrana* actually encouraged the rioters. Troubles continued intermittently until 1884, and about 16 major cities were affected.

Jewish property was burnt, shops and businesses destroyed, women raped and many put to death. Even after the main outbreaks, there were still sporadic pogroms, as in Odessa in 1886. Laws were also brought in which discriminated against the Jews, particularly in the professions, and thousands of Jews emigrated at this time.

The effect of such policies among the Jews who remained in Russia was to drive a disproportionate number of them towards revolutionary groups, and in particular Marxist socialist organisations. In 1897, the General Union of Jewish Workers in Russia and Poland was set up and this was to become involved in the Marxist Social Democratic Movement, playing an important part in the growth of opposition to the autocracy under Nicholas II. Prominent Jews in the revolutionary movement in Russia in the early 20th century included Trotsky, Martov, Zinoviev and Litvinov.

By 1904, Russia was in turmoil. There was widespread unrest in both towns and countryside and Nicholas II seemed to have nothing to offer. At the top there was no leadership and no sense of direction. Although hard-working, the tsar seemed to have no sense of reality and was easily influenced by the reactionary advisers he chose to surround himself with. More competent men like Witte – whom he dismissed as minister of finance and president of the Council of Ministers in 1903 – were treated with suspicion.

Fig. 9 *Unrest spread through the Russian countryside*

The result of all this was to deprive the government of effective leadership or co-ordination during the final years of the tsarist regime. Nicholas was the source of all the problems. If there was a vacuum of power at the centre of the ruling system, then he was the empty space. In a sense, Russia gained in him, the worst of both worlds: a tsar determined to rule from the throne yet quite incapable of exercising power. This was 'autocracy without an autocrat'. Perhaps nobody could have fulfilled the role which Nicholas had set himself: the work of government had become much too vast and complex for a single man; autocracy was out of date. But Nicholas was mistaken to try in the first place. Instead of delegating power, he indulged in a fantasy of absolute power. So jealous was he of his own prerogatives that he tried to by-pass the state institutions altogether and centre power on the court. Nicholas's government was unable to create coherent policies to deal with the mounting problems of society.

The years of the Red Cockerel

The years 1903–04 were particularly turbulent. There were so many instances of arson in the rural communities that the nickname, 'the years of the Red Cockerel', referring to the leaping flames which ressembled a rooster's comb, was coined. The unrest was at its worst in the central Russian provinces, where the landord/peasant relationship was still at its most traditional, but it also spread into Georgia, the Ukraine and Poland. Peasants set fire to their landlords' barns, destroying grain, or vented their anger by attacking landlords and officials or seizing their woodland and pasture.

Industrial strikes escalated in the towns, from 17,000 in 1894 to about 90,000 in 1904. In 1901, the Obukhov factory in St Petersburg saw violent clashes between armed police and whip-carrying Cossacks and such sights became commonplace over the ensuing years. In 1900, in an attempt to control the proliferation of illegal unions, the Moscow chief of the *Okhrana*, S.V. Zubatov, began organising his own police-sponsored trade unions with the approval of the Governor-General of Moscow, the Grand Duke Sergei and the minister of internal affairs, Plehve. The idea was to provide 'official' channels through which complaints could be heard and aid provided, in an attempt to prevent workers being lured into joining the radical socialists. The experiment only lasted until 1903, when Zubatov was dismissed and exiled after one of his unions became involved in a general strike in Odessa. However, another union on the Zubatov model, the Assembly of St Petersburg Factory Workers, was formed in 1904 by Father Georgii Gapon. The Union was approved by Plehve and had the support of the Orthodox Church. It soon had 12 branches and 8,000 members and Gapon tried to expand activities to Kiev and Moscow.

■ Key profiles

Vyacheslav Konstantinovich von Plehve

Plehve (1846–1904) came from a noble German family and was raised in Warsaw. He attended Moscow University, where he trained as a lawyer and entered the Ministry of Justice. In 1881 he investigated Alexander II's murder and was made Director of the Department of the Police, giving him control over the *Okhrana*. In 1902 he became minister for internal affairs. He at first tried to be conciliatory and to work with with the *zemstva*. However, he soon relapsed and abandoned the police-supported trade unions. He was the victim of several assassination attempts, and that of July 1904 succeeded.

Father Gapon

Father Georgii Gapon (1870–1906) studied at the St Petersburg Theological Academy and became an Orthodox priest and prison chaplain, working in the working class districts of St Petersburg. Believing he had a divine mission to help the workers, he began organising workers' unions from 1903, but remained intensely loyal and taught that the tsar was obliged by God to respond to the workers' demands. He escaped with his life after the Bloody Sunday march of 1905, and briefly spent time in exile, supported by Social Revolutionaries. On returning to Russia in December he re-made contact with the *Okhrana*, but was found hanged in March 1906, possibly murdered by Social Revolutionary agents, angered by his double-dealing, or by the *Okhrana*.

Learning outcomes

In this section you have looked at how Russia underwent a rapid programme of industrialisation in the last decade of the nineteenth century and the ways in which this created and amplified social tensions. You have considered life in the towns and the countryside and have read about the conditions in which the Russian proletariat and peasants lived and worked in the years down to 1904. You have also examined the growth of internal opposition, from both liberals and revolutionaries, and have seen how the last two tsars blithely ignored the social changes going on around them, relying heavily on repression in order to uphold the tsarist autocracy. In the next section you will see how these mounting problems eventually provoked a revolution.

Practice questions

(a) Explain why the moderate liberal opposition grew stronger in the years 1881–1904.

(12 marks)

Study tip To answer this question you will firstly need to identify the moderate liberal opposition as that of the intelligentsia – particularly that displayed by the *zemstva* – who wanted constitutional reform. Your answer should provide a set of reasons for the liberals' growth and you will probably want to refer to the position of the *zemstva* and the specific action taken against them, as well as other reasons provoking greater opposition, such as the intransigence of the last two tsars. Don't forget to show how the factors inter-link, and provide a conclusion.

(b) How far was the personality of Nicholas II responsible for the instability in Russia in 1904?

(24 marks)

Study tip In this answer, you will need to set what you know about Nicholas II's personal failings against other factors which were causing instability, such as population growth, economic change, urbanisation, rural problems and the structure of the autocracy. Decide on your argument before you begin to write and ensure that your answer leads to a well-supported conclusion.

5 The Russo-Japanese War and the impact of the 1905 Revolution

In this chapter you will learn about:

- why Russia went to war with Japan in 1904 and the impact of that war

- the causes of the revolution of 1905

- the part played by the different political groups in the revolution of 1905

- the importance of the October Manifesto

- the recovery of tsarist authority by 1906.

Cross-reference

Until January 31st, 1918, the Russians used the Julian calendar, which was 13 days behind the Gregorian calendar used by western Europe. More detail on this is provided in Chapter 8, page 112. This book uses the Julian dates.

Bloody Sunday, January 9th, 1905

It was a bitingly cold January Sunday in 1905 when the priest, Father Gapon, set forth at the head of a procession of unemployed and disgruntled St Petersburg workers anxious for jobs, decent wages and shorter working hours. It was not a spontaneous demonstration. The idea of presenting a petition to their 'little Father', Tsar Nicholas II, in whom they had absolute faith to improve the workers' lot, had been carefully planned and other lines of demonstrators had also foregone the warmth of their homes to join in five separate processions around the city. In total the numbers on the streets reached around 150,000 with many women and children marching alongside their menfolk, crunching through the ice and steeling themselves against the freezing wind that stung their eyes and threw snow into their faces, in order to appeal to their tsar. They held high their precious icons, their lovingly made patriotic banners, their crosses and pictures of Nicholas II and his predecessors, and they kept their spirits up by singing hymns as they marched. Their destination was the tsar's Winter Palace, and all went well until Gapon's group approached the Narva gates. There, blocking the road ahead of them, stood the grim sight of armed tsarist soldiers and mounted Cossacks. It would have been impossible to turn back the dense crowds flooding along the streets, even if the leaders had wanted to, and as those at the back forced the front ranks forward, the guards opened fire and the Cossacks charged.

At Troitskaya Square, not far from the Palace, another group encountered armed guards from the Pavlovskii regiment who similarly opened fire leaving around 150 dead and wounded. As word spread down the ranks and through the city, the panicking crowds fled in the direction of the Winter Palace Square, where they met yet more armed troops – Cossacks, cavalry and even some pieces of heavy artillery ranged against them. Tempers were running high on both sides and as the angry crowds shouted defiance, they were stung by whips and forced back by the blunt sides of the Cossacks' sabres. In the midst of this mayhem, a strange hush suddenly fell as incredulous families watched the troops with bayonets assuming a firing position. Many fell to their knees and crossed themselves, but to little avail. A volley burst forward, straight into the dense mass of protestors and as red blood began to stain the white snow, people turned and fled for their lives.

The events of 'Bloody Sunday, 1905' were the product of a number of factors, not least a war with Japan that had reached its climax a month earlier.

War with Japan and the causes of the 1905 revolution

The Russo-Japanese War

Plehve, Nicholas's minister for internal affairs, is accredited with encouraging the tsar to embark on a *'short swift victorious war'* against the Japanese in January 1904 in order to stem the rising tide of domestic unrest. The origins of the war lay in the weakness of the Chinese Empire. Both Russia, anxious to 'drive to the East' and gain more ports and coastline, and Japan, whose swelling population needed more land and resources, saw opportunities for expansion at the expense of China. Russian penetration had been bolstered by the building of the Trans-Siberian railway. Although the main line ended at Vladivostok, in 1896 the Chinese allowed an additional line to be constructed south from Vladivostok through Northern Manchuria to Harbin. In 1898, a spur line was added to the naval base of Port Arthur on the Liaodong peninsula which Russia was granted on a 25-year lease. Since the Japanese, who were desperate to expand and acquire land and resources for a growing population, had briefly held this peninsula in 1895, the stage was set for the two powers to come into conflict. A Russian 'business venture' with plans to move soldiers into the Liadong peninsular and seize full control may have been the all the provocation the Japanese needed. Their resentment at exclusion from Port Arthur, where the Russians were expanding their influence, and their desire to increase prestige by defeating a European power led to their attack on Port Arthur on January 2nd 1904.

■ Exploring the detail

The authenticity of this remark is in some doubt. It may have been put about by Witte, who disliked Plehve!

Fig. 1 *The Russo-Japanese war*

The tsar, encouraged by his ministers, was determined to fight back. Nicholas regarded himself as an expert on the area, since in 1890 his father had sent him on a grand tour to broaden his political education. This tour had included both Japan and Indo-China and it is said that an incident in Japan, when a mentally deranged terrorist had tried to assassinate him, had left him with a long-lasting hatred for the Japanese. Like many Russians at the time, he regarded the Japanese with racialist contempt, arrogantly referring to them as 'little monkeys' (makaki). He was consequently heartened by the groundswell of patriotic sentiment within Russia for a war against the 'yellow danger'.

■ Cross-reference

Plehve is profiled on page 72.

However, the Russians really had very little idea of their enemy, or the inadequacies of their own forces. Running a war 6,000 miles from the capital was far from easy. Troops had to be sent on a six-day journey across Russia from the west, and the Trans-Siberian railway was only single track. Obviously this placed the Russians at an immediate disadvantage compared with the Japanese with short lines of supply. The organisation was chaotic. Ammunition was in short supply and one officer, having waited for some weeks for reserves of ammunition was disheartened to find the expected train had arrived filled not with munitions but with icons (religious symbols) for the soldiers. A long siege of Port Arthur, plus a series of defeats, turned the initial surge of patriotism into an attitude of hostility and opposition to the government. There was little mourning when Plehve was blown up by a Social Revolutionary bomb in July 1904 and in Warsaw, his home town, crowds turned out to celebrate on the streets. There were renewed cries for a National Assembly, and the moderate Mirskii, who replaced Plehve, reluctantly agreed to allow a group of *zemstvo* representatives to meet – as he said – 'for a cup of tea' and with no publicity, in his own private quarters in St Petersburg in November 1904. However, when Mirskii presented the tsar with an edited version of the Assembly's requests, Nicholas replied: *'I will never agree to the representative form of government because I consider it harmful to the people whom God has entrusted to me.'* All he was prepared to agree to was an expansion of the rights of the *zemstva*.

The 1905 Revolution – Bloody Sunday

The war with Japan provoked internal unrest. Quite apart from the feelings of humiliation and anger, which reached a highpoint on December 20th, when Port Arthur finally surrendered to the Japanese forces, it disrupted the economy, driving up food prices and forcing factory closures.

On January 3rd 1905, a strike began at the Putilov Iron Works in St Petersburg. Many of these strikers belonged to Father Gapon's union and his solution to the troubles was a peaceful march to present a petition to Nicholas II. Their 'humble and loyal adress to the tsar read:

Fig. 2 *The Japanese accept the surrender of the Russian forces at Port Arthur, 1904*

O Sire! we working men of St Petersburg, our wives and children, and our parents, helpless and aged men and women, have come to you, our ruler, in quest of justice and protection. We are beggars, we are oppressed and overburdened with work; we are insulted, we are not regarded as human beings but are treated as slaves who must suffer in silence.

Our first wish was to discuss our needs with our employers, but this was refused us; we were told that we have no legal right to discuss our conditions. We asked that wages of casual labourers and women should be raised to one rouble a day, that overtime should be abolished and that more adequate medical attention should be provided for us with care and without humiliation. We asked that the factories should be rebuilt so that we could work in them without suffering from draughts, rain and snow.

Your majesty! We are here, many thousands of us. We have the appearance of human beings but in fact we have no human rights at all, not even the right to speak or to think. We are turned into slaves by your officials. Any one of us who dares raise his voice in defence of the working class is thrown into prison, sent into exile.

We are seeking here the last salvation. Do not refuse assistance to thy people. Cast away from them the intolerable oppression of officials. Destroy the wall between thyself and thy people. National representation is indispensible. Order immediately representatives from the Russian land from all ranks, including representatives from the working people.

1

Questions

Source Analysis

1 What does the tone of the petition imply about the attitude of the workers to the tsar?

2 List the complaints of the petitioners.

3 How 'reasonable' was the petition?

Gapon was warned to call off the march, but he naïvely went ahead on Sunday January 9th. However, Nicholas himself chose to spend the weekend at Tsarskoe Selo, his summer palace, a little way from the city and the fore-warned authorities drafted 12,000 troops into the city as a precaution.

The situation was tense, even before the fateful march began on Sunday January 9th and the events of that day led to it being known as 'Bloody Sunday'. Probably around 200 were killed and 800 wounded, possibly more. Furthermore, in the chaos which ensued as guards chased workers through the streets, the homes of the rich were ransacked, shops destroyed and pilfered and barricades set up in the streets. Perhaps more ominously, the event hardened the outlook of those who had previously had little political concern. According to one of the crowd:

> I observed the faces around me and I detected neither fear nor panic. No, the reverent and almost prayerful expressions were replaced by hostility and even hatred. I saw these looks of hatred and vengeance on literally every face – old and young, men and women. The revolution had been truly born, and it had been born in the very core, in the very bowels of the people.

Fig. 3 *The desperate workers are driven back by the tsarist forces on 'Bloody Sunday'*

■ The 1905 revolutions: the part played by liberals, revolutionaries and nationalists

The aftermath of Bloody Sunday saw a grim struggle between:

- the authorities, desperate to keep order and regain control
- the demands of liberals, anxious to retain control of the movement for reform

■ radical revolutionaries, determined to press home their advantages

■ nationalist groups, who saw an opportunity to exert their independence.

Nicholas seemed totally unable to come to terms with the situation in which he found himself and acted in a contradictory and indecisive fashion. Although he agreed to meet a few selected workers' representatives at his palace of Tsarskoe Selo in the aftermath of Bloody Sunday, he merely told them that they had been misled and should return to work.

The Putilov strike turned into a general strike through the capital so that by the end of January there were more than 400,000 workers on strike. Furthermore, news of what had happened on Bloody Sunday soon spread through the Empire, and as 1905 progressed, the government steadily lost control of events and the country reached a state bordering on anarchy. By the autumn of 1905 there were around 2,500,000 workers on strike.

The situation was not helped by the news from the East. In March, after 90,000 soldiers had lost their lives, the Battle of Mukden ended in defeat. By April, following the establishment of the 'All Russian Union of Railway Workers', many illegal trade unions had been formed, bringing strikes and demonstrations to all the major cities. There were even a number of workers' councils, or soviets, set up which tried to take control of factories. The first appeared in the Urals in April and in May, this was copied by textile workers in Ivanovo-Voznesensk, east of Moscow. There were soon 60 such (illegal) workers' councils.

Whilst workers were protesting in the towns, peasants in the countryside plundered, burned and looted landowners' property. In August a Peasants' Union was formed which became the first real political organisation of the Russian peasantry, whilst in Moscow, a Peasants' Congress was held which called for an 'All Russian Union of Peasants.'

Adding to the general chaos were the naval mutinies:

■ at Kronstadt, near St Petersburg on the Baltic Coast, in May

■ aboard the battleship *Potemkin*, part of the Black Sea fleet in June.

This spread doubt as to whether the tsar could rely on the loyalty of his armed forces.

A closer look

Mutiny on the *Potemkin*

This battleship had been unable to take part in the Russo-Japanese war since the Straits Convention of 1871 had forbidden Russian warships to sail out into the Mediterranean while Turkey was at peace (another attempt by the British to try to curb Russian influence in the Balkan area). Protest had begun over a meat ration which was considered inedible by the sailors. When one of the sailors' spokesmen was shot, a full-scale mutiny had ensued in which seven officers were killed. Sailing under a red flag, the sailors took the ship into the port of Odessa where they placed the dead sailor's body at the bottom of the 'Potemkin steps' between the city and the harbour. The next day, thousands of townsfolk who had their own grievances against the local authorities, arrived to pay respects and show solidarity with the sailors. When these crowds refused to disperse, troops were ordered to fire at random into their midst. Many jumped into the sea and more than 2,000 were killed and about 3,000 wounded. This was an even worse massacre than that of Bloody Sunday in St Petersburg. The boat eventually sailed off to Romania and was surrendered in return for a safe refuge for the sailors.

Fig. 4 *The mutineers on the deck of the battleship Potemkin*

■ **Activity**

Thinking and analysis

As you read through the following sections, copy and complete the chart below.

	Liberals	Revolutionaries	Nationalists
Leaders			
Demands			
Main activities			
Significance			

Liberals

The liberals grew increasingly anxious as the events of 1905 unfolded. Whilst they were in favour of constitutional change, they were concerned that the initiative was slipping from their hands. Their initial response to the events of January was to pressurise the government once more for a National Assembly as a solution to Russia's problems. Nicholas's immediate response had been to reassert his commitment to autocracy and to dismiss the moderate Mirskii and bring in two new officials who were prepared to follow a hard-line policy : A.G. Bulygin, as his minister for internal affairs, and Major-General D.E. Trepov as the new military governor of St Petersburg. However, he asked Bulygin to prepare draft proposals for some sort of elected consultative assembly, so giving some hope to the moderates that he was prepared to concede change.

A meeting of *zemstva* liberals in Moscow on March 18th urged Nicholas to act swiftly to bring an end to the escalating revolutionary disturbances and a series of congresses followed throughout the year repeating a similar plea. Liberal plans for reform were also discussed in innumerable meetings in the universities which became centres for moderate reformist thinking.

Groups of moderate liberal professionals, including teachers, engineers, doctors, lawyers and others also formed 'unions' of their own, which were rather more extreme in their demands than the *zemstva* liberals. These came together in the creation of a 'Union of Unions' (May 8/9th) led by the liberal politician Pavel Milyukov. They wanted full civil and political rights, **universal suffrage** and nationwide elections to an assembly with full legislative powers.

■ **Key profile**

Pavel Nikolayevich Milyukov

Pavel Nikolayevich Milyukov (1859–1943) studied and taught at Moscow University, where he developed liberal views. He was dismissed because of these and spent some time travelling in Europe and the USA. He returned in 1905 and founded the Constitutional Democratic party (the Kadets) in October. He was a member of the State Duma, and drafted the Vyborg Manifesto, calling for political freedom, reforms and passive resistance to governmental policy. He joined the Progressive Bloc during the war and made a famous speech in 1916, 'What is that? Stupidity or treason?' against the tsarist handling of the war. He wanted to retain the constitutional monarchy but accepted the position of minister of foreign affairs in the Provisional Government until May 1917, when he resigned over his desire to continue the war and gain more territory. He eventually went into exile and died in France.

Bulygin finally published details of his plan for constitutional reform on July 24th. However, this was rejected by a *Zemstvo* Conference held between September 12th and 15th, as not going far enough. Although it proposed the establishment of a *Duma*, or representative parliament, it suggested that this body should simply be for consultation and would have no share in the making of laws and supervising the legality of government. Even for the moderate liberals, this was not enough.

Revolutionaries

As might have been expected, the Social Revolutionaries seized the opportunity afforded by the disturbances of 1905 to perpetrate a further political assassination. On February 4th, the Grand Duke Sergei, the tsar's uncle and commander of the Moscow military region, was blown up by a Socialist Revolutionary (SR) bomb and then on July 11th it was the turn of Shuvalov, the military governor of Moscow. They also encouraged the activities of the peasantry and were behind the attempt to create a council to organise and co-ordinate peasant action, leading to the formation of the All-Russian Peasant Union in May. The council was composed of regional delegates, but it failed to put forwards realistic and coherent demands and proved unable to to co-ordinate the peasant rebellions effectively.

The SRs also led a rising in support of the Potemkin mutiny and a prominent SR, Nikolai Avksentiev, was one of the

Fig. 5 *Grand Duke Sergei is killed by a bomb, December 1905*

main leaders of the St Petersburg Soviet. However, SR intentions were not always clear. Although they wanted the overthrow of tsardom, they were more inclined to support the demands of the liberal reformers than of the Social Democrats and this made for disunity among the opponents of tsarism.

The Social Democrats were taken even more by surprise. Both Lenin and Trotsky were abroad at the beginning of 1905 and although Trotsky secretly returned in February, Lenin missed all the action, only returning in November. The party split had made it harder to co-ordinate activities and although both Bolsheviks and Mensheviks were active in encouraging strike activity and the formation of workers' councils, they lacked direction from the top. Trotsky found his way back as quickly as possible, first to Kiev in the Ukraine and then to St Petersburg, where he tried to push both the Bolshevik Central Committee and Menshevik organisations in a more radical direction. He was forced to flee again, to Finland, in May but returned in October to work on the revolutionary newspaper, the *Russian Gazette*, increasing its circulation to 500,000, and to chair the St Petersburg Soviet, an elected non-party revolutionary organisation representing the capital's workers, but dominated by Mensheviks. This grew out of an earlier soviet established at the beginning of the year and was rapidly reformed in an attempt to co-ordinate the strike action which escalated in October.

■ Cross-reference

To recap on the party split into Mensheviks and Bolsheviks, re-read pages 63–64.

The printers and bakers of Moscow had abandoned work at the end of September, provoking their colleagues in St Petersburg to come out in sympathy. Railway workers had followed and when reports were received that the government had arrested all the leaders of the Railway Workers' Union, the railwaymen were joined by the workers of the post and telegraph offices, the banks and industrial workers from all parts of the country The economy ground to a halt, local government offices were closed and even the imperial ballet refused to dance.

Fig. 6 *The railway strike of 1905 brought the economy to a halt*

This strike had no central leadership and it surprised the revolutionary parties as much as the liberals and tsarist government. The hastily assembled St Petersburg Soviet proved highly effective in maintaining the strike and because it could influence workers to maintain essential services, its authority was even recognised by the government. However, although the Bolsheviks were later to make much of the workers' activity in 1905 and the SD's role in the formation of the soviets, the October general strike was not the result of the revolutionary parties' leadership. Such involvement as they had occurred in response to events, and the attempt of the St Petersburg Soviet to maintain a second general strike in November failed. The 'revolution' of October 1905 was essentially a popular revolt.

Consequently, whilst the events of 1905 were certainly revolutionary in many respects, the part played by the radical revolutionary parties was fairly limited because both the Social Revolutionaries and Social Democrats were fragmented and lacked effective leadership within Russia.

A closer look

The St Petersburg Soviet

According to Trotsky, who was to become its chairman, the first meeting of the St Petersburg Soviet was held on the evening of October 13, 1905 in the Technological Institute and was attended by 30–40 delegates. Known as the 'Soviet of Workers' Deputies', it replaced a 'Soviet of Workers' Delegates', which had already been set up in January/February 1905. It soon had tremendous influence in St Petersburg – organising and co-ordinating strike action and appealing to supporters to refuse to pay taxes and to withdraw their bank deposits to cripple the government. It was made up of 400–500 members, elected by around 200,000 workers, representing five trade unions and 96 factories around the city. However, fearing that the general strike was providing the tsarist regime with an excuse for repression, Trotsky called the general strike off and its importance can be questioned. It broke up in December 1905 when its leaders (including Trotsky) were arrested by the government.

Nationalists

The revolutionary activities of 1905 were especially pronounced in the non-Russian areas of the Empire as nationalist groups with both economic and political grievances seized the opportunity to advance their own position. Such nationalist protest often attracted people of all classes and professions in demonstrations against the demands of the tsarist state. For example, a general strike in Odessa in the Ukraine in June brought people from a wide social background onto the streets.

Nationalist feelings often ran high. There were demands for independence from the Poles, Finns, Latvians and other nationalist minority groups to which the tsarist government responded with force and repression. In June, troops were used against strikers in Lodz in Finland, in the Baltic States and in the Caucasus where inter-ethnic confrontations led to the Armenian-Tartar massacres, causing damage and disruption to the cities and Baku oilfields. In Russian Poland over 400,000 workers became involved in strikes, to the severe disruption of the economy.

Nationalist outbursts in Bessarabia took the form of anti-semitic attacks and these were welcomed by the authorities and right-wing elements who exploited emotions to form the 'Union of the Russian People', which spread the message that non-Russians were deliberately undermining the country.

The Union organised gangs of strike-breakers known as the 'Black Hundreds' to beat up those who caused disruption in the Empire, for example in the Caucasus. Hangings and beatings became commonplace in an attempt to curb nationalist and peasant activity, while Nicholas provided the organisation with moral and financial support.

The events of the first eight months of 1905 unfolded agains the backdrop of war against Japan which dragged on until August. The war exposed the weaknesses of the autocracy and Russia's backwardness, compared to the modernised and progressive Japan, for all to see. In May, for example, the Russian Baltic fleet was sunk by the Japanese in the straits of Tsushima – virtually destroying Russian naval power and provoking the Potemkin mutiny. Thanks to a combination of war and internal unrest, conditions within Russia grew steadily worse. Production fell while prices and taxes rose, aggravating Russia's many social and economic problems.

A closer look

The loss of the Baltic fleet

As the situation in the Far East had deteriorated and the Russian fleet at Port Arthur had been lost, the tsar had agreed to send five divisions of the Baltic Fleet (moored on the Gulf of Finland) to engage the Japanese navy. The fleet set out on October 2nd 1904, but its journey was not without incident. Sailing across the Dogger bank in the North Sea, the *Suvorov* opened fire on two of its own ships, believing them to be patrolling Japanese torpedo boats. In the firing that ensued, a British trawler, one of a small fishing fleet off Hull, was sunk and two English fishermen drowned. This provoked an outcry in Britian and demands for war were only allayed by the payment of a substantial fine by the Russians.

After a seven-month voyage, around Africa and across the Indian Ocean, refuelling with coal from merchant vessels since few ports were prepared to allow the fleet to dock, the Russians sailed northwards towards Manchuria. By the time the ships reached the Straits of Tsushima, where they encountered the Japanese fleet, they were in poor shape. Apart from four new battleships, the Russian ships were old and the long voyage and the lack of opportunity for maintenance meant their hulls were badly fouled, reducing their speed. Whilst the Japanese ships could travel at 16 knots (30 km/h), the Russian fleet could reach only 9 knots (17 km/h) making its ships far less manoeuvrable. Furthermore, the Japanese had more modern rangefinders and superior gunners and shells. These soon wrecked the Russian superstructures and fatefully ignited the large quantities of coal stored on the Russian decks.The battle, which began at 10.00am on May 14th, was over by 11.00am the next day. Only three out of 27 Russian ships escaped, whilst the Japanese, under Admiral Togo, lost only three torpedo boats.

■ Exploring the detail

The Black Hundreds

The Black Hundreds were a subsection of the right-wing 'Union of the Russian People'. Members supported the tsarist autocracy and were devoted to the struggle against revolutionary activity. They were conservative, anti-semitic and believed in, 'Orthodoxy, Autocracy, and Nationalism'. Members were recruited through special church services, meetings and lectures. The gangs used violent tactics, attacking protesting workers, Jews, students and activists. In Odessa, 500 Jews were killed in a three-day pogrom. In Tomsk, the Black Hundreds set fire to a building hosting an anti-government meeting and killed 200. Nicholas associated himself with the Union when he accepted the presentation of its honorary insignia at a public reception in December 1905.

Following the mediation of president Thoedore Roosevelt of the USA the war was finally concluded by the Treaty of Portsmouth (USA), which surrendered less than the Japanese had demanded, but was, nevertheless, a grave blow.

Peace Treaty of Portsmouth (New Hampshire), August 23rd 1905

i   Henceforth peace will prevail between Their Majesties the Emperors of Russia and Japan, and between their respective states and subjects.

ii   The Russian Imperial government, recognising that Japan has predominant political, military and economic interests in Korea, commits itself not to interfere in those measures of guidance, protection and supervision which the Japanese government considers necessary to take in Korea.

iii   The Russian Imperial government cedes to Japan, with the agreement of the Chinese government, the lease of Port Arthur, its surrounding area and territorial waters, as well as all rights, privileges and concessions attached to the lease.

iv   The Russian Imperial government cedes to Japan in perpetuity the southern part of the island of Sakhalin.

This dismal end to the Russo-Japanese War did not create a mood for compromise. On the contrary, the rebels grew more confident and the strikes became better organised and more militant in the months of September and October. However, until the general strike of that month forced him into action, Nicholas continued to spend his days giving tea parties and hunting. He seemed to have had complete faith that Trepov, Governor of St Petersburg, would soon be able to reassert control and it was only when the nation's economy was paralysed, the administration broken down, the government powerless and the people everywhere in a state of open revolt that he was forced to yield. By October, even Nicholas realised that to continue to rely on repression, even if that were possible, would have resulted in *'rivers of blood, and we should only have been back where we started'*.

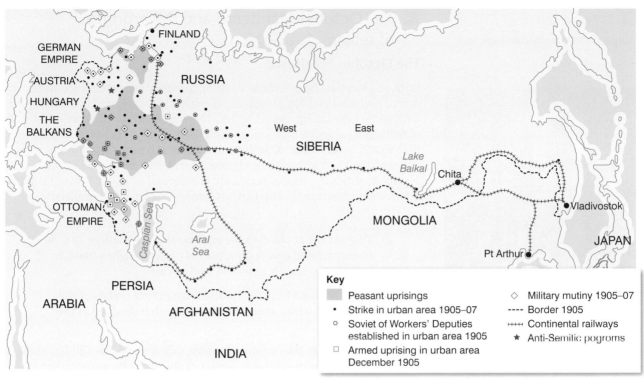

Fig. 7 *Unrest in Russia, 1905*

Key

▨	Peasant uprisings	◇	Military mutiny 1905–07
•	Strike in urban area 1905–07	----	Border 1905
⊙	Soviet of Workers' Deputies established in urban area 1905	+++	Continental railways
▫	Armed uprising in urban area December 1905	★	Anti-Semitic pogroms

Activity

Revision exercise

Copy and complete the summary chart below, using the information given on pages 75–84.

1904/5 Month	Events in Russo-Japanese war	Events in Russia
December		
January		
February		
March		
April		
May		
June		
July		
August		
September		

Question

How far was the political unrest of January–September 1905 the result of developments in the Russo-Japanese war of 1904–1905?

Tip: Use the information in your chart to help you plan your answer. In order to answer this question fully, you will need to balance the impact of the war against other factors, such as economic and social change.

Activity

Constructing a spider diagram

Make a spider diagram to illustrate the long and short-term causes of the revolution of October 1905.

■ Cross-reference

Sergei Witte is profiled on page 45.

Fig. 8 *The promise of reform brought a temporary respite from the troubles*

■ Key terms

Duma: this was the term originally used to denote the elected town councils but it was also to be adopted for the representative parliament set up after the 1905 revolution, sometimes known more formally as the State Duma.

■ Questions

1 In what ways did the October Manifesto go beyond the promises made by Bulygin in July?

2 Which promise ended Nicholas's autocratic powers?

■ The October Manifesto and the promise of reform, 1905–06

The October Manifesto

With the Russian Empire near to total collapse, the tsar agreed to sign a decree on October 17th promising constitutional reform. Even then, he took some persuading. Sergei Witte, the Chairman of the tsar's Council of Ministers, warned that the country was on the verge of a revolution that would 'sweep away a thousand years of History', while even Trepov declared the need for some moderate reform and the Grand Duke Nicholas, the tsar's uncle, reputedly threatened to shoot himself unless refoms were instituted. The tsar's 'October Manifesto' promised:

■ To grant the population the unshakeable foundations of civic freedom based on the principles of personal rights, freedom of conscience, speech, assembly and union.

■ To admit to participation in the **Duma** those classes of the population which at present are altogether deprived of the franchise.

■ To establish it as an unbreakable rule that no law can become effective without the approval of the State **Duma** and that the representatives of the people should be guaranteed the supervision of the legality of the actions of authorities appointed by Us.

There were celebrations on the streets of St Petersburg, as crowds gathered to wave red flags and sing the French revolutionary anthem, the Marseillaise. The General Strike was called off and there was talk of the birth of a new Russia. However, the real radicals, like Trotsky and Lenin, were far from convinced and tried desperately to get the workers to fight on. Lenin's Bolsheviks wrote in their workers' bulletin: *'We have been granted a constitution, yet autocracy remains. We have been granted everything, and yet we have been granted nothing'*. In some ways their view accorded with that of the tsar himself. Nicholas had no intention of becoming a 'constitutional monarch' and few of his ministers had a real commitment to the manifesto promises.

On October 19th, Nicholas was to write to his mother, the Empress Maria:

You can't imagine what I went through before that moment. From all over Russia they cried for it, they begged for it, and around me many, very many, held the same views. There was no other way out than to cross oneself and give what everyone was asking for.

The October Manifesto seemed to offer a number of concessions, but:

■ it stated that the Duma was to be consultative – implying that while it could offer advice, the tsar did not have to accept it

■ it was not to be elected by direct universal suffrage with a secret ballot (as the liberals had wanted) and whilst all social groups would be represented in the suffrage system, this was not equal representative democracy

■ there was no promise of a 'constituent assembly' (again demanded by liberals) with the task of drawing up a new constitution for Russia.

The manifesto was added to by a 'Manifesto to better the conditions of the peasant population' on November 3rd. This promised to reduce by half, from January 1st 1906, and to discontinue altogether, from January 1st 1907, the redemption payments to which peasants were liable and to improve the resources and terms of the Peasant Land Banks. It was an attempt to win back the peasantry and reassure those who feared the government might seize their land because they had fallen behind with their payments during the years of bad harvest.

On April 23rd 1906 a new set of 'Fundamental laws of the Russian Empire' were issued:

■ The supreme autocratic power is vested in the Tsar of All the Russias. It is God's command that his authority should be obeyed not only through fear but for conscience sake.

■ The tsar exercises the legislative power in conjunction with the Council of the Empire and the Imperial Duma.

■ The initiative in all branches of legislation belongs to the tsar. Solely on his initiative may the Fundamental Laws of the Empire be subjected to a revision in the Council of the Empire and the Imperial Duma.

■ The tsar approves the laws and without his approval no law can come into existence.

■ The tsar appoints and dismisses the president of the Council, the ministers themselves and the heads of the chief departments of administration, as well as all other officials where the law does not provide for another method of appointment and dismissal.

6

Activity

Thinking point

Do you think the October Manifesto was a sham, or were its concessions a real breakthrough for the opponents of the autocracy?

Reactions to the October Manifesto

The initial reaction to the manifesto was a wild rejoicing on the streets and a new mood of public optimism which saw many workers return to their factories. The Manifesto had, it appeared, achieved its purpose, even though Witte, one of its architects might say of it, '*I have a constitution in my head, but as to my heart, I spit on it.*'

The more moderate liberals from the *zemstva* tradition, accepted the promises and sought to work with the tsar to make the new Dumas a success. This group became known as the 'Octobrists' and under Alexander Guchkov they created a new party with its own newspaper – *Golos Moskvy* (*The Voice of Moscow*).

However, the left wing liberals were less convinced. They became the Constitutional Democrats, or Kadets, under Pavel Milyukov and, while they accepted the tsar's concessions as a first step, they continued to demand the setting up of a constituent assembly to draw up a fresh Russian constitution. Nevertheless, they supported the government's actions in bringing the radical revolution to an end. Indeed, Pyotr Struve (who moved from the Marxists to join the Kadets) said, '*Thank God for the Tsar who has saved us from the people*'.

Cross-reference

Pavel Milyukov is profiled on page 80, and Pyotr Struve on page 66.

Not all workers and peasants were appeased by the October and November manifestos however and the radical revolutionaries denounced the promise of elections and called for an armed rising to bring tsarism to an end. Trotsky publicly declared the tsar's promises worthless and, on November 8th, Lenin returned to St Petersburg in the hope of winning more support for a revolution. Having grown more politicised during the troubles of 1905, some of the industrial workers, encouraged by revolutionary activists, kept up their strike activity over the following months. November saw a second General Strike in St Petersburg, although the Soviet proved unable to sustain it, and in December there was a Bolshevik-led uprising in Moscow.

In the countryside, some peasants saw the promises as an opportunity to seize land which they believed to be rightfully theirs, and there was actually an increase in peasant risings, after the Manifestos, peaking in November/December. From November 6th – 12th, a second Congress of Peasants' Unions was held, which demanded the nationalisation of land.

There were also continuing troubles in the army and navy. After October, the number of mutinies also increased and at Kronstadt on October 26th and 27th, 26 men were killed and 107 injured when a sailors' rebellion was crushed. A similar rising in Sebastopol led by a retired naval Lieutenant, Pyotr Schmidt, was only suppressed after fierce fighting.

In the East, the Trans-Baikal railway fell into the hands of strikers' committees and demobilised soldiers returning from the Japanese war, and the tsar had to send a special detatchment of loyal troops via the Trans-Siberian railway to restore order. However, the government was not always able to rely on the armed forces and frequently had to turn to the Cossacks and Black Hundreds to restore order.

By November, 10 out of 19 of the largest cities in the Empire were out of control and outbreaks of mutiny continued through the month of December.

■ Repression and the recovery of tsarist authority

Despite the October Manifesto promise of 'full civil rights', repression was extensively used to bring about the recovery of tsarist authority. In St Petersburg, Trepov ordered troops to 'fire no blanks and spare no bullets' in forcing striking workers back to their factories. The Black Hundreds rounded up and flogged peasants, attacked revolutionaries, students and nationalist groups such as the Poles, and in the final months of 1905, in particular, persecuted the Jews, whom the right-wing associated with 'socialists and revolutionaries', in terrible pogroms.

On December 3rd, the headquarters of the St Petersburg Soviet, was surrounded and all 300 members, including Trotsky, arrested. Trotsky was subsequently exiled to Siberia which weakened the revolutionary movement in the capital and helped the authorities to regain control.

The final spasm of revolution was played out in Moscow where the Moscow Soviet assumed the leadership of the revolutionary movement and staged an armed uprising in December. This attempt to mount a General Strike was entirely misjudged. The autocracy was in a position to reassert its authority and heavy artillery and troops from St Petersburg were sent in to restore order. There was bitter street-to-street fighting and the working class Presnaya district suffered an intense bombardment which reduced workers' homes to rubble. Only when a thousand workers had been killed and parts of the city were in ruins, did the militant,

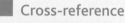

■ Cross-reference

For the Black Hundreds, see page 83 above.

Fig. 9 *Nicholas had survived the events of 1905, but the power of the Russian workers could no longer be ignored. From* L'Assiette au Beurre, *Paris, February 10th 1906*

Bolshevik-inspired workers give in. Although there were sporadic outbreaks of trouble in the countryside for a further two years, the 1905 revolution had been suppressed and the autocracy had survived.

The major events of October–December 1905 are as detailed below:

Table 1 *Events of October–December 1905*

October	**6th** Railway strike begins **10th** Moscow railways brought to halt – General Strike in the city **12th** General Strike in St Petersburg Liberal Kadet party established by the Union of Unions and *Zemstvos* groups **13th** St Petersburg Soviet is set up to direct strikes **17th** October Manifesto is issued pledging a constitution, extended franchise and civil liberties. Witte becomes Prime Minister and issues an amnesty for political prisoners. The General Strike in St Petersburg is called off **18th** Demonstrations for and against the Manifesto – Trotsky publicly denounces it – right-wing violence led by the Black Hundreds and strikers begin to return to work. Pobedonostev is dismissed but the reactionary Durnovo replaces Bulygin as Minister for Internal Affairs Military mutinies continue
November	**3rd** Peasants' redemption payments halved amidst heightened rural unrest **4th–7th** Second General Strike in St Petersburg ended and demand for 8-hour day abandoned **8th** Lenin arrives in St Petersburg **6th–12th** Second Congress of Peasants' Union demands nationalisation of land **14th** Peasant union leaders arrested **14th** Press censorship ended **26th** Head of St Petersburg Soviet arrested – Trotsky takes over
December	**3rd** Government arrests 300 members of the St Petersburg Soviet, including Trotsky **7th** General Strike in Moscow paralyses the city **11th** New electoral law grants wide, but indirect male suffrage Ruthless suppression of rural unrest using the army begins **16th** Durnovo orders mass dismissal of all 'politically unreliable' local government employees Full-scale artillery barrage of working class district (Presnaya) of Moscow by government **19th** last remnants of Moscow revolt crushed

Activity

Group activity

By the end of 1905 the tsarist regime was still intact. Can you suggest reasons why the 1905 revolution failed to topple the tsar? Consider the opposition's aims, methods, and support. Make a list of the strengths and weaknesses of the opposition forces and the tsarist autocracy in order to arrive at a conclusion.

Activity

Thinking point

Does the 1905 Revolution deserve the name 'revolution'?

To answer this you will need to think about what a revolution is.

Learning outcomes

In this section you have seen how the war with Japan brought festering political and social tensions to a head and forced through an incomplete revolution in 1905. You have studied the events of Bloody Sunday and their repercussions throughout Russia as the liberals, revolutionaries and nationalists sought to take advantage of the disturbances to advance their own causes. You have also looked at the tsar's October Manifesto, which, among other promises, agreed to a State Duma and will be aware of the the great weight of expectation attached to this document. You will also have noted that Nicholas II had already recovered some of his authority by the end of 1905 and in the next section you will discover how sincere his promises of change actually were.

Practice questions

(a)   Explain why Nicholas issued the October Manifesto in 1905.   *(12 marks)*

Study tip To explain why the manifesto was issued you will clearly need to provide some context – both of the immediate reasons behind the pronouncement, the general reasons that had provoked revolution in 1905, and the broad opposition to autocracy which had led to demands for constitutional reform. It would probably be sensible to look at these three areas in this order so that it is clear that you understand why the manifesto was issued in October 1905, rather than sooner, or later.

(b)   How successful was the tsarist autocracy in reasserting its authority by the end of 1905?   *(24 marks)*

Study tip To answer this question you will need to balance the restoration of tsarist authority against the ways in which autocratic power had been weakened and authority lost through the events of 1905. You should decide what your argument will be before you begin to write and should guard against presenting a narrative account of the year by considering different aspects of tsarist authority, so as to provide a *thematic* rather than a chronological answer.

6 The Dumas and the work of Stolypin

In this chapter you will learn about:

- the new constitution set up in the aftermath of revolution

- the problems associated with the new Dumas

- Stolypin's attempts to carry through agrarian reform between 1906 and 1911

- the extent of change in the countryside by 1911.

On September 14th 1911, Pyotr Stolypin, Prime Minister of Russia, was enjoying an evening's performance of Rimsky-Korsakov's *The Tale of Tsar Saltan* at the Kiev Opera House. Stolypin was sitting in the stalls, while Tsar Nicholas II and his family were also in attendance, in the royal box. No doubt the troubles of the last few years were forgotten as all relaxed for the evening. However, just after the royal family had left their box, during the second interval, two sounds were heard. Nicholas later said that he thought a glass had been dropped, and he went back into his box to look. Below him, he could see a group of officers and others trying to drag someone along, whilst women were shrieking and Stolypin was standing unsteadily and looking towards him.

Dmitrii Bogrov had shot Stolypin in the arm and the chest but the wounded man had risen from his chair, removed his gloves and unbuttoned his jacket. Nicholas saw his bloodied waistcoat and watched as he raised his left hand to make the sign of the cross to him. Stolypin slowly sank down again crying, '*I am happy to die for the tsar*', Stolypin lived on for four more days and Nicholas visited him in hospital, begging the minister to forgive him for bringing him to this end. Bogrov was hanged ten days later.

Having led a brief administration, which gave rise to a series of major reforms, this was to be the end of Russia's third Prime Minister.

The work of the Dumas

The new constitution

Although the October Manifesto had provided no precise detail as to what the election arrangements for, or powers of, the promised Duma would be, over the following months, a new constitutional arrangement was drawn up with two legislative houses, as shown in Figure 2.

Fig. 1 *The Duma opened amidst great expectation in April 1906*

Government (Council of Ministers under the Prime Minister)	
■ The government (Council of Ministers under the Prime Minister) was to be appointed exclusively by the Tsar. The government was responsible to the Crown, not the Duma	

Lower Chamber (The State Duma)	Upper Chamber (The State Council)
■ Lower Chamber – The State Duma – members elected under a system of **indirect voting** by estates – heavily weighted in favour of the nobility and peasants (who were assumed to be the crown's natural allies). ■ Deputies were to be elected for a five-year term.	■ Upper Chamber – The State Council – half elected by *Zemstva*, half appointed by the tsar – noble representatives from the major social, religious, educational and financial institutions.

The two houses had equal legislative power and all legislation also had to receive the approval of the tsar. Any one of the three bodies could veto legislation.

Fig. 2 *The new Russian constitution and indirect voting*

The Fundamental Laws

Five days before the first Duma met, Nicholas issued a series of Fundamental Laws (April 23 1906) defining his view of power. The laws stated that the tsar:

■ possesses supreme administrative power;

■ is supreme leader of all foreign relations;

■ has supreme command over all land and sea forces of the Russian state;

■ has the sole power to appoint and dismiss government ministers;

- has the sole power to declare war, conclude peace and negotiate treaties with foreign states;
- has the right to overturn verdicts and sentences given in a court of law.

The tsar also had complete control over military expenditure and household expenses and the right to control the Orthodox Church.

> The Emperor of All Russia has supreme autocratic power. It is ordained by God himself that his authority should be submitted to, not only out of fear but out of a genuine sense of duty.
>
> Article 4   To the All-Russian Emperor belongs supreme autocratic power.
>
> Article 9   No legislative act may come into force without the Emperor's ratification.
>
> Article 87   The Emperor may rule by decree in emergency circumstances when the Duma is not in session.
>
> Article 105 The Emperor may dissolve the Duma as he wishes.

 1

Activity

Thinking and analysis

Create a table of two columns. On one side write down the ways in which the new Russian governmental arrangements appeared democratic and on the other write down the ways in which they restricted the emergence of democracy.

Political groupings

There were to be four Dumas. The main political parties which contested the elections (in addition to the independent candidates and fringe groupings) were:

Party	Details
Social Democratic Workers' party (SD) – divided between the Bolsheviks and Mensheviks	Founded 1898. Committed to Marxism. Split in 1903.
	Bolsheviks: Led by Vladimir Lenin. Believed in discipline, centralisation, organisation and the role of the proletariat under party guidance. From 1905 favoured a peasant/proletariat alliance.
	Mensheviks: Led by Yulii Martov. Believed in co-operation with bourgeoisie/liberals rather than peasantry and the use of legal channels of opposition.
Social Revolutionaries (SR)	Founded in 1901; led by Viktor Chernov. Favoured populist ideas of re-distribution of land and nationalisation. Left of party favoured terrorism to achieve aims.
Trudoviks (Labour group)	Non-revolutionary break-away from SR party of moderate liberal views but with no formal programme. Favoured nationalisation of non-peasant land, a constituent assembly, a minimum wage and 8-hour working day. Supported by peasants and intelligentsia.
Kadets (Constitutional Democrats)	Led by Pavel Milyukov (1859–1943). A central liberal party which favoured a constitutional monarchy with parliamentary government; full civil rights; compulsory redistribution of large private estates – with compensation and legal settlement of workers' disputes.
Octobrists (Union of 17th October)	Leaders included Alexander Guchkov (1862–1936). A moderate conservative party which accepted the October Manifesto and opposed further concessions to workers or peasants. Supported by wealthy landowners and industrialists.
Progressists	A loose grouping of businessmen who favoured moderate reform.
Rightists – including the 'Union of the Russian People'	Leaders included Vladimir Purishkevich (1870–1920). The Union of Russian People was extremely right-wing, favouring monarchism, chauvinism, Orthodoxy, pan-slavism and anti-semitism. Promoted violent attacks on the left-wing and pogroms through its street-fighting gangs, the Black Hundreds.
	Other rightists shared conservative views but were less extreme.
Nationalist and religious groupings	Ukrainians, Poles, Georgians, Muslims – all seeking rights and greater independence.

The results were as follows (see Figure 3):

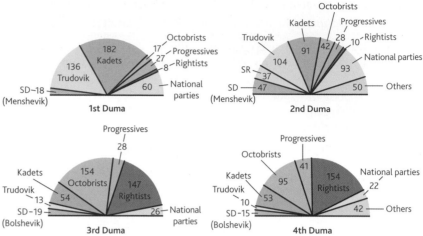

Fig. 3 *Duma election results, 1906–14*

Activity

Statistical analysis

Before reading further, study Figure 3. What changes can you observe in the make-up of these four Dumas?

The four Dumas

The First Duma, May–July 1906

A national election campaign took place through the winter of 1905–06. The Bolsheviks and Social Revolutionaries refused to participate, as did the extreme right-wing Union of Russian People. This meant that the first state duma, optimistically referred to as the 'Duma of National Hopes' was overwhelmingly radical-liberal in composition. The Kadets fought a skilful campaign and won the largest number of seats of any grouping. More than a third of the new deputies (191) were peasants and peasant farmers made up the single biggest professional group. There was also a strong group of deputies to the left of the Kadets, who were strongly critical of the tsar and his ministers.

They met at the Tauride palace in St Petersburg on May 1st 1906.

Maurice Baring, the English journalist writing for the *Morning Post*, attended one of its first sessions:

> I had the good fortune to gain admission to the Duma yesterday afternoon. I think it is the most interesting sight I have ever seen.
>
> One saw peasants in their long black coats, some of them wearing military medals and crosses; priests; tartars; Poles; men in every kind of dress except uniform. When the sitting began I went up into the gallery. The members go to their appointed places, on which their cards are fixed and the impression of diversity of dress and type becomes still stronger and more picturesque.
>
> You see dignified old men in frock coats; aggressively democratic-looking intellectuals with long hair and pince nez; a Polish Bishop dressed in purple; men without collars; members of the proletariat; men in loose Russian shorts with belts and men dressed in the costume of two centuries ago.
>
> They were a motley band and commentators commented on the 'uncivilised' manners of some of the peasant deputies, who threw their smoke ash onto the polished floors and and spat out the husks of the sunflower seeds they liked to chew. It was said that the tsar's mother was upset for several days after witnessing all these commoners in the palace.

2

No sooner had the elections taken place than Sergei Witte, the architect of the October Manifesto and head of Nicholas's Council of Ministers resigned, under pressure from reactionary influences at Court. This was a blow to the hopes of the liberals who no doubt hoped that, under his guidance, a form of government would evolve whereby ministers would take note of the Duma's views and work together with it in the formulation of policies. Witte was replaced by Ivan Goremykin, an old-fashioned conservative, and since the government had been able to negotiate a large loan of 2,250 million gold francs from France in April 1906 to keep it solvent, there was no need for it to rely on the Duma for the approval of the budget.

From the outset, Nicholas found the first Duma too radical. Almost their first act was to pass an 'Address to the throne' in which they requested a political amnesty, the abolition of the State Council, the transfer of ministerial responsibility to the Duma, the compulsory seizure of the lands of the gentry, without compensation, universal and direct male suffrage, the abandonment of the emergency laws, the abolition of the death penalty and a reform of the civil service. Nicholas ordered Goremykin to inform the Duma that their demands were 'totally inadmissible', whereupon the Duma passed a vote of 'no confidence' in the government and demanded the resignation of the tsar's ministers. In the uncertainty as to what to do, the resolution was simply ignored until, 10 weeks later, the Duma was dissolved and Goremykin replaced as Prime Minister by Stolypin, who had a reputation as a hard-liner for his resolute measures when faced with unrest in his Province of Saratov.

Fig. 4 'Oh, how these deputies stink!.' *Tsar Nicholas II holds his nose as the Duma assembles – why do you think this is?*

At this, around 200 delegates (including 120 Kadets, of which Prince Lvov was one) travelled to the Finnish town of Vyborg and issued an appeal to citizens to refuse to pay taxes or do military service. It met with no popular response and the government punished those that had signed the appeal by disenfranchising them and giving them a three month-prison sentence. This deprived the Kadets of their most active leaders, although since the most prominent Kadet, Milyukov, was neither a deputy nor a signatory, he was not involved.

▪ Cross-reference

Milyukov is profiled on page 80.

Fig. 5 *Prince Georgi Lvov*

■ Cross-reference

Stolypin is profiled and his programme of agrarian reform is covered on pages 98–101.

Key profiles

Prince Lvov

Prince Georgi Yevgenyevich Lvov (1861–1925) began his career as a lawyer and worked in the civil service until 1893. In 1905 he joined the Constitutional Democratic Party (Kadets) and won election to the first Duma. He became chairman of the All-Russian Union of Zemstvos in 1914 and was the head of the Provisional Government of Russia, after the tsar's abdication, from March to July 1917. Although later arrested by the Bolsheviks, he escaped and lived out his days in Paris.

Ivan Goremykin

Ivan Goremykin (1839–1917) was a lawyer with strongly conservative political views. He had served as minister for internal affairs between 1895 and 1899, before becoming Prime Minister in 1906. He was soon forced to resign in July, 1906, after disagreements with the first Duma, and was replaced by Peter Stolypin. Goremykin was a close ally of Rasputin and again became Prime Minister in 1914. He retired in February 1916 but was recognised as an ex-tsarist and murdered by mobs in December 1917.

The Second Duma, February–June 1907

Stolypin's government tried to influence the elections to the next Duma, supporting the Octobrists, who more than doubled their representation. However, partly because of the disenfranchisement of the leading Kadets, the more moderate-liberal centre was reduced in size and the more extreme left-wing increased enormously because the Bolsheviks, Mensheviks and Social Revolutionaries decided to participate. Only some 30 representatives from the first Duma were returned and the Duma soon received the nickname, the 'Duma of National Anger' because it was even more oppositional than its predecessor. Neither the left nor the right wanted the Duma experiment to succeed and they succeeded in crippling it as a political force.

Stolypin struggled to find any support for the agrarian reform programme he had drawn up and resorted to passing legislation under the emergency powers granted by Article 87, while the Duma was not in session. When the Duma refused to ratify this, he spread a story about a Social Democrat (SD) plot to assassinate the tsar. When the Duma deputies refused to waive the Social Democrats' immunity from arrest, (a right of all Duma delegates), Stolypin simply dissolved the Duma. The SD delegates were immediately arrested and exiled and and an (illegal) emergency law brought in to alter the franchise. The weight of the peasants, workers and national minorities was drastically reduced and the representation of the gentry increased.

The Third Duma, November 1907–June 1912

Not surprisingly, the groups which favoured the government, the Octobrists and Rightists, won the majority of seats, while the Kadets and socialists were much reduced in size as well as being divided in principles. This time the Duma's nickname in radical circles was the 'Duma of Lords and Lackeys'. Generally, this Duma was far more submissive and it agreed 2,200 of 2,500 government proposals – including important proposals for agricultural reform, presented by Stolypin. However, it is a sign of how unpopular the tsarist regime had become that even this Duma proved confrontational at times. There were disputes over naval staff, Stolypin's proposals to extend primary education and some of his local government reforms. By 1911 the Octobrists had turned into government opponents and the Duma had to be suspended twice, while the government forced through legislation under emergency provisions. Although the Duma ran its course, by 1912 it was clear that the Duma system was not working and had no control over the actions of the tsar or his government.

The Fourth Duma, November 1912–17

The party groupings were broadly similar in the final Duma, although the Octobrists did considerably less well, creating a greater rift between right and left. However, it was a relatively docile body and the new Prime Minister, Kokovtsov, who replaced Stolypin after his assassination in 1911 and remained in this post until 1914, proclaimed, *'Thank God we still have no parliament'*. He simply ignored the Duma and its influence declined. It was too divided to fight back, and in any case, the workers again seized the initiative with a revival of direct action and strike activity in these years down to the outbreak of war.

Activity

Class activity

Convene your own class Duma. Half the class should be Duma deputies, ready to pose questions and the other half can represent the tsar and his ministers and provide suitable replies. Perhaps you might even employ a secretary to take the minutes.

Activities

Class discussion

1 How effective was the Duma experiment?

Complete the following chart which highlights some of the achievements of the Dumas, with balancing criticisms.

Consider the material for and against, and write a speech either in defence of the Dumas or condemning them. Present the best speeches in class and try to come to a balanced judgement.

Achievements of the Dumas	Criticisms of the Dumas
A centre for political discussion which enabled the tsar and ministers to gauge popular feeling	
Helped spread democracy by encouraging public political debate as their activities were reported in the press	
Used their powers e.g. approving the budget and questioning ministers to good effect	
Approved important reforms	
A promising experiment which would have succeeded but was never given enough time to show its true worth	

2 Consider this quotation from the modern historian, Alan Wood

'A tragic drama it certainly was; a revolution it was not. After 1905 there was no real devolution of political power, which still rested in the hands of an irresolute Emperor and his appointed ministers. There was no radical redistribution of property and no realignment of the hierarchical class structure of society. The principles of Orthodoxy, Autocracy and Nationalism still provided the regime with its ideological bedrock. The traditional institutions of the state – bureaucracy, church, military and police – continued to function unaltered. And the Romanov Empire remained – bruised but unbroken.'

In the light of what Wood has written, would you agree or disagree that the events of 1905 deserve to be called a 'revolution'? Explain your answer.

■ The agrarian reforms of Pyotr Stolypin

An outbreak of rural violence following the disastrous harvest of 1901 led to the establishment of a Commission of Agriculture in 1902, on which the most influential member was Pyotr Stolypin, the Governor of Saratov province and himself a landowner.

Stolypin was a hard-liner. When Saratov had been badly hit by peasant disturbances in 1902, and again in 1904–06, he had won a reputation as the only governor able to keep firm control. He developed an efficient police force and used it to build up a profile of every male under his control. His known efficiency and ruthlessness recommended him to Nicholas II; he was appointed minister for internal affairs and in July 1906 replaced Goremykin as Prime Minister.

Although not totally against the idea of Dumas he was determined to ensure that its members were compliant and his dissolution of the first Duma led to uprisings and threats to his own life. In August 1906, he established court-martials led by senior military officers to deal with crimes deemed to be political in intent. In these courts, all cases had to be concluded within two days and the accused was not allowed a defence counsel, while death sentences were carried out within 24 hours. Over 3,000 were convicted and executed by this court system between 1906 and 1909 and the hangman's noose gained the nickname 'Stolypin's necktie' (*stolypinskii galstuk*).

Fig. 6 *Count Pyotr Stolypin*

However, Stolypin combined this intolerance and ruthlessness with a belief in a radical reform of agriculture as the best strategy for resisting revolutionary demands. He strongly believed that the future of Russia depended on building a prosperous peasantry and his motivation for reform was both political and economic. Despite the widespread rural poverty, a significant number of peasants had managed to improve themselves since the emancipation decree by buying up land and farming more efficiently. They had come to form a 'rural upper class' of better-off peasants known as the Kulaks. Stolypin described them as the 'sturdy and strong' and he believed that the future of Russia depended on encouraging men like this to flourish. They would, he believed, act as a bulwark against revolution, since their own prosperity would make them hostile to further change and supportive of the tsar who had made them wealthy. Futhermore, their industry would improve agriculture, and their wealth would be spent on consumer goods, so stimulating industry.

■ Key profile

Pyotr Stolypin

Pyotr Stolypin (1862–1911) came from an aristocratic Russian family and after attending university in St Petersburg had entered government service. He rose to become the youngest ever governor – in Grodno in 1902 – and subsequently was promoted to Governor of Saratov province in 1905. He was the first governor to use police methods to quell disturbances in his province and his reputation for law enforcement brought him to the attention of the tsar who appointed him as Prime Minister in July 1906. He held this position until 1911, during which time he instituted a new court system and carried through a major programme of land reform. He also muzzled the Dumas, changing the electoral law after the Second Duma, and carried through a major programme of health and educational reform. It has been suggested that he was responsible for staving off the disaster threatening the Russian monarchy. He was assassinated in 1911 but the cause gave rise to speculation. Bogrov, the assassin, was both a Social Revolutionary and a member of the *Okhrana*. Some suspected the conservative right were anxious to get rid of him because they were afraid of his reforms and his influence on the tsar, although this has never been proved.

Stolypin's plans, therefore, revolved around the abolition of the *mir*'s communal land tenure, which had proved the main cause of peasant discontent, so making it possible for peasants to become the permanent owners of their land. This land would also be in one piece, rather than a collection of scattered strips around the village. Such ambitions involved no less than the complete transformation of the communal pattern of Russian rural life.

This programme of agricultural reform had begun in 1903, when the *mir*'s responsibility to pay taxes on behalf of all the peasants in the village was removed. However, it was not until after the unrest and violence of 1905 and Stolypin's promotion to the prime ministership that major changes were undertaken. The most important legislation was passed in November 1906 and this was supplemented by further legislation in 1910 and 1911.

■ **Cross-reference**

To review the unrest and violence of 1905, look back to Chapter 5.

The land reforms

Fig. 7 *Russia suffered from widespread rural poverty*

In September 1906, the amount of state and Crown land available for peasants to buy was increased and in October, peasants were granted equal rights in their local administration. In November 1906, peasants were given the right to leave the commune and the collective ownership of land by a family was abolished. This made the land the personal property of an individual (usually the eldest male) who was given the right to withdraw it from the commune and consolidate the scattered strips into one compact farm. Land organisation commissions were set up, containing representatives elected by the peasants, to supervise this procedure and a new peasant Land Bank was also established to help peasants fund their land ownership. (These reforms did not actually become fully operative until approved by the Third Duma – where the Octobrists and Kadets were strong supporters – in 1910.)

Redemption payments were officially abolished – as promised in 1905 – as from January 1st 1907, but in reality they had long since ceased to be paid in full. In June 1910 all communes which had not re-distributed land since 1861 were dissolved. There was also an increase in government subsidies to encourage migration and settlement in Siberia.

The legislation was complex but it encouraged land transfers and the development of larger farms as poorer peasants were encouraged to sell out to the more prosperous ones. Stolypin is said to have claimed that he needed 20 years of peace for his reforms to have an effect and the coming of the war obviously prevented this. However, peasant ownership grew up to 1914 and the hereditary ownership of land by peasants increased from 20 per cent in 1905 to nearly 50 per cent by 1915. A run of good harvests played a significant part in increases in production and rising peasant prosperity, but the development of larger farms able to use more machinery and artificial fertilisers must have played a part. Between 1905 and 1915 Stolypin's encouragement of emigration also took 3.5 million peasants from the over-populated rural districts of the south and west away to Siberia. This move turned the region into one of the Empire's major agricultural regions, particularly for dairy farming, eggs, butter and cereal production.

Limitations

However, there were limitations to the improvements. Only 14 per cent of communal allotment land had passed into private consolidated ownership by May 1915 and changes in the land tenure arrangements took a long time to process. By 1913, only 1.3 million out of 5 million applications for the consolidation and hereditary tenure of individual farms had been dealt with. Furthermore, strip farming persisted, particularly in the central districts of Russia, where conservative peasants were reluctant to give up the security which the *mir* provided for them. By 1914, there were still only around 10 per cent of peasant holdings that had moved beyond the traditional strip farming. There was also the land which remained as the private property of noble landowners, although violence – or the threat of violence – forced many to relinquish their holdings. The opportunity for peasants to build up large farms was, nevertheless, limited by these landowners as well as by cash.

Perhaps the most important limitation of all was that Stolypin's reforms produced a growing class of alienated, poor and landless peasants. Whilst some peasants rose in rank and joined the Kulaks, once again, for every family that improved its status, there was another which descended into deeper hardship and either had to rent land, to be paid for in money or by their own labour, or was forced to join the wandering ranks of the landless, drifting to the cities to work in the factories.

It is impossible to know what the full outcome of Stolypin's programme would have been as it was cut short by the coming of war in 1914. As Russia entered that war, rural poverty was still widespread and considerable tensions remained.

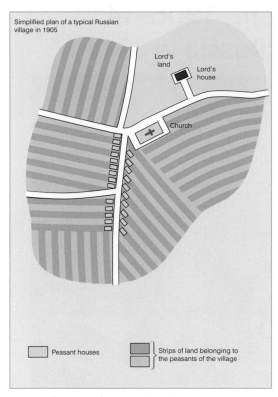

Fig. 8 *Changes in farming, 1905–14*

A closer look

Stolypin's reforms – an assessment

It is difficult to assess the effect of Stolypin's reforms because of the wide variations that existed between areas. In some provinces, peasants owned practically all the arable land by 1914, but in others the proportion was much lower. According to McCauley, although there were a lot of land sales, in Voronezh province 37 per cent of the land bought was purchased by landless peasants, whereas the more prosperous farmers with 20 desyatinas and more acquired only about 4 per cent. This would suggest that these reforms were not helping to create Kulak farmers in that area, but simply ameliorating the lot of the poorer peasants. The historian Shanin has also argued that the reforms did not have the intended effect of concentrating land in fewer hands. He has argued that there was cyclical change. A peasant with a large family who kept the profits within his family prospered, while a peasant with a smaller family could move down the hierarchy. There was, therefore no clear dividing line between rich and poor peasants. A rich peasant's son might work for a poor peasant while a poor peasant might choose to let his land and work in a factory. There is also some dispute as to whether Stolypin's policy could have worked if given more time. Its problem was not only that it required fast industrial growth to provide employment for the surplus rural labour, but also, that a cultural change was required on the part of the peasantry, a desire for self-improvement, a higher level of education and an awareness of the need to think and plan ahead.

Activity

Write an obituary for Stolypin following his assassination in 1911. Decide firstly whether this will be published in a tsarist or radical newspaper.

Summary question

How successful was Stolypin in helping to improve the lot of the peasants in Russia between 1906 and 1911?

7

Economic development, 1906–14 and the condition of Russia in 1914

Fig. 1 *Troubles at Baku: industrial development went through a series of booms and slumps, accompanied by continuing unrest*

As the 20th century began, not all was well in Russian industry. After the boom of the 1890s, Russia had faced a European trade recession by 1900. The slump hit the heavy industries, financed by the state and foreign investment, particularly badly and strikes also caused disruption to the oil industry of Baku and the textile industries in 1902–03.

However, from 1908, the downturn came to an end and there was a new industrial boom.

■ Economic development, 1908–14

Between 1908 and 1913, Russia experienced an industrial growth rate of 8.5 per cent per year. Entrepreneurs prospered as more large modern factories attracted ever larger numbers of industrial workers and there were further increases in overseas investment, although this declined proportionately as Russian businessmen accumulated sufficient wealth to expand their enterprises and found new ones. The state also injected a good deal of money into heavy industry after 1905, to make good the losses of the Russo-Japanese war and re-equip the army. Consequently, heavy industry, such as coal and steel, grew strongly and by 1914 Russia was the world's fourth largest producer of coal, pig-iron and steel. The expanding output from the oil-wells at Baku took Russia to second place in world oil production (after Texas, USA), while the country ranked fourth in gold mining. Furthermore, light industry, which had been neglected by Witte, also grew, fuelled by a growing consumer demand.

The strides made seem impressive and contemporaries certainly thought so. By 1914 Russia was the world's fifth largest industrial power (after Britain, USA, France and Germany). One of the reasons the German generals urged war against Russia in 1914 was because they feared that delaying war any longer would allow Russian industrialisation to reach a point whereby Russia would outstrip the massive German economy.

How strong was the tsarist economy in 1914?

In order to answer this question, first study the following statistics:

(i) *Industrial development, 1908–14*

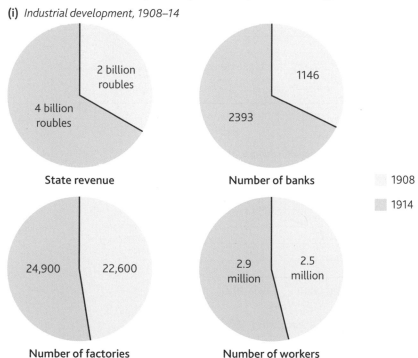

State revenue	Number of banks

Number of factories	Number of workers

☐ 1908
▨ 1914

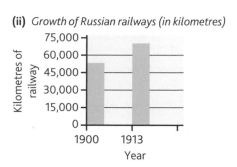

(ii) *Growth of Russian railways (in kilometres)*

Activity

Thinking point

Later Marxist Russian historians suggested that Russia had developed a strong industrial economy by 1914, based on the exploitation of the workers. Why did they make this claim and what truth is there in it?

(iii) *Russian economy (annual production in millions of tons)*

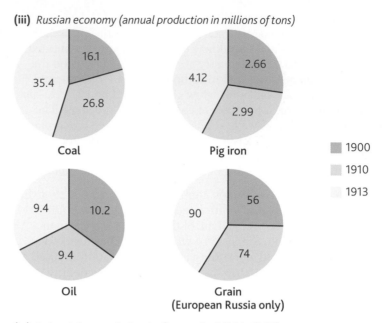

Coal · Pig iron · Oil · Grain (European Russia only)

- 1900
- 1910
- 1913

(iv) *Industrial output in Russia, (base unit of 100 in 1900)*

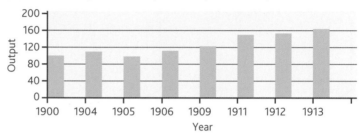

(v) *Russian balance of trade (in millions of roubles)*

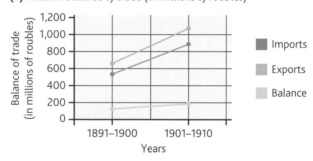

- Imports
- Exports
- Balance

(vi) *Population of Russia, 1897–1913*

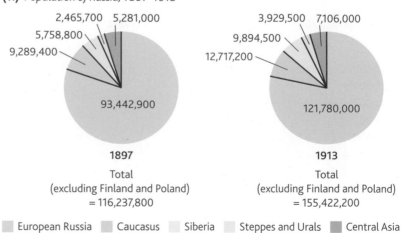

1897	1913
Total (excluding Finland and Poland) = 116,237,800	Total (excluding Finland and Poland) = 155,422,200

European Russia · Caucasus · Siberia · Steppes and Urals · Central Asia

(vii) *Growth of population in Russia's two main cities*

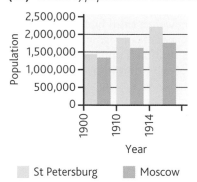

■ St Petersburg   ■ Moscow

(viii) *Comparative growth in national income, 1894–1913*

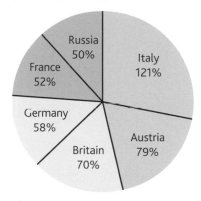

(ix) *Foreign trade in 1913 (in £ millions)*

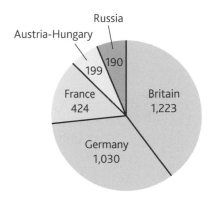

Fig. 2

■ Activity

Statistical analysis

In groups, copy the following chart and beneath each heading fill in as much evidence as you can find from the charts and tables of Figure 2 in support of the claim.

Russia had a strong economy in 1914	Russia had a weak economy in 1914

A full assessment of the strength of the Russian economy in 1914 also needs to take its social costs into account. There was some improvement in the lot of workers in this period. For example, there was an extension of health services provided by the *zemstva* in the provinces and a state system of health insurance for workers was established in 1912. Stolypin promised that compulsory universal education would be established within 10 years from 1908, and, although this had not been achieved by 1914, spending on elementary schools rose from 1.8 per cent of the budget to 4.2 per cent between 1907 and 1912. Overall, there was a 77 per cent growth in the number of pupils and 85 per cent in the number of schools in 1905–1914 and the literacy rate rose from under 30 per cent in 1900 to over 40 per cent by 1914.

However, it would be wrong to suggest that workers gained a great deal from the industrial expansion. Since they lacked effective trade unions and legal protection they remained at the mercy of their employers. The industrial wage rose only from 245 to 264 roubles per month, whilst inflation raised prices by 40 per cent in the same period. Of course, some workers did better than others and wages in St Petersburg were a third higher than those in Moscow, but the general picture was not encouraging. Conditions in factories remained grim and despite the educational improvements, levels of education were low and prospects for self-improvement limited. Furthermore, around four fifths of the population were still peasantry, which discredits any claim that there had been significant industrial development.

A symptom of the frustration of the workers was the revival of a militant workers' movement from 1912. The massacre of 500 striking miners from the Lena Goldfields in northern Siberia provoked sympathetic protest and between 1912 and 1914, around 3 million workers were involved in strike activity.

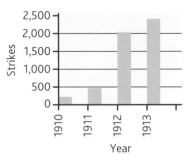

Fig. 3 *Strike activity in Petrograd, 1910–13*

Question

How would you explain these figures and what were their implications for the tsarist government?

■ A closer look

The Lena Goldfields massacre

The gold miners who worked along the banks of the Lena river in northern Siberia worked long hours for low pay in an inhospitable climate. They had long-standing grievances over their accommodation and treatment but the spark which inflamed the 1912 rebellion was the quality of some horsemeat given to one group. When the management took no notice, the miners went on strike and presented a long series of demands. The Bolsheviks helped co-ordinate the spread of the strike to other groups of miners. The management, having gained the support of the local police, arrested some ring-leaders and ordered the miners to return to work. Several thousand converged on one mine to present individual petitions, possibly encouraged by the authorities which were pleased to have the rebels together en masse. The order was given to open fire as they approached and about 500 workers were killed. This set off a wave of sympathetic strikes through Siberia and beyond.

Fig. 4 *Scenes of destruction at the Lena Goldfields in 1912*

Activity

Revision exercise

Refer back to the previous chapter and create your own revision chart like the one below on the economic development of Russia, 1906–1914. You will need to think carefully to complete the final row.

Developments 1906–1914	Industry	Agriculture	Society
Changes which strengthened Russia and its government			
Changes which weakened Russia and its government			
Areas which experienced little or no change			

The condition of Russia in 1914

On the eve of the Great War (World War I), Russia was a country of contradictions. On the positive side, Russia had an elected parliament or Duma, which provided, along with the *zemstva*, a forum for debate about policies and legislation, involving the people in law-making. The autocracy had been weakened and a fairer form of constitutional monarchy seemed to be emerging. The position of the peasantry had also improved, and was still improving, thanks to the work of Stolypin. The *kulaks* had established themselves as efficient, independent and prosperous agricultural producers, increasing Russian output and supporting the country's industrial growth. The economy was much sounder, less reliant on foreign investment and more self-financing. Industrial development had been impressive, in heavy and lighter industries alike and Russia was able to compete on fairer terms with the West. All this had been accompanied by positive educational improvements and some amelioration in the conditions of the workers through state welfare legislation. There had also been an expansion in the number of professionally qualified people – doctors, lawyers and teachers for example – suggesting that Russia was also experiencing important social changes as it modernised. Indeed, in many ways, it looked as though Russia was on an upward curve of development, which could have continued but for the advent of war in 1914.

However, there is another side to the picture. Whilst Dumas had been established, their powers were limited. Witte referred to the parliamentary system as the *'great illusion of our century'*. What is more, the position of the Dumas had been eroded further by Stolypin and the Fundamental Laws had restated the power of tsarist autocracy. Even in the *zemstva*, it was the voice of the well-to-do, rather than that of the mass of citizens, that dominated decision-making. Whilst Stolypin's agricultural reforms were helping some, they were harming others and, in any case, it is difficult to assess their full impact since they had only advanced slowly by 1914. Industrial growth also obscured some major limitations, in comparison with other nations and in the conditions in which workers had to live to achieve these improvements. Socially, all was not well. There was still around 60 per cent illiteracy; many children received no more than the most basic education; there were not enough

Study tip

You should find your chart helpful in completing this essay. Remember you will need to balance points which suggest that Russia was a modern industrial power against those that do not. However, before you begin to write, you will need to establish what constitutes a modern industrial power. Does the existence of a strong rural economy mean that Russia could not be considered 'industrial'? You may wish to debate this issue in class before answering.

 Activity

Thinking and analysis

Before reading this section write down the ways in which you feel Russia had made positive strides forward in the 1906–14 period and the ways in which it had not. Write a few sentences summarising your impression of the position of Russia in 1914. After you have read the following section, return to your list and sentences and see if you wish to revise them.

■ Activity

Research and presentation

Another positive sign within Russia was the flowering of Russian art and culture in the early years of the 20th century. These years, when Russia was at the forefront of European culture, are sometimes referred to as 'the Silver Age'. According to your personal interests, try to find out about one of the following and prepare a short class presentation in which you outline the contribution of one of the following: Blok, Chagall, Chekov, Diaghilev, Gorski, Kandinskii, Pavlov, Rakhmaninov, Scriabin, Stanislavski, Stravinskii.

■ Cross-reference

To see more on the Serbian and Balkan struggles, look at the outbreak of war in Chapter 8.

To review the split between Bolsheviks and Mensheviks, return pages 63–4.

Pyotr Struve is profiled on page 66.

teachers and doctors to provide for neglected rural areas, and there was a huge gap still between the rich and the poor. Furthermore, Russia was ruled by a tsar who failed to appreciate the social and political consequences of economic modernisation. Whilst he, like his predecessors Alexander II and Alexander III, wanted Russia to be a great power which could compete with the West, he was too much a man of the past to be an effective leader at a time of change in the 20th century. The tsarist autocracy was reactionary, oppressive and inefficient. It persecuted national minorities, propped up a Church which was riddled with superstition and allowed administration to be placed in the hands of incompetent leaders – both in the army and the civil government. Consequently, while Russia was, in many respects, modernising, its last tsar was trying to maintain an autocracy little different, after 300 years, from that established by the dynasty's founder, Mikhail Romanov, in the seventeenth century.

In some ways, the future looked promising for the tsar and the governing classes. Since 1905, the liberal, educated classes had grown more conservative in outlook, in their wish to distance themselves from the excesses of the workers and radical groups. The undermining of the Dumas as well as the police activity which, in addition to internal squabbles, helped weaken the revolutionary groups, seemed to bode well for the future of the autocracy. The Marxists were particularly divided between Bolsheviks and Mensheviks and in 1909, Pyotr Struve, one of the original founders of the Social Democrats, condemned the whole idea of revolution. As attention was turned away from internal concerns towards the patriotic call to champion the Slavs in Serbia and the Balkans in their struggles against both Turkey and Austria-Hungary, it might appear that all was well within Russia.

Fig. 5 *Nicholas II surrounded by petitions for reform in 1914; many problems remained unresolved*

However, beneath the surface, there was still much tension since none of the issues which had sparked the revolution of 1905 had been fully resolved. No minister or tsarist official could feel safe after the countless political assassinations, including that of Stolypin, the Prime Minister, in 1911. Between 1905 and 1909 there were 2,828 terrorist assasssinations and 3,332 woundings, even thought the secret police foiled many further activities. Between 1905 and 1909, 4,579 Social Revolutionaries were sentenced to death and 2,365 were actually executed.

There was also a strong anti-tsarist feeling displayed by the Dumas and *zemstva* and an acute restlessness and discontent among the peasants and industrial workers, on whom the country relied. In the towns in particular, this seemed to be getting worse rather than better. After the slaughter at the Lena Gold Mines in 1912, there had been a violent wave of strikes in the summer and autumn of 1913 and by the early months of 1914, there were more workers out on strike than in 1905. Many of these strikes were organised and encouraged by the Bolsheviks, as seen in this government report into strike activity in 1913. The Bolsheviks dominated the largest trade unions in Moscow and St Petersburg, and their newspaper, *Pravda*, established in 1912, sold about 40,000 copies a day.

They (strikes) happen sometimes for the most trivial causes and with extraordinary rapidity embrace wide areas with tens of thousands of workers. But apart from that, the strike movement we are now experiencing has a more threatening social significance. Under the influence of agitators and the Social Democratic press, there has recently developed among the workers a harmony of action such as indicates their close solidarity and organised nature. The places where strikes take place are put under a boycott; those workers who approach are exposed to bitter persecution and are excluded from work. Orders at strike-bound factories and plants are also placed under a boycott, and any factory that might accept them risks a strike among its own workers.

1

As such labour troubles resurfaced, Tsar Nicholas II became increasingly detached. Alexandra and he celebrated the Romanovs' tercentenary in 1913 with traditional pomp and ceremony and allowed Rasputin, a self-styled clairvoyant and 'faith-healer', whose nickname came from the Russian word for dissolute – *rasputnyi* – to gain influence at court. Rasputin's corrupt behaviour and influence over appointments caused resentment within political circles, in the Church and even in the army, but when both Stolypin and the President of the Duma tried, on separate occasins, to present the tsar with a dossier of evidence against him, Nicholas replied, *'there is nothing I can do'* and, after stressing that this was a family matter, *'I will allow no-one to meddle in my affairs'*.

Rasputin's status was thus able to damage the reputation of the tsar with those very people whom he relied upon to prop up the monarchy – politcans inside and outside the court, civil servants, Orthodox bishops and army officers. The Rasputin scandal was probably more a symptom than a cause of the position the monarchy found itself in by 1914, but it certainly showed that whatever the 1905 revolution had achieved, it had failed to alter the outlook of Tsar Nicholas.

A closer look

The Romanov tercentenary

1913 was the tercentenary year of the Romanov dynasty and Nicholas and Alexandra revelled in the jubilee rituals organised to celebrate the permanency of the Romanovs. In St Petersburg, the Emperor and his family left the Winter Palace to drive through the streets in open carriages for the first time since the events of 1905 and crowds flocked to cheer, wave banners, wonder at the decorated streets and thank God for their tsar. At Kazan Cathedral, where an elaborate thanksgiving service took place, a pair of doves briefly flew from the rafters and hovered over the heads of the tsar and his son, which the former interpreted as a sign of God's blessing on his dynasty. After a round of balls and dinners in the capital, the royal family embarked on a three-month tour of 'old Muscovy', the original heartland of Russia where they enjoyed a triumphal entry into Moscow. Nicholas led the way on a white horse, to the adulation of the confetti-throwing crowds who had gathered beneath the Romanov flags that filled the streets.

It is little wonder that Nicholas was to return convinced that *'my people love me'* and that his wife, Alexandra, was to

Fig. 6 *The royal family is greeted by the crowd at the Tercentenary celebrations at the Kremlin, Moscow, in 1913*

complain, *'Now you can see for yourself what cowards those state ministers are. They are constantly frightening the Emperor with threats of revolution and here – you see it for yourself – we need merely to show ourselves and at once their hearts are ours'.*

■ Key profile

Rasputin

Rasputin (1869–1916) was a peasant from Tobolsk province in western Siberia. He had spent three months at Verkhoturye monastery as a young man, although he never became a monk and lacked the education to do so. He also spent time with a mystical sect called the Khlysty, (so-called after a Russian word for a whip as a reference to their practice of holding nocturnal meetings at which members danced naked and whipped one another). They believed redemption came through sin, particularly sexual sin. Rasputin wandered through Russia, living off charity and showed a gift for preaching and faith healing, perhaps the result of his brilliant penetrating eyes, which some suggest exerted a hypnotic power. He arrived in St Petersburg in 1903 at a time when an interest in spiritualism, astrology and the occult was strong among those of high society. He was introduced to the royal family in November 1905 and appeared to be able to lessen the pain of Aleksei, the royal couple's only son (of five children), born 1904, who suffered from the disease of haemophilia, whereby the blood fails to clot and even a small knock can cause internal bleeding, bringing swellings and crippled joints. Alexandra believed he had been sent by God and he soon gained immense power and prestige – but also many enemies. He was eventually murdered in 1916.

Fig. 7 *Rasputin. Does this picture enhance your appreciation of his powers?*

■ Cross-reference

For more on the murder of Rasputin, look ahead to page 115.

■ Activity

Whether Russia was actually close to revolution in 1914, or not, has occupied the thoughts of a number of historians, including Martin McCauley and Michael Florinsky, whose views are reproduced below. Read these two sources and use them, together with the evidence presented above, to draw up a diagramatic response to the question – 'How close was Russia to revolution in 1914?'

Moderate conservatives were taken aback by the refusal of the government to take even their wishes into consideration. Hence, the support base of the autocratic regime was very narrow in 1914. Had war not intervened, the confrontation between the authorities and the rest of the population would possibly have come sooner than 1917. If revolution is taken to mean that the tsar would have to concede much of his power to an elected parliament and educated society, then revolution was inevitable by 1914.

2   *Adapted from: McCauley, M., From Octobrists to Bolsheviks, 1984*

The policy of the Government of the tsar may frequently appear unsound and reactionary; much of it deserves the severest criticism. In spite of that, the fact remains that in the fifty years preceding the War Russia had gone far along the road followed several decades before by other European countries. The venerable structure of the autocratic state had gone through a very remarkable transformation. The general economic progress of the country could not be seriously questioned. In spite of all the imperfections and drawbacks of the new departures, it seems safe to say that they contained the elements for the future progress of the nation along the road that had been followed by other countries.

3 *Adapted from: Florinsky, M., The End of the Russian Empire, 1961*

Learning outcomes

In this section you have seen how the work of the Dumas was undermined by the failure of both sides to work together and how the opportunity to develop a modern constitutional monarchy was lost. You have also examined Stolypin's attempts to reform the agrarian situation and the mixed results that followed from this. By examining the economic and political development of Russia to 1914, you have been able to appraise the strengths and weaknesses of the Russian state as it prepared for war. The consequences of that war will be discussed in the final section.

Practice questions

(a) Explain why Stolypin altered the electoral franchise before summoning the Third Duma.

(12 marks)

Study tip To explain why Stolypin altered the franchise you will need to consider the problems raised by the oppositional Second Duma and also provide some explanation for his frustration, by commenting on the context in which Stolypin was struggling to carry out agrarian reform. Try to produce a range of immediate and more general supporting reasons; stress the reason which you feel was the most important.

(b) How far was Nicholas II's response to the crisis of 1905 'totally inadequate'?

(24 marks)

Study tip The key words, 'totally inadequate', should provoke some debate in your answer. You may, for example, suggest that Nicholas's immediate response was weak, but in the longer term, he responded sensibly – by setting up the dumas. On the other hand, you may agree that he was a faced with a crisis he could not cope with and made innumerable errors of judgement, both at the time and subsequently.

8 The collapse of tsardom and the revolution of February/March 1917

Fig. 1 *In 1914, Russia mobilised for war*

In this chapter you will learn about:

- the impact of the First World War on Russia – militarily, politically, economically and socially

- the events of February 1917 in Petrograd

- the factors leading to the abdication of Tsar Nicholas II

- the setting up of the Provisional Government and Petrograd Duma.

Important note

The Russian Calendar

The Russians used the Julian calendar until January 31st 1918, rather than the Gregorian calendar, adopted by the rest of Europe in the 17–18th centuries. Consequently, by 1918, Russia was 13 days behind western Europe. Some books (including this one) use the old-style calendar, so that the two revolutions of 1917 are given as February 23rd and October 25th. However, others use the 'modern' dating so that the first revolution took place on March 8th and the second on November 7th.

In the event of defeat, the possibility of which in a struggle with a foe like Germany cannot be overlooked, social revolution in its extreme form is inevitable. It will start with disasters being attributed to the government. In the legislative institutions, a bitter campaign against the government will begin, which will lead to revolutionary agitation throughout the country. Socialist slogans will immediately ensue. The defeated army will prove to be too demoralised to serve as a bulwark of law and order. The legislative institutions and the opposition intelligentsia parties will be powerless to stem the rising popular tide, and Russia will be flung into hopeless anarchy, the outcome of which cannot even be forseen.

You might be forgiven for thinking these were the words of a soothsayer, rather than those of the minister for internal affairs Pyotr Durnovo, who died shortly after writing this in February 1914. That Durnovo could forsee, with such accuracy, exactly what involvement in the First World War would mean for Russia and its government, might lead to an assumption that the overthrow of the tsar and the revolution of February/March 1917 were inevitable. However, this is not the case. There were other paths which might have been followed and it was Russia's (and Europe's) misfortune that Tsar Nicholas and his ministers failed to appreciate where their road was leading until it was too late.

The immediate impact of war, 1914

Following Russia's defeat by Japan in the Far East in 1905, and agreements with Britain over Persia and Afghanistan in central Asia in 1907, Russian attention turned to the Balkan area. Encouraged by

Panslavist sentiment in St Petersburg, Nicholas backed Serbia, which sought to carve out a southern Slav nation, and possibly believed that mobilising in support of Serbia, following the dispute between Serbia and Austria-Hungary which arose after the assassination at Sarajevo in July 1914, would divert attention away from the discontent at home.

Ignoring all warnings, including Rasputin's, Nicholas II took Russia to war against Germany and Austria-Hungary in July 1914. As elsewhere in Europe, there was an initial outpouring of popular enthusiasm and patriotic sentiment. The Duma voted **war credits** (August 8th) and the Russian soldiers carried icons of the tsar as they marched to the front. St Petersburg was renamed Petrograd in 1914 at the outbreak of war, because 'Peter's town (burg)' was Germanic. However, this spirit of national solidarity was soon dampened when initial victories against both enemies gave way to defeat at the hands of the Germans in the disastrous Battle of Tannenburg in East Prussia, which left 300,000 dead or wounded in August 1914. Thousands were taken prisoner and a subsequent defeat at the Masurian Lakes in September forced the Russian army into a temporary retreat from East Prussia. Although the Russian troops were rather more successful in the south against Austria, it was soon clear that the war would not end in a quick victory, as had been hoped, and reports of military incompetence inflamed the simmering discontent in the Russian capital.

The Russian economy also quickly showed the strains of war. By Christmas 1914, there was already a serious shortage of munitions and the prospect of a long war, requiring large numbers of men and munitions, was daunting. The army Chief of Staff informed the French ambassador in December 1914:

> Our losses of men have been colossal, though if it were merely a matter of replacing wastage we could soon do so as we have more than 800,000 men waiting in our depots. But we're short of rifles to arm and train these men. Our magazines are nearly empty. The position is hardly less difficult as regards gun ammunition. Our entire reserve is exhausted. The armies need 45,000 rounds a day. Our maximum daily output is 13,000; we hope it will reach 20,000 by about February 15. Until that date, the situation of our armies will not only be difficult but dangerous.

2

Political impact

Even before the end of 1914, there were disputes over the organisation of the war effort. In July 1914 the tsarist government had set up 'military zones' within which all civilian authority was suspended and the military assumed command. This, however, was opposed by the liberal *zemstva* who regarded the government as insensitive to the needs of the people and believed that civilians had a major part to play in running the war. For example, the government's decision to prohibit the sale of alcohol at the end of 1914 was both resented and evaded. Vodka was regarded as a near essential, especially in hard times, so peasants and workers simply distilled their own, whilst the government lost some valuable tax revenue from legal sales.

The *zemstva* established a 'Union of Zemstva' to provide the medical facilities which the state seemed to neglect. Another initiative came from factory owners and businessmen who established a Congress of Representatives of Industry and Business (which included representatives from the Duma and of workers) to help co-ordinate production.

Study tip

It is quite acceptable to use either the Julian or the Gregorian calendar in your examination but you should not mix the two.

Key terms

Panslavism: A belief that Slav races should be united – and look to Russia as the supreme Slav country for leadership.

War credits: the raising of taxes and loans to finance war.

Did you know?

In 1924, St Petersburg/Petrograd was again renamed – Leningrad; however after the break up of the USSR in 1991 it reverted to its original name.

Did you know?

The Durnovos

I .N. Durnovo (1834–1903) was Alexander III's minister of internal affairs from 1889, after Tolstoy, and was blamed for the 1891–92 famine problems. A pun circulated – 'We did not have a good minister – now we've got "*a bad one*" (in Russian, '*durnogo*'). He became Chairman of the Committee of Ministers 1895–1903, under Nicholas II. General P.P. Durnovo (a distant cousin) was Governor of Moscow in 1905, but P.N. Durnovo (1845–1915) was no relation. He became minister of internal affairs (October 1905– April 1906). He helped suppress revolution and led the conservatives in the State Council.

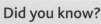

■ Cross-reference

Prince Lvov is profiled on page 96.

In June 1915 existing *zemstva* and municipal dumas joined together to form the All Russian Union of Zemstva and Cities, known as *Zemgor*. It was chaired by Prince Lvov and claimed the right to help the tsar's government in the war effort, but it was never allowed any direct influence and, like the State Duma, soon turned into a liberal focus for discontent. Rather than working with the organisation, Nicholas blamed it for stirring up trouble.

In August 1915, some of the deputies (Kadets, Octobrists and Progressives) from the Fourth Duma, many of them also involved in the Congress of Representatives of Industry and Business, organised themselves into the 'Progressive bloc' and demanded that the tsar change his ministers and establish a 'government of public confidence'. They were effectively asking for a constitutional monarchy, in which they would have a dominant voice. Had Nicholas II been a more astute man, he might well have seized this chance to institute political reform and transfer responsibility for the war effort to a civilian government. However, Nicholas was not prepared to contemplate such a move. Instead, in September, he suspended the sittings of the Duma and it remained officially closed until January 1917, although unauthorised meetings continued.

In September, defeats in Galicia (on the Austro-Hungarian front) led Nicholas II to make the disastrous decision to take on the role of Commander-in-Chief of the Russian Army and Navy and, *'with firm trust in Divine mercy and unshakeable confidence in ultimate victory'* to travel to the front line. The move did nothing to help his cause. Although it had overtones of bravery and heroism, Nicholas had already lost the confidence and support of the Russian General Staff and did not possess the military experience to turn the war effort around. Instead, his new position simply made him appear yet more responsible for the varying disasters which befell his troops and state, whilst distancing him even more from developments in Petrograd.

In Petrograd, Rasputin began to meddle in political appointments and policy decisions, whilst there were rumours that Nicholas's German wife, Alexandra, was deliberately sabotaging the Russian war effort. Whether Rasputin was quite the evil influence some contemporaries made out, or simply the tool of political schemers, we can't be sure. Nevertheless, there were many changes of ministers in the 12 months after September 1915, including three to four changes in some ministries, and these were put down to Rasputin's influence. It was hardly surprising, therefore, that liberals and socialists began to lose patience and demand changes in government. In September 1915 *Zemgor* declared:

> On the path of victory there lies a fatal obstacle; an obstacle created by all the old vices of our political system; we mean irresponsible power, the absence of any link between the government and the country. A drastic change is required in place of our present governors, We must have men who enjoy the confidence of the nation. The work of the Duma should be resumed without delay.

3

Fig. 2 *Rasputin wielded great power over Nicholas and Alexandra. How does the cartoonist convey his views on this?*

The president of the Fourth Duma, Rodzianko, and others warned Nicholas in vain of Rasputin's unpopularity and the damage he was doing the tsarist cause, but it would seem that Nicholas could not bring himself to take action against a person on whom his wife leaned so heavily. It was in an attempt to save the reputation of the monarchy that Prince Yusupov (a nephew by marriage to the tsar) and his accomplice, Purishkevich, who had referred to Rasputin as a '*filthy, vicious and venal peasant*' invited Rasputin to an evening tea at the Yusupov Palace on December 17th 1916 and murdered him. The event came too late, however, and did little to quell the growing discontent.

A closer look

The murder of Rasputin

According to accounts of those not present at the time, but who knew those that were, Yusupov at first tried to kill Rasputin with poisoned cakes, but when these had no effect (probably because his stomach was so well-lined after years of excessive drinking) he enticed Rasputin near him, to look at an Italian Renaissance crucifix. He fired twice into his ribs and Rasputin fell to the floor. Having checked there was no pulse, Yusupov went to get his car, ready to move the body. However, 12 minutes later, on returning to the room, he saw, to his horror, that Rasputin had half risen and was lurching towards him.. He tore the epaulette from Yusupov's shoulder and yelled, 'You wretch! You'll be hanged tomorrow! I'm going to tell the Empress everything'. Yusopov ran from the room and called his waiting accomplices. They entered to find Rasputin gone. He had opened the door to the garden and was dragging himself away through the snow. Purishkevich fired a bullet into his neck and another into his body while Yusupov fetched a bronze candlestick and battered his skull. Finally they bound his body and threw him into the river – just to be sure that if he was not already dead, he would drown.

Nicholas seemed unaware of, or unconcerned about political demands. His letters to Alexandra, whom he addressed with such terms of endearment as, 'my own lovebird', showed more anxiety about the children's measles than (as Alexandra wrote in a message on February 25th 1917) '*young boys and girls running about and screaming that they have no bread*'. Nicholas reassured his wife that '*this will all pass and quieten down*'.

Military problems

Although the Russian government managed to mobilise around 15 million men between 1914 and 1917, mainly conscript peasants, it proved unable to provide for them. The problems of the early years grew steadily worse so that soldiers were sent to fight not only without suitable weaponry, but also lacking basic warm clothing and properly fitting, waterproof footwear. In 1914, the infantry had only two rifles for every three soldiers and in 1915 it was not unusual for Russian artillery to be limited to two to three shells per day. In these early years, the soldiers had to rely on the weapons of fallen comrades in order to fight at all.

By 1916, some of the most glaring deficiencies in equipment had gone. The winter months of 1915–16 had been relatively quiet for the Russians so the time had been spent ensuring that soldiers were better trained and rifles were being produced at a rate of 10,000 a month. By the time the Brusilov offensive was launched in June 1916, most front-line units had a reasonable complement of machine guns and artillery shells. However, the army had a serious lack of experienced officers since most been killed in the early stages of war.

Activity
Research task

Use a variety of sources to find out more about Nicholas II – his background, personality, strengths and weaknesses. Do you feel sympathy or dislike for Nicholas? Using evidence to support your views, present your character profile to the rest of your class.

Exploring the detail

The Brusilov offensive

Named after General Brusilov, this was a Russian attempt to push westwards from the area of the Ukraine and break through the Austro-Hungarian lines. It succeeded in destroying the Austro-Hungarian armies, which had to rely on German reinforcements, but within three months it had ground to a halt.

Fig. 3 *Nicholas II encouraging his army officers*

The Brusilov offensive secured some advances but the armies soon experienced communication problems as they advanced west. The Germans, with their superior railway network, were able to move men forward more quickly than the Russians and by August the Russian advance had come to a halt. Morale in the army plummeted and soldiers lost faith in the declared goal of annexing more territory for Russia.

From October 1916, the effectiveness of the Russian army started to decline, partly because of the deteriorating economic and political situation within Russia itself, and partly because of the heavy casualties it suffered. That year thousands of soldiers deserted the army and many more did so in 1917.

Economic and social costs of war

The war proved an economic disaster. The direct cost of war rose from 1,500 million roubles in 1914 to 14,500 million in 1918 but the losses were actually greater. Although only 9 per cent of the Russian population was mobilised for war (compared with 20 per cent in Germany and France), 15 million conscripts and volunteers were enlisted for military service between 1914 and 1917 and this was, of course, at the expense of the rural or industrial workforce. Whilst women and children took on some of the men's work, production slumped and, in any case, in time of war, the country needed to to be producing more, not less, to feed and supply its armies. Poland and other parts of western Russia were overrun by the Germans, removing important industrial capacity, while naval blockades of the Baltic and Black Sea ports, together with the loss of overland routes to Europe, brought Russian trade to a virtual standstill.

In the countryside, although the loss of young sons and husbands was a cause of despair, the departure of many men into the army actually helped relieve some of the population pressure. Peasants who had horses that could be used by the military could also make money, whilst their grain was in high demand to feed the troops. However, the prices offered by the government were too low to allow them to make essential purchases of tools and equipment – which were in short supply. It became a struggle to buy essential household goods. As a result, some hoarded what grain and foodstuffs they produced, exacerbating an already difficult situation.

Even when the grain was released for the market, inefficiencies of distribution meant that it did not always reach the town workers who desperately needed it. Railways had been taken over to transport men and goods to the front, railway locomotive production halved between 1913 and 1916 and there were acute fuel shortages. Foodstuffs that should have found their way to the cities were left to rot beside railway sidings or huge cargoes of grain would be sent to the front leaving none for the desperate townsfolk. This made life hard for the town populations which swelled as factories sought more workers for essential war industries. This recruitment drive meant that though armament manufacture improved in 1916, when rifle production doubled and heavy artillery production quadrupled, this was all at the expense of civilian needs.

In urban centres, particularly in Petrograd and Moscow, unemployment soared as non-military factories, deprived of vital supplies, were forced

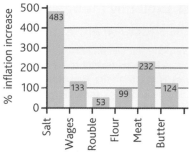

Fig. 4 *Inflation; Percentage increase from pre-war figures*

to close. Lock-outs and strikes (some directly encouraged by the German government in a deliberate attempt to foster industrial unrest and undermine the Russian war effort) financially crippled what little industry survived. A 300 per cent rise in the cost of living, rising death rates because of the workers' insanitary lodgings and the inadequacies of their diets left thousands living on the brink of starvation. In such circumstances, in January 1917, 30,000 workers went on strike in Moscow and 145,000 in Petrograd.

The February revolution and the abdication of Tsar Nicholas II

By the winter of 1917, the streets of Petrograd were tense with the the pent-up frustrations of the unemployed, the starving and the desperate. In January, 150,000 workers demonstrated in Petrograd on the anniversary of Bloody Sunday and by February 14th, there were 100,000 workers from 58 different factories on strike in Petrograd. The reassembled Duma heard speeches arguing that the Tsar had to go, but it was not to be the Duma, nor the disgruntled Army High Command that actually forced Nicholas's hand.

News that bread would be rationed from March 1st increased the long queues at the bakeries, and the city's womenfolk waited around the clock to buy the black bread which was the staple sustenance of working families through the freezing winter. Taut nerves sometimes led to angry and violent exchanges, as the desperate jostled for the limited supplies and the police who struggled to keep order were attacked. When, on February 22nd a further 20,000 workers from the Putilov engineering works went on strike following an argument over pay, the situation deteriorated still further.

Events turned particularly sour on International Women's Day, Thursday February 23rd, when the traditional march of women from the Petrograd suburbs to the city centre turned increasingly political. Although women, including striking female textile workers, took the lead (and some local Bolsheviks even tried to persuade them to return home, fearing premature action might jeopardise Bolshevik plans for a May Day protest march) the demonstration was joined by many different groups. These included the Putilov strikers, militant students, other workers from other factories, 50 of which abandoned work in the course of the day, and even some of the women from the bread queues, who became caught up in the militant mood of the protestors. The city fell into chaos as female drivers refused to drive their trams and deliberately left them to block the city streets, whilst some male drivers were forced to stop and had their keys taken away to prevent them re-starting their electric motors. It has been estimated that as many as 240,000 came out on the streets that day and order was only restored by a desperate police force in the early evening, although the day saw no loss of life.

Over the next three days, the crowds swelled in number and became more brazen in their demands and behaviour. They overturned tsarist statues, waved red flags, wore red rosettes, shouted revolutionary slogans calling for an end to tsardom and sang the Marseillaise. These demonstrations appeared to be spontaneous and there was no obvious organisation from any of the radical political parties, although members of such were no doubt helping to keep up the pressure by distributing emblems and banners which demanded an end to the war and to the autocracy rather than simply pleading for food.

Activity

Make a chart to illustrate the impact of the First World War on Russia. You will need to include military, economic and social, and political factors.

Fig. 5 *By February 1917, events in Petrograd moved beyond Nicholas's control*

Exploring the detail

International Women's Day

The first International Women's Day took place in USA in 1909. In 1910 around 100 women from 17 countries gathered for a socialist conference in Denmark and agreed to an annual women's day to campaign for female suffrage. Russian women, demanding peace, not war, observed their first International Women's Day on the last Sunday in February 1913. They were led by Alexandra Kollontai who also helped organise the women's march of February 1917. See page 140 for key profile on Alexandra Kollontai.

Did you know?

The Marseillaise was the French National Anthem and derived from the singing of the soldiers from Marseilles as they went to war on behalf of revolutionary France. To sing it is to show support for the ideals of the French Revolution – 'Liberty, Equality and Fraternity'.

Sergei Mstislavsky, a Social Revolutionary leader in Petrograd during these 'February days', described events as follows:

> The Suvorov Prospekt is black with people. A dray cart has been unhitched and orator follows orator on to this shaky platform which towers above the crowd. My wife returns from the centre of the town. She says it is the same thing there. Everywhere there are automobiles and crowds. The arsenal has been taken. They say that about 20,000 automatic pistols alone have been handed out. There is a lot of firing in the streets, but it all seems to be for show. Mostly it is adolescents who are doing the shooting. The area continues to be a bubbling cauldron of activity. A boy whistles and all at once everyone turns. The crowd surges towards the pavement – a mad crush follows. Pushing their way forward come armed students and workers. An artilleryman on a magnificent stallion rides up to the human chain and salutes the crowd. Everyone crowds around the horse and rider. Street urchins escort him through the crowd, holding on to his stirrups. Caps are thrown in the air. The youths on the pavement madly fire their pistols into the air. Slowly, with a dancing step, the officer rides by. The Guards Artillery must have mutinied.

4

By Saturday February 25th, after three days of demonstrations, 200,000 people (over half the capital's workforce) were on strike and Petrograd was at a virtual standstill. Almost all the major factories and most of the shops and restaurants were firmly closed and no-one seemed able to control the many incidences of looting, violence, vandalism and drunkenness. Violence escalated as Shalfeev, in charge of the whip-wielding police which was trying to control the masses, was set upon, dragged from his horse, beaten and shot. The same day, a band of civilians was killed by soldiers on the Nevskii Prospekt. However, some soldiers identified with the people and opted to join the demonstrators, making it much harder for the authorities to curb the unrest.

On Sunday 26th Nicholas ordered the Duma to close down, but it refused and Rodzianko sent the Tsar a telegram:

> The situation is serious. The capital is in a state of anarchy. The government is paralysed; the transport service has broken down; the food and fuel supplies are completely disorganised. Discontent is general and on the increase. There is wild shooting in the streets. Troops are firing at each other. It is urgent that someone enjoying the confidence of the country be entrusted with the formation of a new government. There must be no delay. Hesitation is fatal.

5

Nicholas deliberately ignored the message. He noted in his diary, '*That fat bellied Rodzianko has written some nonsense to which I shall not even bother to reply*'. The next day, Major-General Khabalov, Commander of the Petrograd military district, received a direct order from the tsar to restore order by military force. He promptly ordered the soldiers onto the streets to fire at the protestors and around 40 demonstrators in the city centre were killed. This turned what had been riots into revolution.

Activity

Thinking point

This account was written some years after the events it describes in 1923. Do you find it valuable for your understanding of the 'February days'? Why?

Cross-reference

For a letter written by Tsarina Alexandra to Nicholas II on 25th February 1917 see page 115.

Many of those ordered to shoot the demonstrators were themselves of peasant or worker background. They were were the young and newly enlisted, who had joined the Petrograd garrison to await the dreaded call to proceed to the front line. Furthermore their junior officers included men from the middle-ranking 'intellectual' class, rather than from the traditional 'noble' background. These were men who had joined the army from a sense of patriotism inspired by war and their sympathies, like the sympathies of those they commanded, lay with the masses.

A mutiny among the soldiers of the Volynskii regiment, some of whom had been involved in the shootings, was followed by similar refusals to issue or obey orders elsewhere. In all, around 66,000 men mutinied and joined the protestors, arming them with 40,000 rifles. Virtually all the soldiers in Petrograd, including the Cossack regiments, were not only refusing to obey orders but acting against the police by attacking police stations, opening prisons and forcing police snipers to abandon their look-out points on the rooftops.

The same day, Monday 27th, three important developments took place:

1 The Duma, which was meeting at the Tauride palace, formed a special committee comprising representatives of the main political parties to debate Russia's future. A group of members, led by Mikhail Rodzianko, set up the the Provisional Committee of the Duma, and demanded the tsar's abdication.

2 The generals of the army's High Command, which had already ordered troops to march to the capital to restore stability, changed their minds and ordered them to halt and give support to the Duma Committee. The Duma Committee ordered all soldiers to return to their barracks, but many gathered in the capital in support of governmental changes.

3 A body of socialists, calling itself the Soviet of Workers' Deputies or 'Petrograd Soviet', also took up residence in the Tauride Palace. Dominated by Mensheviks, they invited factories to elect representatives to attend a full meeting, which took place on February 28th when a Provisional Executive Committee was elected.

Also on February 28th, Nicholas II left his military headquarters at Mogilëv and started to make his way back to Petrograd. His intentions were uncertain and in any case, he never arrived. His train was diverted by rebellious railway workers and forced to stop at Pskov, 200 miles south of his destination. Whilst Nicholas fretted over his future, the Kronstadt sailors mutinied and the Petrograd Soviet agreed, under pressure from the soldiers, that each regiment should elect committees which would send representatives to the Soviet. This would subsequently become known as the 'Soviet of Workers' and Soldiers' Deputies'. The same day, 'Order No 1' – a charter of soldiers' rights – was produced.

Exploring the detail

Soviets

Soviets had appeared in 1905 and were literally 'councils'. They were not necessarily supportive of any one particular party and it was not originally a political term. Following the revolution of February 1917, Soviets sprang up in many cities and towns in Russia but the one in Petrograd, often known simply as 'The Soviet', was the most important. By March 10th it had 3,000 members but because it was so large, most of its work was done by the executive committee which was dominated by socialist intellectuals.

A closer look

Order No 1

- Every unit to elect a soldiers' committee.
- All units to elect a deputy to the Soviet.
- All units to be subordinate to the Soviet – i.e. the army was placed under the political control of the Petrograd Soviet.
- The Military Commisssion of the Duma was to be obeyed, only if it agreed with the Soviet's orders.
- All weapons to be controlled by the soldiers' committees – not the officers.

- All soldiers to enjoy full citizens' rights when off duty – e.g. no requirement to salute or stand to attention.
- No honorific titles to be used for officers – only Mr General, Mr Colonel etc.
- Officers were not to address soldiers in the '*ty*' form (like '*tu*' in French. This second person singular form was used to address children, pets and serfs).

The Tsar was under pressure from the Chief of General Staff, General Alekseev, to resign. Alekseev was reassured by an agreement on March 1st that the Petrograd Soviet would recognise a Provisional Government formed by members of the Duma, and felt able to suggest that the Tsar resigned both his military and imperial positions in favour of his son, Alexis, with Nicholas's younger brother, Mikhail, acting as regent. Other officers of the General Staff, on Alekseev's instructions, also sent messages of support for the tsar's abdication, so leaving Nicholas with little choice.

Приложеніе къ № 18 Под. Губ. Вѣд. 1917 г.   Цѣна 6 коп.

Высочайшій Манифестъ.

БОЖІЕЮ МИЛОСТІЮ

МЫ, НИКОЛАЙ ВТОРЫЙ,

ИМПЕРАТОРЪ И САМОДЕРЖЕЦЪ

ВСЕРОССІЙСКІЙ,

ЦАРЬ ПОЛЬСКІЙ, ВЕЛИКІЙ КНЯЗЬ ФИНЛЯНДСКІЙ,

И ПРОЧАЯ, И ПРОЧАЯ, И ПРОЧАЯ.

Объявляемъ всѣмъ вѣрнымъ Нашимъ подданнымъ:

„Въ дни великой борьбы съ внѣшнимъ врагомъ, стремящимся почти три года поработить Нашу Родину, Господу Богу угодно было ниспослать Россіи новое тяжкое испытаніе. Начавшіяся народныя внутреннія волненія грозятъ бѣдственно отразиться на дальнѣйшемъ веденіи упорной войны.

Судьба Россіи, честь героической Нашей Арміи, благо народа, все будущее дорогого Нашего Отечества требуютъ доведенія войны во что бы то ни стало до побѣднаго конца. Жестокій врагъ напрягаетъ послѣднія силы и уже близокъ часъ, когда доблестная Армія Наша, совмѣстно со славными Нашими Союзниками, сможетъ окончательно сломить врага. Въ эти рѣшительные дни въ жизни Россіи почли мы долгомъ совѣсти облегчить Народу Нашему тѣсное единеніе и сплоченіе всѣхъ силъ народныхъ для скорѣйшаго достиженія побѣды и, въ согласіи съ Государственной Думою, признали мы за благо отречься отъ Престола Государства Россійскаго и сложить съ Себя Верховную Власть. Не желая разставаться съ любимымъ сыномъ Нашимъ, Мы передаемъ наслѣдіе Наше брату Нашему ВЕЛИКОМУ КНЯЗЮ МИХАИЛУ АЛЕКСАНДРОВИЧУ и благословляемъ Его на вступленіе на престолъ Государства Россійскаго. Заповѣдуемъ Брату Нашему править дѣлами государственными въ полномъ и ненарушимомъ единеніи съ представителями народа въ законодательныхъ учрежденіяхъ на тѣхъ началахъ, кои будутъ ими установлены. Принеся въ томъ ненарушимую присягу во имя горячо любимой Родины, призываемъ всѣхъ вѣрныхъ сыновъ Отечества къ исполненію своего святого долга передъ нимъ, повиновеніемъ Царю въ тяжелую минуту всенародныхъ испытаній и помочь Ему вмѣстѣ съ представителями народа вывести Государство Россійское на путь побѣды, благоденствія и славы.

Да поможетъ Господь Богъ Россіи.

На подлинномъ Собственною Его Императорскаго Величества рукою написано:

„НИКОЛАЙ".

Данъ 2 марта 15 часовъ 1917 г.
Городъ Псковъ.

Скрѣпилъ Министръ Императорскаго Двора Генералъ-Адъютантъ Графъ Фредериксъ.

Fig. 6 *Nicholas II announces his abdication*

On March 2nd, Nicholas agreed to their demand but feared that Alexis's health was too delicate and in the end the abdication pronouncment named Grand-Duke Mikhail as the new tsar (even though he had not been consulted). Nicholas gave, as the reason for his abdication:

> It has been God's will to visit upon Russia a new and grievous trial. The internal disturbances which have begun among the people threaten to have a calamitous effect on the future conduct of a hard-fought war. The whole future of our beloved fatherland demands that the war be carried to victory. In these decisive days in the life of Russia, we have deemed it our duty in conscience to help our people draw closer together and to unite all the forces of the nation for a speedier attainment of victory. Consequently, in agreement with the State Duma we have judged it right to abdicate the throne of the Russian state and to lay down the supreme power.
>
> Not wishing to be parted from our beloved son, we hand over the succession to our brother, the Grand Duke Mikhail Aleksandrovich and bless him on his accession to the throne of the Russian state.

6

Nicholas went on to add that Mikhail should lead the country

> '*in complete union with the representatives of the people in the legislative bodies on principles to be established by them and to take an inviolable oath to this effect*'.

By the time Vasilii Shulgin and Alexandr Guchkov – members of the Duma Committee – arrived at Pskov station on the evening of March 2nd, the terms of Nicholas's abdication had already been agreed, although in the event Mikhail refused the offer of the throne.

The tsar and his family were placed under house arrest, as were most of the members of the tsar's Council of Ministers. All the administrative apparatus of the old tsarist regime (the bureaucracy, the police, the provincial governors and local councils) was dismantled, where it hadn't already collapsed. A fire engine was even sent out to tour Petrograd and remove such tsarist symbols as the excited workers, soldiers and young people had left in their determination to rid Petrograd of whatever imperial emblems and statues they could lay their hands on. Thus 304 years of the Romanov dynasty came to an end.

 Activity

Creative thinking

Take on the role of one of the following people and write your view of the events of February 1917, including whether your reaction to what happened, who or what you feel should be blamed or praised and your hopes for the furture were:

■ A soldier at the front.

■ A tsarist minister of noble rank.

■ A middle class member of the Duma.

■ A worker in Petrograd.

■ A peasant in Western Russia.

Present your views to your class and decide, which person would have been most/least hopeful for the future and why.

 Activity

Thinking point

In what ways does Nicholas II's abdication declaration suggest he has misunderstood the real reasons why he had to give up the throne?

■ **Exploring the detail**

Beyond Petrograd

Revolutionary disturbances spread beyond Petrograd – to Kronstadt naval base, Moscow and other industrial cities and rural areas. In cities, workers seized control of their factories, set up workers' committees and deposed their former bosses – sometimes dumping them in a nearby river! Everywhere, rebellious peoples set up their own elected regional assemblies and soviets. The army, technically under the command of the Petrograd Soviet, disintegrated into semi-independent bodies and soldiers' soviets without clear leadership and coordination. In the countryside, peasants attacked landlords' properties and felled trees illegally. In the provinces such as Finland, Poland, the Ukraine and the Caucasus, national minorities declared their independence.

 Activity

Thinking point

Look back at Chapter 7. At the end of that chapter you considered the state of Russia in 1914. Make two columns. On the left record the position in 1914 and on the right the position in 1917.

How far did the war undermine Russia, politically, economically and socially?

Fig. 7 *The royal family in exile*

A closer look

The fate of the Romanovs

Nicholas, his family, two servants and the family doctor were placed under house arrest in their summer palace at Tsarskoe Selo. After the October Revolution which brought the Bolsheviks to power they were transferred to Tobolsk in western Siberia. After the outbreak of civil war in early 1918, they were moved again to prevent the tsar becoming a rallying figure for the White armies which opposed the Bolsheviks. They were sent to Ekaterinburg in the Urals where a merchant's house was commandeered for their use. On July 17th at 2.00am the group were woken up, marched to the cellar and shot – probably on Lenin's orders. The bodies were disfigured with acid to prevent recognition and buried in makeshift graves. In the 1990s their remains were discovered and were DNA tested. This was designed to put an end to the many stories of miraculous escapes – particularly those of individuals who had claimed to be Alexis and even more convincingly, Anastasia. (The last claimant of that position, calling herself Anna Anderson, died in USA in 1984.) The authenticity of the bones was verified and they were taken to a side chapel in the Cathedral of St Peter and Paul in St Petersburg to be reinterred. In 2000 Nicholas was canonised by the Russian Orthodox Church and became known as Nicholas the Martyr. Even this did not quell all the rumours but further more sophisticated tests in July 2008 confirmed that all members of the Romanov party were indeed killed at Ekaterinburg.

A closer look

The revolutionary opposition

Soviet historians (writing after the Bolsheviks came to power), interpreted the events of February 1917 as the result of the inevitable class struggle between the bourgeoisie-proletarian forces on one side and traditional aristocratic forces in St Petersburg, on the other. They alleged that it was the Bolsheviks who inspired the revolution and the setting up of the Petrograd Soviet. However, rather as in 1905,when the revolution broke out, most of the revolutionary leaders, not only of the Bolsheviks, but also of the Mensheviks and Social Revolutionaries were either in prison or in exile, in Siberia or abroad. The Bolsheviks were in no position to provide leadership and co-ordinate the risings of February 1917. The revolution itself would appear to have been largely spontaneous and the result of the peculiar circumstances of war. Whilst it overthrew the tsar, it did not overthrow all 'aristocratic forces'.

Activity

Pairs discussion

Discuss the views of the soviet historians with a partner. How far was the rising of February 1917 the work of the revolutionary opposition?

Summary activity

Explain why Tsar Nicholas II abdicated in Februrary 1917.

You will need to consider a range of factors and show the links between them. The following three diagrams in fig. 8 show different ways of doing this. Complete them and compare your ideas with those of the rest of your group.

Explain why . . . ?

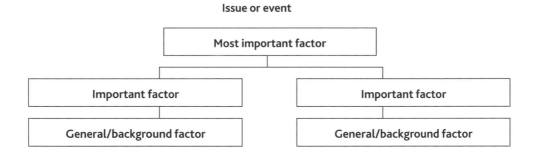

Issue or event

Most important factor

Important factor

Important factor

General/background factor

General/background factor

Long term

Short term

Explain why . . . ?

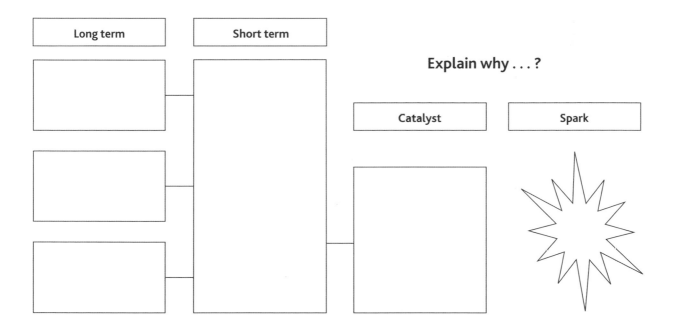

Catalyst

Spark

Explain why . . . ?

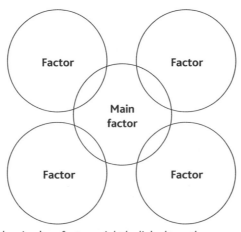

Factor

Factor

Main factor

Factor

Factor

Fig. 8 *Models for 'Explain why' answers showing how factors might be linked together*

Russia under the Provisional Government and the revolution of October/November 1917

In this chapter you will learn about:

- the attempt to rule Russia through a dual power

- the problems which faced the Provisional Government and how it dealt with these

- the return of Lenin and the growth in Bolshevik support

- the Bolshevik seizure of power.

Fig. 1 *An idealised picture of the storming of the Winter Palace, Petrograd. Soldiers, sailors and workers all wanted a part in the new Russia*

The Provisional Government

Whilst news of the tsar's abdication was being celebrated, not least by the peasants, who assumed that the land would now be theirs, and the thousands of soldiers who deserted their regiments and began hurrying home to take their share of the spoils, the Duma Committtee set about trying to restore some sort of order.

On March 2nd, a Provisional Government was formed after negotiations between the Duma Committee and the Petrograd Soviet. It was known as 'Provisional' as it intended to rule only until a Constituent Assembly could be elected under an equal, direct and secret ballot, which would then draw up a new constitution for Russia. Prince Lvov, who had formerly headed the *Zemgor*, was to become the Prime Minister and a new committee of 'commissars' was appointed to replace the tsarist ministers. This government was mainly composed of liberals – Octobrists and Kadets. Alexander Kerensky was the only socialist and the only minister to sit on the executive committee of the Petrograd Soviet as well.

Cross-reference

Prince Lvov is profiled on page 96 and the Zemgor, pages 113–4.

■ Key chronology

The October Revolution, 1917

March	Provisional Government announced its programme of reform and civil liberty.
3 April	Lenin returned and the April Theses were compiled over the next few weeks.
3 June	The first All-Russian Congress of Workers' and Soldiers' Deputies met.
2 July	Trotsky joined the Bolsheviks having previously failed to take sides within the Social Democratic grouping.
3–4 July	The 'July Days' were marked by anti-government demonstrations in Petrograd.
5–7 July	Bolshevik leaders (including Trotsky) were arrested and Lenin fled to Finland.
16 July	Kornilov was appointed Commander in Chief of the Russian forces.
18 July	Kerensky (Socialist) became first minister.
26–30 August	Kornilov's coup failed and the Bolshevik Red Guards were given arms.
9 September	Trotsky became chairman of the Petrograd Soviet and the Bolsheviks commanded majorites in both the Petrograd and Moscow soviets.
10 October	Lenin attended a meeting of the Bolshevik Central Committee and his call for a Bolshevik-led revolution was agreed.
20 October	The Military Revolutionary Committee of the Petrograd Soviet met for the first time.
24–25 October	Armed workers and soldiers led by the Bolsheviks and organised by the Military Revolutionary Committee took over key buildings and communication centres in Petrograd.
25–27 October	The remaining members of the Provisional Government were arrested by the Bolsheviks. The 'revolution' was announced at the second Congress of Soviets.
	The Congress adopted Lenin's decree on peace and decree on land and appointed the first Soviet government, The Council of People's Commissars, with Lenin as Chairman.
December	Establishment of a secret police force – the *Cheka*.

Chief Members of the Provisional Government

Prince Georgii Lvov – Prime Minister – a wealthy aristocratic landowner and former liberal Kadet leader who had served in the First Duma and had been leader of the Russian Union of *Zemstva* in 1914 and leader of Zemgor in 1915. He had helped organise the war effort under the tsarist regime. He favoured decentralised government but was essentially traditionalist in outlook. He retired on July 4th having found it impossible to control the mixture of liberals and socialists.

Pavel Milyukov – Minister of Foreign Affairs – was a liberal academic who had become leader of the Kadets. He had served in the State Dumas and had been part of the Progressive bloc of 1915, pressing for constitutional change during the war years. He had favoured a constitutional monarchy and had no sympathy with the socialists. He was determined to continue the war effort. But, following his 'note' to Britain and France in April 1917, promising continued support, he was forced by the military to resign in May.

Alexander Guchkov – Minister of War – came from a capitalist/business background. He was an Octobrist and had served at the head of the independent Military-Industrial Committee during the war. He was one of the Progressive bloc of 1915 and had gone with Shulgin to persuade the tsar to abdicate in March 1917. He supported strong government and was forced to resign after supporting 'Milyukov's note'.

Alexander Kerensky – Minister of Justice – was a member of the Social Revolutionary party and his position on the executive of the Petrograd Soviet, where he was Vice Chairman, made him an invaluable link between these two bodies. He was made Prime Minister in July.

■ Key profile

Alexander Kerensky

Alexander Kerensky (1881–1970) was a lawyer born in Simbirsk, like Lenin. Kerensky's father was Lenin's headmaster. Kerensky became involved in radical politics as a teenager but was not attracted to Marxism or terrorism. He ran an office in Petrograd to advise workers (free of charge) on their rights. In 1905 he published a socialist newspaper and was arrested. He served four months in prison. In 1912, he was elected to the Duma and joined the Trudoviki group of left-wing socialists. In February 1917 he joined the Social Revolutionaries and sat as their representative in the Petrograd Soviet and as minister of justice in the Provisional Government. He was a good orator, trusted by workers and very popular with women. He was an energetic man, but also rather arrogant, seeing himself as the man destined to save Russia. He lived in Alexander III's rooms in the Winter Palace and had a red flag raised and lowered as he went in and out. In May he became minster of war and in July, Prime Minister. He took action against Kornilov's coup but was deposed by the Bolsheviks in October and fled to France. He finally moved to the USA where he wrote extensively on the Russian Revolution.

Fig. 2 *Alexander Kerensky*

It was essential that the Petrograd Soviet gave the new government support since it controlled the factories, essential services and the military, without which government could not function. This was achieved in an uneasy compromise, whereby the Soviet did not press for the redistribution of land or state control of industry, while the Provisional Government promised to carry out most of the Soviet's other demands, allowing:

- a complete amnesty for all those charged with religious, terrorist or military crimes
- freedom – of speech, of the press, to form trade unions, to hold meetings and to strike (civil liberties)
- soldiers to enjoy the same civil liberties as civilians
- self-government for the army
- the establishment of a citizen militia to keep order, under the control of local authorities elected on a universal, equal, direct and secret franchise
- the abolition of all legal restrictions based on class, nationality and religion
- a promise of independent judges, trial by jury and the abolition of capital punishment and exile
- the garrison of St Petersburg (Petrograd) to retain its weapons and remain in the city (i.e. not to be sent to the front).

■ Activity

Thinking and discussion

Look through this list of promises with a partner. For each try to account for why the Soviet made this demand and what the likely significance of the promise might be.

Power was thus shared between the new government and the Soviet in a 'dual power' arrangement. The Provisional Government 'ruled' while the Soviet acted as a sort of watchdog to protect the interests of the workers and soldiers and guard against any attempt to return to the old tsarist ways. The Soviet comprised up to 3,000 members and was not dominated by a party. Its leading orators were the socialist Kerensky and the Mensheviks, Chkeidze and Skobelev.

However, for the first two months of the Provisional Government's existence, as reforming measures were passed, tsarist officials rounded up, arrested and imprisoned and the secret police disbanded, there was an air of optimism. It looked as though stability had been restored. Even the Bolsheviks, led by the recently returned Stalin and Kamenev (Lenin was still out of the country), joined the other socialist parties in giving the government support.

Outside Petrograd

In the weeks after the tsar's abdication, the government tried to strengthen its control in the rest of Russia. Provincial governors were replaced by Commissars (mostly old *zemstvo* chairmen and landowners) but in many areas, 'Committees of Public Organisation', formed from old *zemstvo* personnel supplemented by workers, soldiers and others, wielded greater authority. Soviets were also established in towns to represent the workers and copied by peasants in rural areas. However, in the more distant parts of the Empire, the government struggled to control the national groups. Only Poland received an official recognition of independence – and that was because it was behind the German lines. The other nationalities were ordered to wait until a Constituent Assembly could be elected. Indeed, the Provisional Government only ever really controlled Petrograd, Moscow and the central European provinces.

Early reactions to the Provisional Government

Although the Provisonal Government had been propelled into power in a spirit of excitement and optimism, it is hardly surprising, given the difficult situation in which both the country and government were placed, that it soon had to cope with disappointments and opposition. The Provisional Government took the line that major decisions had to wait until the election of a Constituent Assembly. However, many Russians, not least the peasants, expected immediate change. Furthermore, since the revolution had led to the removal of censorship, the government found itself attacked by innumerable opposition articles, and could not itself control propaganda in an attempt to win loyalty.

Peasants

The peasants had believed that, with the collapse of the tsardom, the rich landowners would be forced to hand over land to the peasantry. However, to their frustration, this did not happen. Although the Provisional Government finally set up land committees in April, to collect information on land-holding prior to a reform, for many peasants the months of waiting produced huge frustration. They were also disappointed by the provisions of the new grain requisitioning scheme, which offered higher payments than in tsarist times, but still provided less than they needed or felt entitled to. Peasants refused to hand over grain and seized landlords' property, livestock and machinery. The nobility, the Church and even those wealthier *kulaks* who had their own farms all suffered from the peasant disturbances.

Activity

Thinking point

Why was the Petrograd Soviet prepared to support the 'middle class' Provisional Government?

In small groups, consider the following factors and try to decide your answer to this question by placing the factors in order of importance.

- The Soviet was aware of the need for the experience of the Provisional Government to maintain the economy.
- Their leaders feared working class anarchy and were uncertain of their ability to control their own followers.
- Their leaders feared counter-revolution, whereby supporters of the old regime might try to seize back power if events appeared to be going too far too quickly.
- Their leaders' Marxist views were founded on the belief that a middle class revolution had to precede a working class one.

Exploring the detail

Peasant activities

The 1917 revolution revived the *mir* once again as it defended the interests of its peasants against 'outsiders' – landowners, townsfolk, merchants, state officials and even peasants from other communities. The *mir* organised seizures of land, rent strikes and boycotts. Until May, demands remained fairly moderate but they intensified once it was clear that tsarism would not return. Encouraged by the return of army deserters, acts of vandalism increased in number and intensity.

In the aftermath of February 1917, workers demanded greater respect from their foremen and managers. They became more aware of themselves as citizens and offensive remarks might lead to an official being beaten up and dumped in a canal or cesspit. Even domestic servants insisted that they should be addressed in the formal 'you' form (rather than the more familiar form previously used to address serfs). Refuse collectors renamed themselves 'house directors', women demanded equal pay and waiters marched in Petrograd demanding respect, not tips. There were 'festivals of liberation' and labour organisations and political meetings expressing collective solidarity proliferated.

■ **Key terms**

Conciliation chamber: This was composed of an equal number of elected representatives from management and workers and was responsible for settling all misunderstandings arising from management–labour relations. No foremen or members of management could be removed without its approval.

■ **Did you know?**

The Women's Death Battalion

In an attempt to prevent defeat on the Eastern Front, Kerensky encouraged the formation of the Women's Death Battalion in May 1917. Its leader was Maria Bochkareva, who commanded 2,000 women. They fought for three months on the front-line, by which time their numbers had fallen to 250. On October 25th, Bochkareva and the remaining members of the Women's Death Battalion attempted to defend the Winter Palace against the Bolsheviks. They were very badly treated, arrested and held until November when the battalion was dissolved.

In the new atmosphere of local involvement and representation, the village commune (*mir*) and parish (*volost*) became the centres of rural activity. Peasants arrested local officials and made their wishes clear through their peasant representatives, in councils, sometimes called soviets. Sometimes these made the decision that a whole parish would set off with their horses and carts to demand grain, equipment and livestock from a neighbouring landowner. A report from Saratov province showed the state in which the peasants might leave landlords' property:

> As far as the manor buildings are concerned, they have been senselessly destroyed, with only the walls left standing. All forms of transport have been destroyed or taken; cumbersome machines like steam threshers, locomotives and binders were taken out for no known reason and discarded along the roads and in the fields; agricultural tools were also taken. Anything that could be used in the peasant households has simply disappeared from the estates.

With strength in numbers, the peasants inflicted brutal punishments on stewards that refused to meet their demands. However, the government was forced to authorise the use of armed force against the peasants themselves, in an attempt to control their activities.

Workers

The government was determined to get the factories producing again, despite the shortages of fuel and raw materials. Factory committees were set up which tried to represent the interests of the workers but the Provisional Government supported the efforts of employers to restore discipline. They allowed owners to dismiss workers and to refuse an 8-hour day, wage rises or improvements in conditions. **Conciliation chambers** and factory committees were set up, allowing workers to negotiate directly with their employers, but workers were given no say in the management of their work-places and the new committees were banned from meeting during working hours. Living standards remained poor and the soviets set up to manage housing accommodation simply encouraged a greater sense of working class grievance. Food shortages, inflation and unemployment continued and workers consequently felt let down. As more factories were forced to close in the worsening economic situation, there were some fierce clashes between the workers and the authorities, and the number of strikes escalated, to reach 175,000 by the month of June. This unrest also had the effect of alienating the factory owners, who felt the Provisional Government had not done enough for them.

Soldiers

Continued conscription and wartime failures left a demoralised and war-weary army. Soldiers' committees were formed in the different army units and there was some improvement in soldiers' positions and a reduction in the aristocratic control of the army, but because there were insufficient trained officers to replace the old elites, for many, everything seemed to be continuing much as before. The military committees often took matters into their own hands, ignoring the government's and even the Soviet's demands and between March and May 1917 there were 365,000 desertions from the army (compared with 195,000 August 1914 – March 1917). Although discipline held until the summer months, there were those in the army command that wanted the government to bring back the death penalty and curb the activity of the committees. However, the Provisional Government was torn between the need to restore order and the fear that a strong army might try to mount a right-wing military coup.

Fig. 3 *Kerensky urged troops to show their heroism*

Attitude to war

In addition to the specific grievances of the workers, peasants and soldiers, there was also a widely shared hostility to the Provisional Government's commitment to continue the war. Milyukov talked of *'prosecuting the war until victory'* and even Kerensky urged the soldiers to show their heroism, although, unlike his colleagues, he did not favour fighting for territorial gains.

Lenin's return – April 1917

Lenin returned to Russia on April 3rd, helped by the Germans who expected him to seize power and make peace. He had travelled in a railway carriage (which had been locked and sealed as it passed through Germany), from exile in Switzerland, through Germany to Sweden (neutral) and thence to Finland and Petrograd.

Fig. 4 *Map of Lenin's sealed train route*

He greeted the crowds at the Finland station, where he arrived with a rousing speech, prepared during his long journey. The gist of his words were later written down in the so-called 'April Theses', although some of these were actually written in May, after Trotsky's return to Russia. They were published in the party's official newspaper – *Pravda*. Lenin wrote:

> The specific feature of the present situation in Russia is that the country is passing from the first stage of the revolution – which placed power in the hands of the bourgeoisie – to its second stage, which must place power in the hands of the proletariat and the poorest sections of the peasants.
>
> No support should be given to the Provisional Government. The utter falsity of its promises should be made clear. The masses must be made to see that the Soviets of Workers' Deputies are the only possible form of revolutionary government.

The April Theses demanded that:

- power should be transferred to the soviets
- the war should be brought to an immediate end
- all land should be taken over by the state and re-allocated to peasants by local soviets.

These demands have often been summed up as a demand for 'Peace, bread and land' and 'All power to the Soviets'. Lenin argued that the Russian middle class was too weak to carry through a full 'bourgeois revolution' and that to allow the middle classes to continue in power, was to hold the inevitable proletarian revolution back.

The initial reaction was mixed.

- The Bolsheviks had only 26,000 members and were still in a minority among the socialists.
- The Bolsheviks were divided over whether to co-operate with the Provisional Government or not.
- Some Bolsheviks feared that Lenin had grown out of touch and that his radical proposals would do more harm than good.
- There were allegations that Lenin was in the pay of the Germans (to some extent true).
- The Mensheviks feared Lenin would undermine what they had been doing, and by stirring up discontent would provoke a right-wing reaction.

However, Lenin gradually won over suppport with his speeches – which largely recognised much that was already happening. The peasants did not seize land because Lenin told them to – it was already happening, but Lenin could claim the credit! By the end of April, Lenin had won over the majority of the Central Committee of the Bolshevik party to his view that the Bolsheviks had to lead the opposition to the Provisional Government.

The broadening of the Provisional Government and a new offensive

The socialist influence in the government increased in May, following the resignations of Milyukov and Guchkov over their attitude to the war. Five socialist leaders from the Petrograd Soviet came in, including:

- Skobelev (Minister of Labour)
- Tsereteli (Minister of Posts and Telegraphs), the leader of the Mensheviks
- Chernov (Minister of Agriculture), the leader of the Social Revolutionaries.

This had two important consequences. It alienated those property owners and army leaders who had hoped the government would grow more right-wing and supportive of their needs, yet also associated certain socialists with the continuance of war, something which the Bolsheviks were able to play on. Furthermore, the socialist ministers themselves could do little in an assembly with an overwhelmingly liberal majority and when Chernov tried to pass a measure that would have allowed the peasants to use land from private estates, the liberals blocked it.

However, when the the first All Russian Congress of Soviets met in Petrograd on June 3rd, it passed a vote of confidence in the new government – 543 votes to 126 – with the Bolshevik representatives being the only substantial group voting against. This confidence was put to the test when the Provisional Government chose to launch a new offensive in mid-June, in an attempt to rally support. Even some socialists hoped that a successful offensive would enable them to gain better terms from the Germans in bringing the war to an end.

Alexander Kerensky, who had become minister for war in May, masterminded a huge recruitment drive to persuade civilians to join the 'shock battalions' that were rapidly formed, but he was less successful in persuading the existing soldiers to fight. Thousands deserted and others deliberately sought **fraternisation** with German troops on the front lines.

The offensive in Galicia lasted from 16–19th June but it did not hold. Soldiers deserted in their thousands, killing officers and commandeering trains to get home and a counter-attack forced a major retreat. The failure had repercussions within Russia once again. The month of June saw nearly 700 complaints about peasant attacks on landed property while in Petrograd, there followed series of riots and demonstrations which have become known as the 'July Days'.

The July Days, 3rd to 5th July 1917

The uncontrolled rioting of the July Days was essentially an explosion of the frustrations and disappointments of the workers, soldiers and sailors with the policies of the Provisional Government and in particular the continuation of the war.

Shortages of fuel and raw materials had forced 586 factories to close in Petrograd between February and July, with the loss of 100,000 jobs. Furthermore, the 1917 harvest had been poor and grain prices in the city had doubled between February and June. All the Provisional Government had done was to send 'punishment brigades' into the countryside to force requisitions, but this had just made the situation worse. The workers were demanding price controls but the government was frightened to act against the industrialists.

Soldiers and 20,000 armed sailors from nearby Kronstadt joined workers in the streets chanting slogans, such as 'All power to the Soviets', attacking property, looting shops and seizing the railway stations and other key buildings. No doubt encouraged by activists, some marchers went to the Tauride Palace demanding that the Petrograd Soviet take power, and when Chernov went out to calm them, he was seized and bundled into a car – to be rescued by Trotsky who climbed on to its bonnet!

Key terms

Fraternisation: behaving like brothers and forming friendships.

Did you know?

For almost a month Lenin lived in hiding in the forest along the shore of the Razliv Lake under the guise of a hay-maker. His 'home' was a hay barn which Lenin jokingly called his 'green office'. His 'kitchen' a crossbeam over a campfire was nearby. However, he continued to work, preparing materials for the Sixth Bolshevik Party Congress and writing *The State and Revolution*. Lenin eventually left for Finland beardless, in make-up and wearing a wig, with documents in the name of a worker from an arms factory, K. Ivanov. Lenin's beard had not grown back by October 1917 so any pictures which suggest he was bearded at the time of the Bolshevik coup could not have been produced at the time.

The Provisional Government issued warrants for the arrest of the Bolsheviks, whom they blamed for stirring up the troubles, and several, including Trotsky, were sent to gaol. It is quite possible that the rebellion was fomented by Bolsheviks – possibly those in the lower ranks of the party – and it was a grave miscalculation, although Lenin, who had actually been on holiday when the rioting broke out, always claimed that the demonstrations were spontaneous. He immediately returned, but just as quickly fled into exile in Finland, minus his beard which he had to shave to disguise himself as a working man.

Lenin's attitude to these July Days appeared ambivalent. On his return he urged the Central Committee of the Bolshevik party to restrain the workers and call off a rising planned for the next day. However, he did not condemn the rebellion either and it may have been that he was waiting to see how things turned out. He later claimed that the Bolsheviks had risen too soon and had failed to wait for his own direction, but this observation could easily have been the product of hindsight and self-justification.

Certainly the affair did not do the Bolshevik cause much good. Troops loyal to the Soviet dispersed the crowds and the Soviet newspaper *Izvestia* denounced the role of the Bolsheviks, suggesting that Lenin was working in the pay of the Germans and against Russia's best interests. Bolshevik propaganda was burned and the offices of the Bolshevik newspaper *Pravda* closed. Lenin's reputation fell, for fleeing rather than leading, whilst other leaders languished in gaol. Some believed their moment had passed.

Kerensky replaced Prince Lvov as Prime Minister on July 8th as he seemed to be the only man who could bring the various factions together. He was anxious to stop a drift to civil war. Whilst the balance in the Provisional Government had moved to the left, which is where he stood, he nevertheless wanted to keep a coalition which included the liberal Kadets in an attempt to provide stable government.

Activity

Thinking point

What were the options open to Kerensky? How might he halt the escalating political and economic troubles in Russia?

The Kornilov Affair, 26th to 30th August, 1917

General Lavr Kornilov was appointed as Commander-in-Chief of the Army on July 16th, by agreement with Kerensky, who assumed the position of Prime Minister two days later on July 18th. Kornilov was well known for his toughness and as a condition of his acceptance he asked for the reintroduction of death penalty and courts martial for the army. However, this would have contravened the Soviet Order No 1 and was vigorously opposed by the Soviet. Those who opposed the Bolsheviks, including the Kadets and liberals, welcomed his appointment as a chance to restore military discipline and he was also seen by Russia's British allies, who provided the Rusians with additional finance, as a suitable man to get the war effort moving again in the East.

Fig. 5 *General Kornilov reviewing his troops in 1917*

General Kornilov

General Lavr Kornilov (1870–1918) came from a family of a Siberian Cossacks. His father was a small-holder which made him an unusual candidate for high military office. Although known as a brave soldier, he had risen no higher than a Divisional Commander before March 1917, and was said to have the 'heart of a lion and the brains of a sheep'. The right-wing adopted him, since he favoured strong military discipline, but whether he personally wanted a military dictatorship is unclear. It is likely that Kerensky fabricated the story and the Bolsheviks supported it, to reinforce their role in saving Russia.

In August, the regiments involved in the July Days were disbanded and disarmed and the Kronstadt base was reduced to just 100,000 men. Kornilov also made other demands. He wanted the government to impose tougher sanctions against workers who failed to maintain the production of war materials. He suggested strikes and factory meetings should be banned and troublesome workers sent to the front. He suggested that the railways should be placed under the control of the army and he prepared to bring loyal troops into the capital to enforce these tough measures and suppress any further soviet-inspired disturbances. He later claimed he had an agreement with Kerensky to do this, but this was a claim that Kerensky vigorously denied.

The Provisional Government was in a very difficult position. Kornilov's demands would have helped curb the disruptive strikes and restored military discipline, but there was the grave danger that he would not stop at these demands but might go on to assume control of the government, destroying much of that which the government believed in. The situation was not helped by news that the town of Riga had fallen to the German armies and that the enemy was now in a position to advance towards Petrograd.

What actual negotiations had taken place we shall never know, but when Kornilov demanded that martial law be proclaimed in Petrograd, Kerensky clearly panicked. He ordered the removal of Nicholas II and family to Tobolsk amidst fears of a right-wing reaction in the aftermath of the July Days and he called on the Petrograd Soviet to help him defend the city from counter-revolution. The soldiers, sailors and workers again took to the streets, this time, supposedly in defence of the Provisional Government. The Bolsheviks seized the opportunity to organise armed bands of workers commanded by their '**Red Guards**', a militia they had trained in secret to act in support of the Bolsheviks. Kerensky even supplied them with arms.

As bands of Russian cavalry troops began to advance towards Petrograd on August 27th, Kerensky ordered Kornilov to surrender his command. He claimed that Kornilov was planning to use the troops to seize control and set up a military dictatorship. After several tense days, railway workers halted the trains carrying Kornilov's troops and persuaded them to desert. Kornilov and his fellow generals were arrested on September 1st.

Key terms

Red Guards: these were not crack troops but were loyal, volunteer soldiers which had been recruited from the factory workers in the city. They included young and old alike.

Activity

Thinking point

What do you think would have happened if Kornilov had successfully brought troops to the capital? Explain your ideas to your class.

Exploring the detail

Kornilov's arrest

Kornilov, with 30 fellow officers, was placed under arrest in the Bykhov Monastery near Mogilev. Conditions were lax and Kornilov was allowed to retain his bodyguards. Officers' families visited twice a day and officer Denikin's fiancée practically lived on site. These officers were to become the founding nucleus of the White Army which fought against the Bolsheviks in the Civil War of 1918–21. Other officers, not in captivity, were less fortunate. Soldiers were suspicious of the involvment of their superiors in the plot and hundreds were killed – often brutally – by their own men.

Results

The Kornilov episode proved seriously damaging to Kerensky's reputation, whilst it helped to bolster that of the Bolsheviks once again. Kerensky and the Menshevik and Socialist leaders' association with him lost both Soviet and army support. Army officers, who felt that Kerensky had betrayed Kornilov, were not prepared to support him, whilst the army rank and file, who were furious that he had appointed such a man in the first place, were equally hostile, although much of their anger was taken out on their own officers, many of whom were murdered in the aftermath of this affair.

The Bolsheviks, on the other hand, were able to bask in the reputation of having been the only group to have opposed Kornilov consistently. Lenin sent orders from Finland urging his followers to keep up the pressure and 'Committees to save the Revolution' were set up throughout the country. Kerensky was compelled to release those Bolsheviks imprisoned in July, including Trotsky, and he relaxed the curbs on their activities.

Consequently, Bolsheviks were elected in increased numbers to soviets throughout urban Russia and in the Duma elections in Moscow, Bolshevik support increased by 164 per cent between June and December. The Bolshevik membership, which had stood at 23,000 in February, had reached 200,000 by the beginning of October, by which time the party was producing 41 newspapers and maintaining a force of 10,000 Red Guards in the capital's factories. By September, when new elections were held to the Petrograd Soviet, the Bolsheviks won a majority, which together with their control of the Moscow Soviet placed them in a powerful position. On September 21st Trotsky even became chairman of the Petrograd Soviet.

It looked as though Lenin's tactics were paying off, but it must be remembered that the Bolsheviks were not, at this time, a tightly organised or discplined group. They tended to go along with events rather than initiate change and although, from mid-September, Lenin (still in hiding in Finland) bombarded the 12-man Central Committee of the Bolshevik Party with demands to stage a revolution and seize power, the Central Committee and, in particular its two most prominent members, Zinoviev and Kamenev, fearing that Russia was not yet economically ready for revolution, urged restraint and even burnt some of Lenin's letters.

On September 12th Lenin wrote claiming that *'History will not forgive us if we do not assume power now'*, but three days later the Committee voted against a coup.

Again on September 16th he sent a letter arguing:

> If we were to attack at once, suddenly from three points, Petrograd, Moscow and the Baltic fleet, the chances are a hundred to one that we should succeed with smaller sacrifices than in the July days, because the troops will not advance against a government of peace. Even though Kerensky has loyal cavalry in Petrograd, he would be compelled to surrender since we enjoy the sympathy of the army. If, with such good chances, we do not take power, then all talk of transferring power to the soviets becomes a lie. It is my profound conviction that if we let the present moment pass, we shall ruin the revolution.

3

However the Central Committee wanted to wait. Kamenev and Zinoviev believed that they should not act before the results of the Constituent

Assembly elections (the date of which was still undecided) were known, while Trotsky suggested they should work through the Petrograd Soviet and wait for the Congress of Soviets which was due to be convened on October 26th. He believed that, at this Congress, they could win the support of all socialist parties for a soviet government without having to resort to violence.

■ A closer look

The Bolshevik Central Committee Headquarters

The Central Committee of the Communist party and the Petrograd Soviet had set up their Headquarters in Petrograd's Smolny Institute, a former Convent School for the daughters of the Russian nobility. It stood adjacent to the picturesque Smolny Convent building and still bore the imperial arms carved in the stone above the entrance. Within its 100 or so huge rooms, linked by vaulted corridors and lit by rare electric lights, the swarming throngs of workers and soldiers in their heavy boots must have looked hopelessly out of place. Everywhere were notices imploring cleanliness and on the doors, which still bore enamel plaques with notices such as 'ladies' classroom no 2', newer handwritten signs such as, 'Central Committee of the All-Russian trade unions' or 'Central Executive Committee' had been added.

This information comes from the article, 'Scenes at the Smolny Institute', October 24th 1917, by John Reed, an American journalist who was in Russia at the time. Reed's writings, and in particular his book, *Ten Days that Shook the World*, provide a valuable account of the momentous days surrounding the Bolshevik takeover of power.

■ Activity

Research task

Try to get hold of Reed's *Ten Days that Shook the World* and read about events at first hand for yourself.

■ The Bolshevik Revolution of October 1917

On October 7th Lenin secretly returned to Petrograd to attend a meeting of the Central Committee and try to win them over in person to the policy of taking power immediately.

Kerensky was well aware that the Bolsheviks wanted to seize power. He responded by sending some of the more radical army units out of the capital. This provided an excuse for the Bolshevik-controlled Soviet, which claimed that Kerensky was abandoning the capital to allow it to fall to the Germans, to set up a 'Military Revolutionary Committee' under Trotsky and Dzerzhinsky on October 9th. This comprised 66 members – 48 of them Bolsheviks – and it appointed Commissars to military units, to issue orders and organise weapon supplies. The Committee controlled 200,000 Red Guards, 60,000 Baltic sailors and 150,000 soldiers of the Petrograd Garrison and while its declared purpose was to control troop movements (in the face of a German threat) its existence also seemed justified by the fears that government ministers might support a right-wing coup.

On October 10th Lenin harangued the Central Committee of the Bolshevik party all night and finally succeeeded (with a vote of 10 to 2) in persuading them that *'an armed rising is the order of the day'*. Zinoviev and Kamenev refused to agree and published their own views in a newspaper – *Novaia zhin* – declaring that, *'If we take power now and we are forced into a revolutionary war, the mass of soldiers will not support us'*.

Activity

Thinking and debate

Why do you think the members of the Central Committee were so reluctant to act in October 1917? One half of the group could give a speech, such as the one Lenin might have given to persuade the committee. The other half should listen, question and point out the problems.

Key profiles

Lev Borisovich Kamenev

Lev Borisovich Kamenev (1883–1936) was the son of a Jewish railway engineer, who joined the Social Democrats in 1901. Arrested many times, he became a propagandist overseas until 1914, when he was arrested and deported to Siberia, where he met Stalin in 1915. He returned in April 1917 and edited *Pravda*, opposing the April Theses. With Zinoviev, he voted against an armed uprising in October 1917, preferring a coalition with the socialists. Nevertheless he was made a member of Lenin's Politburo and joined Trotsky at the Brest-Litovsk negotiations, making peace terms with the Germans in 1918. He was forced from power by Stalin, expelled from the party in 1932 and executed in 1936.

Gregory Zinoviev

Gregory Zinoviev (1883–1936) was of Jewish origin. He joined the Social Democratic party in 1901 and was a member of the central committee from 1907–27. He was close to Lenin in exile and returned with him in 1917 in the sealed train but then supported Kamenev against the October Revolution. Zinoviev was against the idea of the Bolsheviks seizing power on their own, and wanted to work with other socialist groups. He became the head of the party's Petrograd organisation. He too was expelled from the party by Stalin and was executed in 1936.

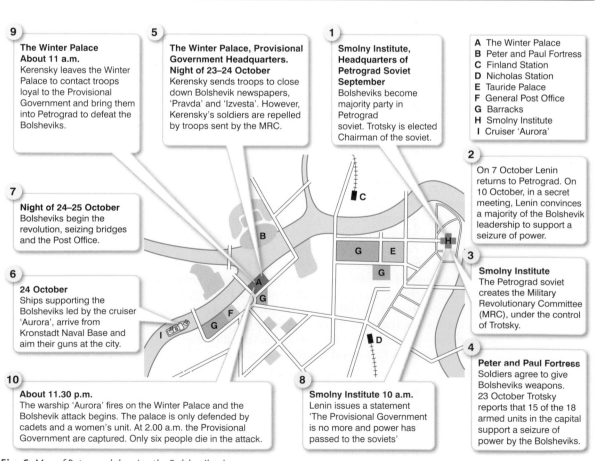

9
The Winter Palace
About 11 a.m.
Kerensky leaves the Winter Palace to contact troops loyal to the Provisional Government and bring them into Petrograd to defeat the Bolsheviks.

5
The Winter Palace, Provisional Government Headquarters.
Night of 23–24 October
Kerensky sends troops to close down Bolshevik newspapers, 'Pravda' and 'Izvesta'. However, Kerensky's soldiers are repelled by troops sent by the MRC.

1
Smolny Institute, Headquarters of Petrograd Soviet
September
Bolsheviks become majority party in Petrograd soviet. Trotsky is elected Chairman of the soviet.

A The Winter Palace
B Peter and Paul Fortress
C Finland Station
D Nicholas Station
E Tauride Palace
F General Post Office
G Barracks
H Smolny Institute
I Cruiser 'Aurora'

2
On 7 October Lenin returns to Petrograd. On 10 October, in a secret meeting, Lenin convinces a majority of the Bolshevik leadership to support a seizure of power.

7
Night of 24–25 October
Bolsheviks begin the revolution, seizing bridges and the Post Office.

3
Smolny Institute
The Petrograd soviet creates the Military Revolutionary Committee (MRC), under the control of Trotsky.

6
24 October
Ships supporting the Bolsheviks led by the cruiser 'Aurora', arrive from Kronstadt Naval Base and aim their guns at the city.

4
Peter and Paul Fortress
Soldiers agree to give Bolsheviks weapons. 23 October Trotsky reports that 15 of the 18 armed units in the capital support a seizure of power by the Bolsheviks.

10
About 11.30 p.m.
The warship 'Aurora' fires on the Winter Palace and the Bolshevik attack begins. The palace is only defended by cadets and a women's unit. At 2.00 a.m. the Provisional Government are captured. Only six people die in the attack.

8
Smolny Institute 10 a.m.
Lenin issues a statement 'The Provisional Government is no more and power has passed to the soviets'

Fig. 6 *Map of Petrograd showing the Bolshevik takeover*

Kerensky tried in desperation to close down two Bolshevik newspapers and restrict the Military Revolutionary Committee's power. He even ordered the bridges linking the working class areas to the centre of Petrograd to be raised. However, his actions, which Bolshevik propagandists suggested were a betrayal of the Soviet and an abandonment of the principles of the February Revolution, gave the Bolsheviks an excuse to act.

It therefore just remained for Trotsky, with his tremendous power and influence on the Military Revolutionary Committee, supported by fellow Bolshevik Yakov Sverdlov, to organise the final stages of the Bolshevik revolution. Through the night of October 24th, with the support of the Petrograd Military Revolutionary Committee, and in the name of the Second Congress of Soviets, 5,000 sailors and soldiers from Kronstadt moved into the city and Bolshevik Red Guards seized key positions around the capital. These included the telephone exchange, post office, railway stations, news agency, state bank, bridges and power stations. Although they encountered some resistance at the main telegraph office, the troops on duty generally gave in without resistance. In the morning a further 3,000 troops arrived.

Since Kerensky could not rely on the Petrograd troops to defend the Provisional Government, he left for the Front – borrowing a car from the American Embassy and disguising himself as a nurse. He hoped to be able to make contact with loyal troops who would march to the city and defend it. The rest of the government met in emergency session in the Winter Palace where on the evening of October 25th, as Red Guard soldiers and sailors surrounded the palace, a blank shot from the guns of the battleship *Aurora* was heard. This was the signal for the beginning of the Bolshevik attack. Further shots followed, including some from the St Peter and Paul fortress, the headquarters for the Military Revolutionary Committee, across the River Neva from the palace. However, only one shot hit the palace and most went into the river.

Fig. 7 *A Soviet painting of the storming of the Winter Palace.* In what ways is this picture an effective piece of propaganda?

S.L. Maslov, the minister of agriculture, who was one of those within the Winter Palace, recalled the events of October 25th:

> At 7.00pm Kishkin [appointed that day to control defence] was handed a note signed by Antonov [Bolshevik] demanding the surrender of the Provisional Government and the disarming of its guard. The guard of the Winter Palace was made up of some cadets, part of the Engineering School, two companies of Cossacks and a small number of the Women's Battalion. At around 10pm, a shot was fired in the palace, followed by cries and shots from the cadets. About 50 hostile sailors and soldiers were arrested and disarmed. In the meantime more and more sailors and soldiers arrived, until the guard seemed helpless.
>
> At about 2.00am, there was a loud noise at the entrance to the Palace. The armed mob of soldiers, sailors and civilians, led by Antonov, broke in. They shouted threats and made jokes. Antonov arrested everyone in the name of the Revolutionary Committee and proceeded to take the names of all present.
>
> We were placed under arrest and told we would be taken to Peter-Paul fortress. We picked up our coats, but Kishkin's was gone. Someone had stolen it. He was given a soldier's coat. A discussion started between Antonov and the others as to whether the ministers should be taken in automobiles or on foot. It was decided to make them walk.
>
> Each of us was guarded by two men. As we walked through the Palace it seemed as if it were filled with insurrectionists, some of whom were drunk. When we came out on the street, we were surrounded by a mob, shouting and threatening. At the Troitsky Bridge the mob shouted, "Throw them in the river!" The calls were becoming louder and louder. Just then a machine gun opened fire from the other side of us. We threw ourselves down, while some of the mob ran – and with them one of the arrested men.

4

Questions

1 What can you learn from this source about the Bolsheviks' seizure of power?

2 Why might the Bolsheviks wish to put about a different story?

Did you know?

Within the Winter Palace lay an unexpected treasure – the ex-tsar's enormous wine cellar. Thousands of bottles of antique wines were found and fuelled a frenzy of drunkenness. The Bolsheviks posted guards around the cellar, but they turned suppliers to the waiting crowds, and when a Commissar was appointed as guard, he got drunk too. Plans were made to move the hoard but came to nothing. Hundreds of drunken townsfolk were thrown into jail, and anarchy reigned for several weeks. When in desperation, some of the wine was poured away on the streets, crowds gathered to drink it from the gutters.

A closer look

The storming of the Winter Palace

Once the Bolshevik Communists were in power in Russia, they spread the myth that the storming of the Winter Palace by the Red Guards, supported by the massess, was an act of great bravery and heroism. On the tenth anniversary of the event in 1927, a famous film entitled *October* was made by Sergei Eisenstein. This made the attack appear a desperate feat undertaken against the odds by committed crowds desperate to ensure their revolution was carried through. The dramatic pictures of the masses breaking down the gates and storming in were entirely fictitious. Such troops as there were at the palace gave in easily. When the *Aurora* fired, the Women's Battalion became hysterical and all agreed they should leave whilst most of the cadets used little resistance and preferred to lay aside their arms and go home rather than fight. Some of the Red Guards simply walked in through back doors where there was no-one on guard and wandered around until they found the remaining members of the government. There was never a real 'break-in'. Originally, some sort of attack had been planned for the afternoon, but, thanks to Bolshevik inefficiency, nothing happened until the evening and by then several government members had already departed, unnoticed, out of the building's many exits.

Activities

Thinking and analysis

1 Using the source and 'Closer look' case study information, list the ways in which the Bolshevik seizure of the Winter Palace was more shambolic than heroic.

2 How far did the revolution of October 1917 differ from that of February 1917? Copy and complete the following table:

	February 1917	October 1917
Participants		
Spontaneity		
Leadership		
Programme		
Actions		
Results		

Fig. 8 *Lenin addressing the 2nd Soviet Congress. How does the painter suggest that Lenin enjoyed widespread support?*

On the evening of October 26th , the second 'All Russian Congress of Soviets' held its first session. The chairman, Kamenev, informed them that the Petrograd Soviet had seized power in their name and that a new governing committee was to be set up, headed by Lenin. He read out the list of proposed Commissars who would form the Soviet Council of People's Commissars or **Sovnarkom** – and they were all Bolsheviks or left-wing Social Revolutionaries and included one female, Alexandra Kollontai. The delegates, who were made up of a mixture of socialists, were not in full agreement. Whilst the 390 Bolshevik representatives were happy to accept the proposals, the 80 Mensheviks and 180 right-wing Social Revolutionaries as well as more than 30 others were not and these formed the majority. They claimed that the action was a Bolshevik coup and that power had not been taken in the name of the soviets – which was essentially correct. Trotsky taunted: *'You are miserable bankrupts,*

Key terms

Sovnarkom: means the cabinet – important ministers who, between them, would run the country.

Fig. 9 *The new* Sovnarkom, *1917. All members were Bolsheviks*

your role is played out; go where you ought to be – into the dustbin of History'. Rather than staying to fight it out, many stormed out of the hall and this left only those prepared to support Lenin, who consequently claimed majority support for his new government. He announced, *'We shall now proceed to construct the socialist order'* and by the following day had issued a:

- Decree on Peace – calling for immediate peace; and a
- Decree on land – announcing that all land was the property of the people and was to be redistributed by village soviets.

Key profiles

Josif Vissarimovich Djugashvily (Stalin)

Josif Vissarimovich Djugashvily (Stalin) (1879–1953) was the son of a peasant/cobbler and washerwoman from Georgia and was thus one of the few leading Bolsheviks who could claim genuinely lowly roots. He had trained to become an Orthodox priest but was attracted by the social democratic movement in 1898 and expelled from his seminary in 1899. Over the following years, he was repeatedly arrested and exiled to Siberia, but he escaped several times. In 1903, he took the Bolshevik side when the party split and he organised fighting squads who raised money by robbing banks. He was again in Siberia from 1912 to 1917 but he returned with Kamenev and others in 1917 and became the editor of *Pravda*, the Bolshevik newspaper. He played only a minor role in the October revolution but was made Commissar for Nationalities because of his background. He eventually took the leadership after Lenin's death and established himself as a dictator within Russia.

Alexandra Kollontai

Alexandra Kollontai (1872–1952) came from an aristocratic family and she first became interested in the lives of the peasants while staying on her grandfather's estates in Finland. She studied the works of Marx and Lenin and became well-known in revolutionary circles for her own writing. She joined Gapon's march of 1905 and was subsequently forced into exile. She joined the Bolsheviks in 1914 and in 1915 toured in the USA, making speeches against

World War I. She inspired the International Women's Day marches in Russia, although she did not return until after the women's march in February 1917 which inspired the first revolution. She was arrested after the July Days. As the first woman elected to the Party's Central Committee, Kollontai was popular but controversial. She favoured the simplification of marriage and divorce procedures and improving the position of illegitimate children. She lost some favour with Lenin but went on to become the first ever female ambassador under Stalin.

■ Cross-reference

For more on International Women's Day marches see page 117.

The October Revolution in Petrograd, whereby power passed to the Bolshevik Communists, thus proved a relatively small-scale affair. Trotsky claimed that 25,000–30,000 'at the most' were actively involved (this would mean around 5 per cent of all the workers and soldiers in the city) and this broadly tallies with other calculations based on the mobilisation of the Red Guards and others. There may have been 10,000– 15,000 in the square in front of the Winter Palace on the evening of the 25th, but many would have been bystanders and not actually involved in the so-called 'storming'. The few surviving original photos suggest that forces were quite small, but it did, of course, suit the Bolsheviks to claim they were larger, as the legitimacy of their regime was based upon the fact that it emerged from a 'popular' revolution.

Much of Petrograd remained unaffected by the disturbances – trams and taxis ran as normal and restaurants, theatres and cinemas remained open. Even Trotsky had to admit that the revolution was essentially a series of *small operations, calculated and prepared in advance'*.

However, the Bolshevik revolution was not entirely peaceful. After his hasty departure, Kerensky had set up headquarters at Gatchina not far from Petrograd, and had rallied forces to defeat the Bolsheviks. Many commanders had refused to co-operate – fearing being branded as counter-revolutionary by their soldiers – but Krasnov provided 18 Cossack regiments and the Social Revolutionaries also raised a small force of cadets and officers. Against this threat, the Bolsheviks looked weak. Many of the Petrograd garrison had returned to their homes in the countryside, and since Lenin had no direct contact with troops at the front, his forces were smaller in number than those of his opponents.

As he prepared to defend the city, there were 10 days of fighting in Moscow between those who remained loyal to the Provisional Government and the Bolshevik revolutionaries. There was particularly heavy fighting around the Kremlin and many Muscovites were frightened to leave their homes. In Kiev, Kazan and Smolensk there was also strong resistance to the imposition of Bolshevik control. However, Lenin thwarted some opposition by agreeing to inter-party talks and, thanks to Bolshevik agitators who persuaded some of Kerensky's troops to defect and a contingent of workers and soldiers who repulsed the rest on the outskirts of the city, the Bolshevik revolution was saved. It was, however, to take four more years of bitter civil war before the Communists could claim full victory and military control of the country.

Research task

Try to dip into the works and articles of different historians of the Russian Revolution and decide for yourself which interpretations you consider the most convincing.

A closer look

Problems of interpretation

The part played by Lenin himself in the October revolution has been subject to different interpretations. In the aftermath of the Communist seizure of power, it suited Soviet historians to idealise his role and treat him as a hero. The British historians E.H. Carr and E. Acton also accepted the view that Lenin was the central directing force. Such an interpretation is based on Lenin's part in winning over the masses with his April Theses, building up Bolshevik membership, spreading propaganda and, above all, persuading the Central Committee to take action in October. However, Lenin's contribution is open to question. It could be argued that Trotsky was far more important, organising the Red Guard, taking command in the Petrograd Soviet, dominating the Military Revolutionary Committee and organising the actual seizure of power. Another view, as expressed by the British historian Robert Service, is that Russia was heading for a socialist takeover anyway. Lenin merely ensured that this was a Bolshevik takeover. Critics of the 'heroic Lenin' school argue that since he was not even in Russia for most of 1917, he simply reacted to events and constantly deferred to the Central Committee (which was not united behind him), and that he can hardly have been the driver of revolution. They also point out that, when in Russia, he stayed in Petrograd rather than trying to create a truly 'Russian' revolution. If this interpretation is accepted, it might be felt that the Provisional Government's failures were more important than Lenin's leadership in bringing the Bolsheviks to power.

Another difficult issue concerns whether the October Revolution was, as Soviet historians suggested, a popular rising or whether, as Richard Pipes has claimed, it was, *'a classic coup d'état, the capture of governmental power by a small minority'*. During the years of Cold War, westerners tended to favour the latter interpretation but more recently some historians such as Sheila Fitzpatrick have adopted a more liberal view, accepting that there was at least some radicalism and spontaneous rebellion which the Bolsheviks were able to exploit.

Activities

Revision exercises

1 Look back through the momentous events of the year 1917 in Russia and make a month by month (and where necessary day by day) timeline of events.

2 Copy and complete the following chart by expanding on the points listed in the columns to summarise your ideas.

Weaknesses of the Provisional Government	Strengths of the Bolsheviks
Political position	Political manoeuvres
Policies	Policies
Kerensky's mistakes	Lenin and Trotsky as leaders

Other factors	Other factors
Defeat in the First World War	Pressure from workers and peasants

Learning outcomes

Through your study of this section you have considered how the tsarist regime was finally toppled by the experience of the First World War which threw into relief many of the inadequacies of the tsarist autocracy. You have seen how lack of equipment, poor leadership and appalling casualties, combined with food shortages and high inflation, created the ingredients for revolution, and how, in February 1917, the defection of the military forced Nicholas's abdication. You have also learnt how the Provisional Government, sharing power with the Petrograd Soviet, failed to cope with the critical problems facing the country – the war, the land hunger, workers' unrest and nationalist hopes. You have been invited to assess the part played by Lenin in exploiting these weaknesses and preparing for a Bolshevik takeover in October 1917 and have seen how the Bolsheviks propelled themselves into power. In the conclusion, you will have the opportunity to reconsider why the tsarist autocracy collapsed and from what point its demise became just a matter of time.

Practice questions

(a)   Explain why the tsar was forced to abdicate in March 1917.   *(12 marks)*

Study tip In (a) you will need to divide your answer into long-term and short-term factors. It would probably be better to start with the latter and explain the circumstances surrounding the tsar's abdication in February/March 1917, before reflecting briefly on what had brought the tsardom to this point. Remember your answer will need to be concise and well focused.

(b)   How far was Lenin responsible for the Bolshevik seizure of power in October 1917?   *(24 marks)*

Study tip In (b) you will need to balance Lenin's contribution against a range of other factors. The chart you have prepared on page 142 should help you to decide what you wish to argue and you may decide that the Provisional Government's weaknesses were more important. Whatever your view, ensure you state it clearly at the outset and support it throughout your answer, showing a balanced evaluation of a range of reasons. Remember that your answer should lead naturally to a well-supported conclusion which provides some judgement on Lenin's part in the coming of the October Revolution.

Conclusion

Тов. Ленин ОЧИЩАЕТ землю от нечисти.

Fig. 1 *With the arrival of Lenin, tsardom, the Church and the old capitalist bourgeoisie were destroyed. But what would the future bring?*

In 1855, Alexander II and his ministers would scarcely have been able to picture the Russian government of October 1917. Secure in the knowledge that the Romanov dynasty had the weight of nearly 250 years behind it, they would have been hard-pressed to imagine a Russia run by a motley assortment of individuals, from a middle class and even peasantry background, who claimed to rule in the name of the workers. Yet, beneath this vast change, there were still elements with which Alexander II would have been only too familiar: a backward and rebellious peasantry; a malfunctioning economy; an inadequate communication system; demanding national minorities; determined opposition groups and the need to use force and repression to maintain control. Alexander II, just like Lenin, was also aware of the humiliation and demands created by wartime defeat and the need for swift action to keep a restless population in check.

Just as Alexander II would have been amazed to have learned that there would be a Communist government in Russia just 36 years after his death, he might well have been surprised that some of the problems which he had tried to tackle in his reign had still not been solved. Alexander II set out to reform in order to preserve. He appreciated the need to compete with western powers and develop a stronger industrial economy, just as he understood that Russia needed a society based on the rule of law with stable local government and a sound education system.

The modernisation of the sprawling state thus began in Alexander II's reign. The serfs were emancipated, the *zemstva* established, schooling extended, railways developed. It was a sound beginning, but only a beginning, and in trying to transform the autocracy into something ressembling a modern western state, he had released forces of opposition which were destined to grow over the coming years. Some felt threatened by their loss of power and believed that Alexander had tried to steer Russia in the wrong direction, while others were frustrated by the tentative nature of many of his reforms. Some were content to keep their thoughts to themselves, others were determined to take action – as Alexander II found to his cost when an assassin's bomb brought his reign to an abrupt end.

Alexander II's dilemma proved to be Russia's dilemma through the later 19th and early 20th centuries. Like his successors, Alexander III and Nicholas II, Alexander II had frequently found himself having to choose between two conflicting policies – encouraging reform and modernisation by relaxing the controls of the autocratic state – and maintaining firm political control in order to protect that state from the forces that were threatening it. Such forces included the liberal intelligentsia and university students, the Populists and Social Revolutionaries, and the Marxist Social Democrats, who divided between Bolsheviks and Mensheviks.

Alexander III swayed towards the path of repression and reaction and yet, even during his reign, the forces of modernisation were in progress, as Witte helped to propel Russian industry forward and in so doing created a new industrial proletariat. Nicholas II oscillated between the two. Although naturally conservative and inclined to rely on repression, when faced with the test of the 1905 revolution, he gave in to the demands for political reform from both the liberal professional classes and rebellious workers and peasants. A Duma was established and whilst he tried hard to rein in the changes he had permitted, a crack had opened up in the previously solid armoury of the autocracy which was to prove impossible to close.

Whether the Russian autocracy collapsed in 1917 because it refused to change, or whether because it changed too much, is an interesting conundrum. Certainly, the decision to allow some powers to be passed to a State Duma from 1905 is a good example of the difficulties faced by the last Russian tsars. Although, in 1905, the opposition had focused on the establishment of a representative body, once that body had been set up, it was no longer enough. The Duma became a forum for debate and opposition, and in so doing, its existence worsened, rather than improved the relationship between the tsar and his people. When the first two Dumas were closed down and Stolypin changed the electoral system to try to produce a more amenable body, it simply made matters worse.

The work of Stolypin himself further outlines the contradictions of Russia in the early twentieth century. Stolypin tried to stabilise the regime through a series of agrarian and administrative reforms. He understood all too well Russia's desperate need to develop the rural economy, to solve the long-standing problem posed by the huge peasant population and create stability and prosperity in the countryside to support the developments taking place in the towns. Yet to achieve this and to quell endemic rebellion, he resorted to measures of the utmost ruthlessness. In the countryside, Stolypin, whose own death came through assassination, was to be remembered for his 'necktie' rather than his reforms.

In the years leading up to World War I, the tsarist regime seemed to reach a point of 'no return', although Nicholas II, absorbed by his family problems and tercentenary celebrations, seemed unable to grasp this fact. Although it was not until the demands of the First World War split the crack wide open, that the autocracy collapsed, the strikes, rebellions, assassinations and widespread discontent, which even permeated the court circles where Rasputin held sway, gave some forewarning of what was to come.

February 1917 brought Romanov rule to an end as the hungry, demoralised and unemployed took to the streets of Petrograd in mass riots and demonstrations. There had been riots before, but by 1917 it was the attitude of the military that was crucial. Although he tried, Nicholas discovered that the army could no longer be relied upon to obey orders and disperse the crowds. Thus, the long tradition of resorting to repression in order to maintain autocratic control was broken and the tsar had to go.

The sudden end of tsarist rule left a vacuum at the top. Throughout the previous 60 years, it had always proved easier to challenge, oppose and destroy than to change, support and reform, and despite the excitement surrounding the prospect of a new tsar-less Russia, the Provisional Government found it no easier than the discredited autocracy to reconcile the many different demands which it faced. The threat of rebellion never went away, and its own authority, curbed by the demands of the ever-watchful Petrograd Soviet, was never fully secure. The continuation of the war was to prove ruinous, whilst its inability, or unwillingness, to offer instant solutions to the demands of the peasants and workers was to prove fatal.

By the autumn of 1917, with the country once again in military, economic and political turmoil, the hungry urban masses and desperate army deserters were ready to turn to the group who, with the weight of Marxist theory behind them, promised liberation in the form of, 'peace bread and land'. Lenin, Trotsky and other Bolshevik leaders found themselves in a position to force through the revolution for which they had been striving for years. It might have taken the form of a coup rather than a spontaneous proletariat rising, but the outcome was the same; it established the Bolsheviks in command of Russia and opened the way to a new Communist future.

Thus, it seemed as though the country had changed beyond all recognition since 1855 and no doubt many genuinely believed in October 1917 that they were living at the dawn of a new and glorious future. However, in some respects, the wheel had simply turned full circle. Communist rule was not to be the panacea for all ills which the idealists had hoped for. To enforce his control, Lenin turned to repression. He replaced the tsarist *Okhrana* with the Communist *Cheka*, he abolished the freedom of the press, abandoned many hard-won civil rights and ruled by decree. When elections for a Constituent Assembly in January 1918 produced a result which he did not approve of, he had the body closed by force. The 'voice of the people' in local self-government – the *zemstva*, soviets and local committees – disappeared as such bodies were dismantled or subordinated to Bolshevik control. Worse still, in his determination to repress the national minorities, prevent a tsarist comeback and ensure the permanence of one-party Soviet power, Lenin plunged the country into a bloody civil war from 1918 to 1920. Whether the end justified the means is a different story and would require broader knowledge of developments in Russia after 1917, but in response to the underlying theme of this book, of how rulers could achieve modernisation whilst still maintaining political control over society, Lenin's methods were to prove little different from those of the tsars he had so decried.

Glossary

A

Autocracy: this is when all power is in the hands of one man.

B

Bolshevism: when the Social Democratic Workers' party (qv) split in 1903, Lenin led the faction which believed that the party should be spearheaded by a small group of determined revolutionaries, These became known as the Bolsheviks and they seized power in Russia in October 1917.

C

Cheka: the Bolshevik secret police set up in December 1917.

Communism: communism is derived from Marxism and refers to an economic and social system in which everyone works together for the common good. In a perfect communist society, all would be equal and there would be no need for any money. Government and states would wither away and society would be classless. Communists saw this 'perfect' state as the ultimate stage in human history.

D

Dual Power: this was the name given to the power-sharing agreement between the Provisional Government and the Petrograd Soviet in February 1917. The Provisional Government was tolerated so long as it did not infringe the 'peoples' rights' which the Petrograd Soviet sought to protect.

Duma: this is the Russian term for an elected council. Originally a Duma was a municipal council but between 1905 and 1917 the Duma became the elected legislative council of state.

G

Gold Standard: this is when the amount of money in circulation is strictly limited by that country's reserves of gold. It makes a currency more stable and more respected abroad.

I

Intelligentsia: the educated, usually middle class elites who were often critical of the tsarist regime.

L

Land Captain: an institution set up by Alexander III to restore power to the nobility in the provinces of Russia. Land Captains had extensive powers, including an ability to over-rule the local *zemstva*.

Liberalism/Liberal: liberalism was a political concept spread by the French revolution that encouraged personal and economic freedom. Personal freedoms included the right to property and the freedom of speech, of religion and of participation in politics. Economic freedoms included free trade and non-interference in working relationships. The term 'liberal' came to imply those in favour of representative, elected government.

M

Marxism/Marxist: this refers to the political ideology deriving from the theories of Karl Marx who taught that all history is driven by economic forces which create class struggles. In the 19th and early 20th centuries, most Marxists wanted to further the stage of history whereby the proletariat (workers) would rise against the bourgeoisie (capitalists).

Mensheviks: when the Social Democratic Workers'party held its conference in 1903, Martov led the Mensheviks in arguing that the party needed a broad membership and should await a middle-class (bourgeois) revolution before a communist (proletarian) revolution could take place.

Mir: this is the Russian word for the village commune where the peasants worked. After 1861, the peasants were not allowed to leave the mir until their redemption dues were paid.

N

National Minorities: these were people of different ethnic backgrounds, such as Poles, Finns, Ukrainians and Jews, who lived within the state of imperial Russia.

O

Okhrana: the Okhrana was the name given to the tsarist secret police force, which replaced the Third Section in 1880.

P

Peasants: these were mainly former serfs which made up the bulk of the Russian population. They lived in the countryside and worked the land in primitive conditions which improved little across the 1855–1917 period.

Pogrom: this was an attack on Jews – often involving extreme violence, burning homes, raping and looting.

Populism: this was a belief in the power of the people – which effectively meant the peasants – to bring about change in Russia by working together in the commune to create a new society. This protest movement was popular in the 1870s but split in 1879 into the Black Partition and the People's Will. The Social Revolutionary Party emerged from this tradition in 1901.

Pan-Slavism/Pan-Slav: the Pan-Slavist movement favoured uniting all Slavs into a single country. Pan-Slavists felt sympathy for their fellow Slavs elsewhere and wanted to help them.

Protection: this involves placing duties on goods to protect home industry and prevent unwanted foreign imports.

Provisional Government: this was the name given to the government which emerged out of the Duma and held power in a dual power arrangement with the Petrograd Soviet in Russia from February until October 1917. It was called Provisional as its declared aim was to arrange for elections to a Constituent Assembly which would draw up a new constitution for Russia.

R

Right-wing/left-wing: in politics it is quite normal to talk about 'the left' and the 'right' or left- and right-wing. This division derives from the time of the French Revolution when deputies who supported the monarchy sat on the right, while more radical opponents, who wanted change, sat on the left in the Assembly. Thus 'right' has come to mean conservative – and, at its most extreme, authoritarian and in favour of strong rule – while left means pro-reform, in favour of the workers and, at its most extreme, Communism.

S

Serfs: there were various categories of serfs in Russia before 1861, including state serfs, household serfs and privately-owned serfs. All were the personal property of their masters and could be bought and sold. They were required to serve their masters in various ways and had to apply for permission, for example, to marry or to travel. After 1861 there were technically no serfs in Russia.

Slavophiles: these were 19th century thinkers who believed that western European models were not applicable to Russia and that the country should seek a basis for its future development in its native traditions.

Social Democratic Workers' Party: this was the Marxist Party founded in Minsk in 1898. In 1903 it split into the two factions, Bolsheviks and Mensheviks.

Social Revolutionary Party: this was a political grouping founded in 1901 which primarily championed the cause of the peasants and land re-distribution (following the Populist tradition) but also believed that the urban proletariat could lead revolution. It advocated terrorist methods including assassination.

Socialism: socialism seeks to achieve greater equality by reducing private profit, extending opportunities and spreading welfare reforms. Socialism was embraced by both the Social Revolutionaries and Social Democrats in Russia.

Soviet: a Soviet was an elected council, usually of workers, soldiers, sailors and perhaps peasants, which controlled a local area. It was a left-wing body and one was set up in St Petersburg (by Trotsky) in 1905 and many more in different parts of Russia in 1917. Their leadership was not always Bolshevik. The Petrograd Soviet shared dual power with the Provisional Government.

Synod: the governing body of the Russian Orthodox Church. It was effectively controlled by the tsar through his representative, the Procurator of the Holy Synod.

T

Tariffs: this is another word for customs duties. (*See* Protection.)

Trade unionism: trade unions are organisation of employees set up to lobby employers and the governing powers for better conditions of both work and living for their members. Before 1905 these were illegal in Russia.

tsar: this derives from the Latin word 'Caesar' and refers to an Emperor. It was the title given to the Emperor of Russia.

W

Westernisers: this section of the 19th century Russian intelligentsia believed in the development of Russia along the lines followed by western nations.

Z

Zemstva: this was the name given to the elected local government assemblies set up in Russia by a decree of 1864. They were the first type of 'democratic' institution to be established in Russia but while often effective in their local areas, their tendency to criticise central government led Alexander III to rein in their powers and restrict the popular vote to these in 1890/92.

Bibliography

General coverage

D Evans and J Jenkins, *Years of Russia, the USSR and the Collapse of Soviet Communism*, Hodder Arnold (2nd edn), 2001

C Corin and T Fiehn, *Communist Russia under Lenin and Stalin*, Hodder Murray (Hodder Murray), 2002

D Murphy and T Morris, *Russia 1855–1964*, Collins, 2008

A Wood, *The Romanov Empire 1613–1917*, Hodder Arnold, 2007

M Lynch, *Reaction and Revolutions:Russia 1881–1924*, Hodder Murray (2nd new edn), 2005

J Bromley, *Russia 1848–1917*, Heinemann, 2002

G Darby, *The Russian Revolution 1861–1924*, Longman, 1998

J Hite, *Tsarist Russia 1801–1917*, Causeway Press, 2004

J Laver, *The Modernisation of Russia 1856–1985*, (1856–1917 sections), Heinemann, 2002

A Wood, *The Russian Revolution*, Longman (2nd edn)

S Fitzpatrick, *The Russian revolution*, Oxford University Press (3rd edn), 2008

S J Lee, *Russia and the USSR*, Routledge, 2005

Biographies and first hand accounts

D Lieven, *Nicholas II Emperor of all the Russias*, Pimlico, 1994

R Service, *Lenin: A Biography*, Pan Books, 2002

B Williams, *Lenin (profiles in power)*, Longman (2nd edn, revised), 2000

Other useful reference books

H Rogger, *Russia in the Age of Modernisation and Revolution 1881–1917*, Longman, 1983

P Oxley, *Russia 1855–1991*, Oxford University Press, 2001

G Freeze, *Russia, A History*, Oxford University Press, 2002

O Figes, *A Peoples Tragedy: The Russian Revolution,1891–1924*, Pimlico, 1997

J Hutchinson, *Late Imperial Russia*, Longman, 1999

D Offord, *Nineteenth-century Russia. Opposition to Aristocracy*, Longman, 1999

P Waldron, *The End of the Imperial Russia*, Macmillan, 1997

M Lynch, *Reaction and Revolutions: Russia 1881–1924*, Hodder Murray, 2nd new edn, 2005

R Service, *The Russian Revolution 1900–1927*, Macmillan, 1991

W Mosse, *Alexander II and the Modernisation of Russia*, B Tauris (2nd edn), 1995

N Rothnie, *The Russian Revolution* Palgrave Macmillan, 1989

R Pipes, *Russia under the old regime*, Penguin, 1995

S A Smith, *The Russian Revolution, a very short introduction*, Oxford University Press, 2002

J N Westwood, *Endurance and Endeavour*, Oxford University Press, 3rd edn, 1987

Useful websites

www.fbuch.com/posters.html (Visual material on the Revolution)

www.marxists.org.archive/lenin/index.html (Lenin)

www.hsc.csu.edu.au/modhist/courses

Photographs

B Moynahan, *Russian Century: A Photographic History Weidenfeld*, 2000

P Kurth, *Tsar: The Lost World of Nicholas and Alexandra Back Bay*, 1998

Acknowledgements

The author and publisher would like to thank the following for permission to reproduce material:

Source texts courtesy of:

p3, *Years of Change 1890–1945*, R. Wolfson, Edward Arnold 1978; p8, *The Reign of Rasputin; an Empire's collapse*, Boris Chicherin, M V Rodzianko, London, 1927; p10 'Rech' Aleksandra II predvoditelyam Moskovskogo dvoryanstva' in 11, *Khrestomatiya po istirii SSR* vol II, S S Dmitriev (ed.), Moscow, 1948; p12 from *Father and Sons*: Norton Critical Edition, Second Edition by Ivan Turgenev, translated by and edited by Ralph E. Matlaw. Copyright © 1989, 1966 by W.W. Norton & Company, Inc. Used by permission of W.W. Norton and Company, Inc; p15, p30, *Scenarios of power*, Richard Wortman, Princeton University Press, 2000; p26, p67, *Years of Russia, the USSR and the Collapse of Soviet Communism*, David Evans and Jane Jenkins, Hodder, 2001; p17 *Turgenev*, Henry Troyat, Allison & Busby, New Ed edition, 1991; p30 *Emperor Alexander II* Tatishchev, Moscow, 1903; p31 *Russia Under the Old Regime*, Richard Pipes, Orion, 1974; p33 *The Russian Empire 1801–1917*, Hugh Seton-Watson, OUP, 1967; p3. Society is at present divided (98 words), Extract from 1882 manifesto 'Young Russia' p34, *A sourcebook for Russian history from earliest times to 1917*, G Vernadsky et al (eds), Yale University press, 1972; p34, 'Catechism of a Revolutionary' Mikhail Bukunin and Sergey Nechayev, Berne, 1871; p39 *Russia 1815–1881*, R Sherman, Hodder, 1991; p45 *Russia 1855–1991*, Peter Oxley, OUP, 2001; p52, p67, p71, p76, p77, p109, p110, p141, *A People's Tragedy*, Orlando Figes, Jonathan Cape, 1996; p53, p57, p68, p76, p84, p86, p86, p94, p103, p113, p114, p115, p121, p128, p130, p134, p138, *The Russian Chronicles*, J. Ryan (ed.), Bramley Books –Quadrillon publishing ltd, 1998; p86, *Ocherki diplomaticheskoy istorii RusskoYaponskoy voyny, 1895–1907*,., B. A. Romanov, Moscow-Leningrad, 1947; p87, *Jahrbuch des offentlichen Rechts* (1908) quoted in *Reading modern European History (1909)* by J H Robinson and C A Beard; p87, *Europe Transformed 1878–1919*, Norman Stone, Blackwell, 1999; p97, p115, *The Romanov Empire 1613–1917*, Alan Wood, Hodder Arnold, 2007; p97, *The Romanov Empire 1613–1917*, Alan Wood, Hodder Arnold, 2007; p110, *Octobrists to Bolsheviks: Imperial Russia, 1905–1917* (adapted), contributors: Martin McCauley, Peter Waldron, Edward Arnold, 1984; p111, *The End of the Russian Empire* (adapted), Michael T. Florinsky, Yale University Press., 1931; p112 *Readings In Russian Civilisation*, 2 vols, Thomas Riha (ed.), Chicago, 1964; p134, p135, p139 *Communist Russia under Lenin and Stalin*, Chris Corin and Terry Fiehn, Hodder, 2002; 'Scenes at the Smolny Institute, 24 October 1917' by John Reed, 'Witnesses to the Russian Revolution', Roger W Pethybridge, Allen and Unwin, 1982; p140, *Russia 1855–1964*, Murphy, Harper-Collins, 2008; p142, *The Russian Revolution 1988–1919*, Richard Pipes, Vintage books; Table 1, pp84–85 *Russia 1855–1964*, D Murphy & T Morris, Collins, 2008; Table 9, 11, 12, 13, 15, *Reaction and revolutions in Russia*, Michael Lynch, Hodder 1992; Table 1, p98–101, *Octobrists to Bolsheviks*, McCauley, Edward Arnold, 1984.

Photographs courtesy of:

Topfoto; 0.1, 0.2, 1.4, 1.8, 2.3, 2.4, 4.5, 6.5, 7.2, 8.2, 8.5, 8.6

Edimedia; 1.1, 1.7, 3.2, 5.7, 6.3, 6.4, 7.1, 10.1

World History Archive; 1.3, 2.1, 3.5, 3.6, 4.2, 4.3, 4.4, 4.6, 4.7, 5.1, 5.6, 7.3, 7.5, 8.1, 8.3, 8.4, 9.2, 9.3, 9.6

Grantham Bain Collection; 1.5

Mary Evans Pictures; 1.6, 2.5, 4.8, 5.5, 6.2

Ann Ronan Picture Library; 1.2, 2.2, 3.1, 3.3, 3.4, 9.1

Photo12; 2.6, 4.1, 5.2, 5.3, 5.4, 6.1, 9.5, 7.4.

Index